Puerto Rico | *A Socio-Historic Interpretation*

For Carmen Sara,
    my little comrade. . .
because she represents the
future of the liberated
fatherland.

Manuel
Maldonado-
Denis

PUERTO RICO:

A SOCIO-HISTORIC INTERPRETATION

Translated by Elena Vialo

Random House
New York

FIRST AMERICAN EDITION

Copyright © 1972 by Manuel Maldonado-Denis
Translation Copyright © 1972 by Random House,
Inc.

All rights reserved under International and Pan-
American Copyright Conventions. Published in the
United States by Random House, Inc., New York,
and simultaneously in Canada by Random House
of Canada Limited, Toronto. Originally published
in Mexico as *Puerto Rico: Una interpretación histórico-social* by Siglo veintiuno editores,
s.a., Mexico City.

Library of Congress Cataloging in Publication Data

Maldonado-Denis, Manuel, 1933–
  Puerto Rico: a socio-historic interpretation.

  Translation of Puerto Rico: una interpretación
histórico-social.
  Bibliography: p.
  1. Puerto Rico—History.   2. Nationalism—
Puerto Rico.   I. Title.
F1975.M2713   1972   972.95   71-37062
ISBN 0-394-47347-7

Manufactured in the United States of America by
American Book–Stratford Press.
2 4 6 8 9 7 5 3

Translator's Preface

In translating *Puerto Rico: A Socio-Historic Interpretation,*
I made a few decisions which I wish to clarify here. I chose
to follow the Hispanic practice of saying "North American"
instead of "American" because this term conveys the
awareness of the existence of more than one America,
which is important to the South and Central Americans,
and should also be to the "North Americans."

In the footnotes, I did not translate the Spanish titles, as
it is the Spanish editions of these works which are available
to researchers.

I wish to thank Professor Haydee Rivera for her help and
encouragement, and the author of this book, Dr. Manuel
Maldonado-Denis, for the many clarifications of the text
which he so kindly sent me. I hope the reader will find this
translation, above all, clear and readable.

ELENA VIALO

Author's Prologue
to the English Edition

This book was originally written for a predominantly Spanish-speaking public, composed mainly of Latin Americans and Puerto Ricans living on the island of Puerto Rico. One of its main shortcomings was its relative silence concerning that one-third of our people who at the present moment live in the United States. It is perhaps a reflection of the alienation that exists between Puerto Ricans living on the island and those exiled on the mainland that until very recently we had practically forgotten about the existence of one another. This gap is gradually being overcome, particularly by the postwar generation of Puerto Ricans born in the United States, who have become increasingly aware of the need for roots in a society that rejects them because of their ethnic origins. Although I must confess my ignorance of what it really *means* to be a Puerto Rican in New York, I have tried to deal with the subject, albeit in a very preliminary fashion.

The addendum to the English edition of this book is thus a first and admittedly incomplete attempt to deal with the very complicated subject of Puerto Ricans in the United States. I hope it will be the beginning of a more serious study on the subject, which I intend to carry out during the span of my appointment as Visiting Professor of Puerto

Rican Studies at Queens College of the City of New York during the academic year 1972–73.

As for the book itself, I have decided to let it stand as it is. An essay of this nature is not meant to be just a journalistic account of Puerto Rican reality. Hence it is bound to be overtaken by events. In this sense, the author must always resist the temptation of bringing the book up to date, since it is practically impossible to do so.

Whether or not this social and historical interpretation of Puerto Rican society will be considered accurate will be determined by the forces that ultimately prevail—not only in Puerto Rican society as such, but throughout the world. In other words, the validity of this interpretation will ultimately be tested, not merely by its theoretical accuracy, but also by its practical—i.e., political—bearings. The ultimate test of social theory—as Marx so brilliantly demonstrated —is its ability to correctly analyze the forces and tendencies within a society struggling to achieve hegemony within it, and to predict—no matter how loosely—the shape of things to come.

Seen from this viewpoint, this book pretends to be no more than a dissenting view of Puerto Rican history and society—dissenting because it goes against the grain of what passes for interpretations of Puerto Rican reality in Puerto Rico, Latin America, and on the mainland. At the same time, this book pretends to be nothing less than the voice of an ever-increasing sector of the Puerto Rican population which is presently struggling for our independence and liberation. It is a voice reaching out to both the Puerto Rican population living in the United States and the American public itself.

I suppose that no author is ever really satisfied with a translation of his work. I must confess that I am not altogether satisfied with this one. I have personally revised the translation to see that it reflects accurately what I want to say. On the whole I would say that I am satisfied with the outcome.

I would particularly like to express my profound debt to John Simon of Random House, who became interested in translating my book in the first place, and my heartfelt thanks and appreciation to Susan Rabiner of Random House for her sympathy and understanding in the revision and handling of my book. To both of them I say with Hispanic zest: "Salud, compañeros."

MANUEL MALDONADO-DENIS
HATO REY, *Puerto Rico*
February, 1972

Author's Prologue
to the Spanish Edition

Alejo Carpentier has said that the mission of the writer is always the same: to say what he means. In this essay I have attempted to meet the standard criterion set down by this great Cuban writer. I have tried to say what I mean without mincing words or beating around the bush, guided by a desire to make available both in and out of Puerto Rico an interpretation of our history and our society other than that offered by those who defend the colonial condition from which our country suffers.

Through almost a decade of teaching at the University of Puerto Rico it has been my students who have most contributed to the writing of this essay. Their perplexities, their questions, their discussions, both in and out of the classroom, have made me see the need for these young people to have a book that would help to rid their minds of much of the mental confusion produced by our colonial status. This, then, is my humble repayment to each and every one of them—as much to those in disagreement as to those in agreement with my view of Puerto Rican reality.

My colleagues and companions in the College of Social Science and at the University of Puerto Rico have also contributed to the successful conclusion of this work. I appreciate particularly the economic aid and the material and moral encouragement given me by the Center of Social

Research at the University of Puerto Rico and its present
director, Dr. Luis Nieves Falcón. I believe it is only just to
further thank him for everything he has offered me—his
books, articles and lectures—to enrich my knowledge of
Puerto Rican society. Also, I must thank Dr. Thomas G.
Mathews, Director of the Institute of Caribbean Studies at
the University of Puerto Rico, for the valuable help he has
always given me through his economic and moral support.

My colleagues, Professors Milton Pabón, Justo Méndez
Colón, Eugenio Fernández Méndez, Eduardo Seda Bonilla,
José Emilio González, Pablo García Rodríguez, Robert W.
Anderson, Gordon K. Lewis, Rubén Berríos Martínez,
Gamaliel Ortiz, Isabel Gutiérrez del Arroyo, Margot Arce
de Vázquez, Nilita Vientós Gastón, as well as the Puerto
Rican writers René Marqués, Pedro Juan Soto, and Emilio
Díaz Valcárcel have sustained a prolonged dialogue
throughout these years with me on the Puerto Rican prob-
lem, a dialogue which has doubtlessly enabled me to obtain a
clearer vision of the Puerto Rico that grieves us all. Naturally
I alone am responsible for the ideas expressed in this essay.

A work of this kind could never have been finished were
it not for the infinite patience within a capacity for impatience the author's companion exercised day by day.
Her patience at my being continually shut up with my work
as well as her impatience at my occasional impulses of
indolence were what made of Alma, my companion in the
struggle and beyond it, the consolation as well as the stimulus that spurred me on toward the conclusion of my essay.
It is not a mere figure of speech to say that this small book
belongs to her as well as to that domestic cyclone, our
daughter Carmen Sara.

MANUEL MALDONADO-DENIS
December, 1968

Contents

Puerto Rico | *A Socio-Historic Interpretation*

Introduction

The real man goes to the root. That's what a radical is: someone who goes to the root. One who does not see things in depth cannot be called a radical.

MARTÍ

We are now more than one hundred years into the struggle for Puerto Rican independence. On September 23, 1868, the Republic of Puerto Rico was proclaimed. This great, though unsuccessful, event—celebrated as the Cry of Lares —continues to set the tone and the ultimate goal of the struggle of the Puerto Rican people. Sadly, this initial fleeting triumph of one hundred years ago still stands as the high-water mark of Puerto Rican independence. Today, our people continue to live under a colonial regime—though this regime attempts to disguise itself beneath the pompous title of "Commonwealth of Puerto Rico."

But the will for independence of the Puerto Rican people is strong; and events in the twentieth century will continue to demonstrate the degree to which our will will be indestructible—even when faced with continuing repression by our most powerful opponents.

Nevertheless, this effort, this struggle, so often mute and generally thankless, which has been waged by those of our people who are battling to defend the Puerto Rican from those who would negate him, has not received the attention it deserves from many historians. On the contrary, a glance at the historiography of this century under North American domination, a superficial look at what passes for Puerto Rican history in high school and even university texts, reveals just how ambitious has been the attempt to rewrite our country's history to make it fit the mold imposed by the ruling regime. Thus do others attempt to belittle, ridicule, and often ignore all that has been part of the direct struggle against a system predicated on the submission of our people to another. Thus the young person who studies in our high schools learns that Hostos was a great sociologist and De Diego a great poet and orator, but he is not told that both men fought tenaciously to achieve independence for Puerto Rico.

Of course none of this should take us by surprise. Cynics say that history is written by the conquerors and the survivors. But the victory of those who have given us political inferiority, first under Spain and now under the United States, is pyrrhic, and is intelligible only to those who look in the historical process for the triumphant sign of the conquerors whom they serve. According to the accommodating interpretations of the officious historians of the regime, the true history—to distinguish it from the prehistory of Puerto Rico—begins in 1940 with the coming to power of the Popular Democratic party (PPD). The invasion of the island by the North Americans in 1898 is merely the backdrop to the "change of sovereignty" from Spain to the United States.

It is not surprising that the two best books of this century on Puerto Rico were written in the decade of the thirties: *Insularismo,* by Antonio S. Pedreira, and *Prontuario histórico de Puerto Rico,* by Tomás Blanco. Both are short essays, great syntheses of our historical development. Those students of our history not blinded by the dazzling show of the "era of Muñoz Marín" should continue to read Pedreira and Blanco in spite of the fact that Pedreira, in particular, suffers from an aristocratic—and we might almost say racist—conception of our evolution which in many respects undermines his sharp observations.[1] It is noteworthy that the best book on Puerto Rico in a long time has been written by the British professor, Gordon K. Lewis, in his monumental work, *Puerto Rico: Freedom and Power in the Caribbean* (1963).

The subject might perhaps be discussed in terms of generations. Many intellectuals, seduced by Muñoz Marín's oratory, were unable to see the true implications of his actions and followed him along the path which has made Puerto Rico an island increasingly less Puerto Rican. Reaching their intellectual maturity in the decade from 1930 to 1940, these intellectuals were the ones who supplied the necessary rationalizations for the turn toward the right of the leader who before had demanded our independence. They thus became apologists for the "Commonwealth" as the "showcase of democracy." A reading of what was written in Puerto Rico in the fifties would illustrate how Jaime Benítez, Arturo Morales Carrión, Teodoro Moscoso, Rafael Picó, and others sang in unison a hymn of praise periodically echoed by partisan voices in the colonial power, such as Friederich, Wells, Galbraith, Hanson, etc. The best illustration of this "celebration of Puerto Rico" is found in a special issue of the *Annals of the American Academy of Political and Social Science,* published in

[1] The author of this book has made the criticism of Pedreira in his essay "Visión y revisión de *Insularismo,*" *Asomante* (San Juan, P.R.), Vol. XLX, no. 1 (1963).

1952. It was necessary in this illustration, however, to offer an interpretation of our history in which the *independentistas'* contribution was made to appear insignificant and in which the true direction of the desires of our people was interpreted as autonomism. The term "autonomism" has meant many things to many people. In the specific case of Puerto Rico in the twentieth century, however, it has meant simply and directly what Muñoz Marín himself—in times of greater patriotic candor—called "freedom with a long chain."

Autonomism thus defined came to be an important support of the ideologists of colonialism. Hence some have attempted to establish a greater historical continuity between the autonomism advocated by Baldorioty, who during the nineteenth century demanded a complete break with the colonial power and was thus the most radical among the Puerto Rican autonomists; that of Muñoz Rivera, who supported the two organic laws passed by the U.S. Congress—which conceded very little autonomy to our nation —in order to govern in Puerto Rico; and that of Muñoz Marín, who fostered autonomism by perpetuating the political situation he inherited from his father. This continuity—which in fact has been not just a continuity but also, as we will try to show, a continuation of colonialism in Puerto Rico—served, then, as the touchstone for all those attempting to justify our political condition. Though they deny it, deep down the autonomists really believe that the Puerto Rican people are a people who have not merely accepted colonialism but who have desired it.

This book is based on the premise that the above assumption is not true, although one crucial fact is accepted: that throughout our history, power in the colony has oscillated between the unconditionalists or annexationists and the autonomists. Consequently, in this essay the central axis of the historical analysis will be the struggle waged throughout our nation's development between the forces competing for power under the ruling colonial system and the forces opposing the system. I will also assert that in the historical evolution of our country, the pro-independence forces have been the only ones to have fought using all means possible for the liquidation of colonialism in Puerto Rico, while the annexationist and autonomist forces have retarded our people's achievement of their independence. I will therefore interpret our history as the scene of a struggle between these two forces: those who are in agreement with the demise of colonialism as a world historical trend, and those who are antihistorical and retrogressive in their support of colonialism.

I am aware that in outlining for myself a work of this kind I will be accused of partiality and lack of objectivity. To this I reply that no historian is really impartial—unless he is not an historian, but a mere compiler of facts. History is not chronology, although regrettably it seems to be so for those who see in the past only dead material, only the past. . . . Nor is it, as Ranke used to say, "what really happened," although he was not completely incorrect in this observation. Every historical work is a work of interpretation of that primary material which is furnished us in the form of the "historical fact." Like his fellow scholar, the sociologist, the historian must be selective, must assign certain facts greater significance than others. That is to say, he maintains certain criteria by means of which he determines x issue to be more important than y. Every historian conscious of his craft makes manifest to himself and to his reader these criteria, this cross section of concepts within which he links together that which he considers of greatest historical meaning. This means that, to be valid, every work of historical investigation must be guided by a theory of historical reality. This does not mean, of course, that the historian ignores the facts before him. If he does, he easily falls into fictional literature. No. But it is also necessary to organize the facts within a certain perspective or theory. Both things go hand in hand.

The problem becomes complicated when that which you are attempting to analyze and describe is something still alive, something which touches the researcher very closely. Here it is difficult to relinquish a given ideological position in order to see things in a cold and dispassionate atmosphere. This is true for any historian or sociologist, not merely for the social scientists whose interpretations differ from those of defenders of the status quo. No one is perfectly impartial or perfectly objective because before anything else, the historian is a man: as such, he is a being living in a certain society and having a certain vision of the world, a particular social position, etc.

Each epoch, each generation, reexamines its history. And what once seemed an insignificant fact or a utopian action may sometimes become a significant fact or an action preceding future changes. Great historical events—like great social revolutions—force a reexamination; they impose on those who study the historical-social world the necessity of seeing its development in a new perspective.

The present world—our world—is a world in effervescence, in revolution. The entire universe is the setting for this struggle between possessors and dispossessed, colonizers and colonized, humanizing and dehumanizing forces. In periods like this, praxis serves as a goad to theory, and theory to praxis. New social movements arise that crystallize the demands of new human groups. To the degree that social action becomes radical, revolutionary, social theory does the same—and vice versa. Old idols fall and carefully fabricated myths crumble. There then arises the necessity for a radical criticism of the existing order.

We can feel this rebirth of a radical consciousness today in the United States,[2] in Santo Domingo,[3] and in Cuba[4] (as could be expected). Although only in the case of Cuba can it be said that social revolution has triumphed, I mention all three countries because in Quisqueya a revolution was undertaken but frustrated, while in North American society one is being born.

Although the same cannot be said of Puerto Rico when speaking of revolution, our island cannot remain on the margin of what is happening in the rest of the world.

[2] See in this regard the interesting collection of essays edited by Barton J. Bernstein, *Towards a New Past: Dissenting Essays in American History* (New York: Pantheon Books, 1968). The development of what has been called the North American new left has given rise to a whole series of books that question the official interpretations of the cold war and the international role of the United States. In this respect the following works deserve to be singled out: David Horowitz, *The Cold War Colossus,* Gar Alperovitz, *Atomic Diplomacy,* Oglesby and Shaull, *Containment and Change,* to mention only the most significant.

[3] In Santo Domingo a group of professors of the Universidad Autónoma de Santo Domingo has undertaken this reexamination of Dominican history, putting in its proper perspective the historiography previously considered sacred. Deserving mention in this respect are the works of Dr. Hugo Tolentino Dipp, *Orígenes, vicisitudes y porvenir de la nacionalidad dominicana* (1962), *Perfil nacionalista de Gregorio Luperón* (1963); of Professor Franklin J. Franco, *República Dominicana: clases, crisis y comandos* (1965); and the works of Dr. Francisco Antonio Avelino. Almost all these works have been published in the magazine *Ahora,* which thus becomes a rich documentary source for every student of Dominican society.

[4] Naturally the work of reexamining the history of Cuba is titanic. In the journals *Unión* and *Casa de las Américas* the reader can find material of great value in this regard.

Because although it is true that, as Marx said, "the tradition of past generations weighs like an incubus upon the mind of the living," it is no less certain that many, especially our university youth, are already beginning to shake off the incubus which hangs over their heads. The policy of the colonial powers that have governed us for centuries has always been to isolate us from the rest of the world, to limit us to the narrow scope of the colonial power/colony relationship. But when winds of profound changes are blowing in the colonial power, when its once invincible might is mired down by the indescribable courage of a small, heroic nation, the effect is felt in the colony—belatedly, more slowly than in other places, but unfailingly, inexorably.

In the historic moment in which we live, it is indispensable to fight against the asphyxiating tendency of the anti-historical forces seeking to overwhelm our country while she lies prostrate from a long amnesia that prevents her from recognizing herself in the past. For if separated long enough from her historical roots and the cultural symbols that might identify her as a nation, she will in time be culturally assimilated into the North American nation.

This essay attempts to rescue our libertarian struggles from the obscurity to which they have been relegated by the official historians serving the regime. At the same time, it attempts to outline the pertinent historical responsibilities. Going to the root of our problems as a people, this essay attempts to bring into the open all acts of compliance, collaborationism, and surrender never mentioned in our official history. This will not, of course, be to the liking of many. But at least it will contribute to the cause of historical justice, although true justice will be complete only if our fatherland achieves its final liberation. When that occurs— and it will occur—all those who have known how to suffer and to die for our fatherland will finally be vindicated.

Part I | *Under Spanish Colonialism (1493–1898)*

I | Puerto Rico, Puerto Pobre: The First Three Centuries of Spanish Domination

> What centuries ago was Puerto Rico, Should now be called Puerto Pobre; For whoever seeks gold, silver, or copper there, Will surely find damned little.
> MANUEL DEL PALACIO,
> *Spanish poet of the nineteenth century*

When Christopher Columbus set foot on Borinquén* on November 19, 1493, he found an island with exuberant vegetation, a beautiful bay, and an indigenous population later calculated to be approximately 50,000 by Salvador Brau and some 70,000 by Ricardo Alegría.[1] That the aborigines populating our territory during that period were in a state of civilization inferior to that of the most ad-

---

* Borinquén was the original Taino name for Puerto Rico. (Translator's note)

[1] Concerning this matter, see the note of Dr. Isabel Gutiérrez del Arroyo in her annotated edition of Salvador Brau, *La colonización de Puerto Rico* (San Juan: Instituto de Cultura Puertorriqueña, 1966), p. 134, note 62. This book by Brau was originally published in 1907.

vanced indigenous cultures of the New World is demonstrated by the fact that "no West Indian cultural group knew the architectural use of stone, nor how to work metals, and therefore monumental construction and the technique and richness of gold and silver work were skills alien to all of them."[2] Possessing a rudimentary social organization, the native inhabitants of Puerto Rico belonged to the cultural group of the Tainos. Their origin was South American Aruacan. They had a fundamentally agrarian culture, their economy based primarily on the cultivation of yucca and the manufacture of cassava.

Once colonization began, a regime based on the exploitation of the indigenous population was not long in coming. Bent on the exploitation of Puerto Rico's meager gold resources, the Spaniards made the Indians their principal instrument of labor. A European population that in 1510 did not exceed three hundred people immediately converted the Indian into the object of merciless exploitation. With the characteristic brutality of the colonizer, the Spanish colonist imposed on the Indians the iniquitous and painful condition of being strangers on their own soil. In regard to the Spaniards, Brau says: "Received as guests, they made themselves absolute lords. To the cordiality of feeling with which they had been greeted on their arrival, they responded by taking possession of the land, which, after all, being virgin and exceedingly fertile would have provided sufficient food for all; but with the possession of the land came the thirst for gold, and with it the forced labor of the natives, disturbance of their family life, alteration of their

[2] Felipe Pichardo Moya, *Los aborígenes de las Antillas* (México: Fondo de Cultura Económica, 1956), p. 12. See also in this regard the *Relación* of Brother Ramón Pané about the antiquities of the Indians (1505), published as a fragment in E. Fernández Méndez, ed., *Crónicas de Puerto Rico* (San Juan, 1957), Vol. I.

simple customs, scorn for their beliefs—the loss, in short, of all that which constituted the human personality in its exercise of the free functions granted it by the Supreme Creator."[3] The result of these acts was a sudden decline in the native population. There occurred what Pichardo Moya calls "the early extinction of the West Indians," due primarily "to the clash with the new civilization and the cruelty of the conquest."[4] But it did not happen without the natives first rebelling against the colonizers, with whom they engaged in bloody battles before giving up, overwhelmed by a technology more advanced than their own. The insurrections led by the chieftains Gueybaná and Guarionex in defense of their legitimate rights deserve special mention. Although their rebellions were crushed, they established as of that moment that the native inhabitants of Borinquén were not in the least docile.

The extinction of the natives around the middle of the sixteenth century made the introduction of a new type of labor—that of black slaves—indispensable. With the depletion of the Puerto Rican gold deposits and the discovery of rich beds of the precious metal in Perú and México, the economy of Puerto Rico came to depend primarily on the cultivation of sugar cane and the creation of sugar refineries. Black slavery was adopted as the mode of production. As a matter of fact, in the instructions given by Ferdinand and Isabella to the governor of the Indies, Nicolás de Ovando, on September 16, 1501, "the entrance of black slaves into the overseas colonies was authorized for the first time in American history."[5]

[3] Brau, *op. cit.*, p. 141.

[4] *Op. cit.*, p. 28.

[5] Luis M. Díaz Soler, *La esclavitud negra en Puerto Rico* (Río Piedras: Editorial Universitaria, 1965), p. 20. "In regard to the slave trade," says Díaz Soler, "a *license* was an authorization by the king to transport

The substitution of black for Indian labor established the slave system of production in Puerto Rico. Social classes were soon structured on the principle of the master-slave relationship. It was not until 1873 that slavery was abolished in Puerto Rico. From 1501 to 1873 was a period of penury for the black slave, while during this period the slave-owning minority sought by all means possible to perpetuate the regime of privilege which guaranteed them the forced labor of large contingents of workers.

Thus does Brother Íñigo Abbad y Lasierra, the first historian of Puerto Rico—writing in his *Historia geográfica, civil y natural de la isla de San Juan Bautista de Puerto Rico* in 1796—describe the situation of the blacks under the slave system of production:

Some of the blacks on this island were brought from the African coasts, others are creoles, descendants of the former, without any racial mixture: the first are all sold as slaves; in the second group there are many free men; when all is said and done there is nothing more ignominious on this island than to be a black or one of their descendants: a white insults any of them with impunity and in the most contemptible terms; some masters treat them with despicable harshness, getting pleasure out of keeping the tyrant's rod always raised and thereby causing disloyalty, desertion, and suicide; others regard them with excessive esteem and affection, making them tools of luxury and vanity, employing them only in domestic service; but even these blacks eventually suffer the harshness of slavery when their master dies and they are passed on to another, or because he has become fond of something else. Then a narrow, miserable hut serves him as a dwelling, his bed is a cot of cords or slats, more appropriate for torturing the body than for resting it;

slaves for the purposes of increasing the population, supplying the work force necessary for mining and agricultural development and providing overseas subjects with servants." *Ibid.*, p. 27.

the coarse cloth which covers part of his bare body neither defends him from the heat of day nor from the harmful night dew; the food that is given him—cassava, sweet potatoes, bananas and such things—scarcely suffices to sustain his wretched existence; deprived of everything, he is condemned to continuous labor, always subject to experiencing the cruelty of his greedy or fierce master.[6]

From this description one can see what the condition of a black slave was a little less than a century before his emancipation.

After the slave, the next instrument of labor was the free day laborer. At the top of the social pyramid was the owner of land and labor. The economic situation was such that even for the landowner it entailed great hardship. Let's take a look at some figures. The first census undertaken in Puerto Rico (1530) showed the following balance: whites, 369; free "protected" Indians,* 473; Indian slaves, 675; black African slaves: males, 1,168; females, 355. Total, 3,040 inhabitants.[7] With the discovery of gold in Perú, the colony ran the risk of becoming almost totally depopulated, and the governor had to take drastic measures to prevent any future exodus. Confronted with Spain's commercial monopoly, obliged to trade only through the port of Seville, deprived of rich gold deposits, and subject to the implacable onslaught of hurricanes, the island was practically abandoned to its fate by the colonial power.

[6] I refer here to the edition put out by the Editorial Universitaria de la Universidad de Puerto Rico (1959) with a preliminary study by Dr. Isabel Gutiérrez del Arroyo. I quote from page 183.

* The "indio encomendado" was free largely in a euphemistic sense, as he was entrusted for his welfare to a Spanish colonist, who was also responsible for his religious and secular education. He was often, as a matter of fact, used as a laborer by his "protector." (Translator's note)

[7] Salvador Brau, *Historia de Puerto Rico* (San Juan: Editorial Coquí, 1966), pp. 70–71. This book was originally published in 1904.

Twenty years after colonization had begun, says Brau, "the gold was giving out in the mines; two cyclones in one year razed the countryside, leveled the huts, and destroyed livestock and cultivated fields; misery was devastating the country and panic was invading the spirits of the people."[8]

In 1582, a military garrison was established at El Morro, thus converting Puerto Rico into a military base. In 1586, the so-called Mexican allowance* was set up to provide the island with an annual sum from the treasury of México. During the sixteenth and seventeenth centuries the isolation and economic indigence of Puerto Rico did not prevent the English as well as the Dutch from attempting to take over the island, although both failed. Contraband flourished as a means of avoiding the Spanish commercial monopoly. In 1673 a tax list of San Juan revealed the following figures: 820 whites, 667 slaves, 304 free mulattoes. Total: 1,791 inhabitants. The population was so small that the governor found it necessary to ask the mother country for a shipment of white people to the island.

By this time the Spanish Empire was already in open decadence. While capitalism and the bourgeoisie had already appeared as historical forces in England, France, Holland, and Belgium, Spain remained on the margin of capitalist development and consequently on the margin of the economic development which with the passing of time would make of Europe the world center of the capitalist system. Referring to the Spanish Empire and the causes of its early decadence, Brenan informs us:

Too easily and with excessive rapidity Spain went through an immense inheritance without possessing sufficient economic

---

[8] Brau, *La colonización*, p. 395.
* *situado* in Spanish. (Author's note to the English edition)

or cultural preparation; and this acted like a drug. Spanish pride, belief in miracles, scorn for work, impatience, and a taste for destruction, although they already existed in Castilla, received a powerful impulse at that time. From 1580 on, the few woolen mills which existed in the country disappeared, and the Spanish became a nation of people living on a fixed income, a nation of gentlemen who lived in parasitic dependence on the gold and silver which came to them from the Indies and from the industry of the Netherlands.[9]

This mentality of a people living off others, maintained by the shipment of wealth from colonies to the mother country, would allow Spain to watch the rest of the world plunge into an intense economic activity that would undermine the foundations of the *ancien régime* of Europe and would profoundly affect reactionary Spain, the standard-bearer of Catholicism and of the Counter Reformation.

The eighteenth century was the century of two great revolutions: that of the United States (1776) and that of France (1789). This century saw the germination and growth of the forces which in the nineteenth century would give the final checkmate to the Spanish Empire in America. For Puerto Rico, the eighteenth century was characterized by a long period of peace during which, in the words of Tomás Blanco, "the foundations of Puerto Rican society were laid down."[10] San Juan became the second stronghold of America: commerce was liberalized, the cultivation of coffee was introduced, smuggling was intensified, and the population increased considerably. According to O'Reilly's Memorandum of 1765, the total population was figured at

[9] Gerald Brenan, *El laberinto español* (Paris: Ediciones Ruedo Ibérico, 1962), p. 11.

[10] Tomás Blanco, *Prontuario histórico de Puerto Rico* (San Juan: Biblioteca de Autores Puertorriqueños, 1935), p. 43.

44,883, with 5,037 slaves. By 1776 it had increased to 70,000, by 1786 to 96,000, 1796 to 133,000 and in 1800 the island had to reckon with 155,426 inhabitants.[11]

In the work previously cited, Brother Íñigo Abbad verifies that at this time (1782) the Puerto Rican economy revolved around sugar cane, cotton, tobacco, and coffee.[12] The economic and political frameworks were the same. All power resided in the governor of the island, "from whom come all the orders, as the military and political governor, and as superintendent of the branches of the public treasury and the royal vice-patronate. He may intervene in the affairs of parishes, in the accounts of personal income, factories, and churches; he disposes of troops and militia for defense, reviews them, arbitrates in their disputes, presides over the commissions of the public treasury, and is the superior judge over all the justices on the island."[13] In short, all authority—political and economic as well as military—was concentrated in the hands of the governor. This condition of centralized authority would characterize Spanish colonialism throughout the years of its existence. In fact, militarism and authoritarianism would march hand in hand in the government of the colony until almost the last moment.

In *Insularismo,* Pedreira calls the first three centuries of Spanish domination a period of "formation and passive accumulation" in the development of our nation.[14] As a matter of fact, the sixteenth, seventeenth, and eighteenth centuries were a period of gestation for our nation; they

11 *Ibid.,* pp. 48–49.
12 *Op. cit.,* p. 161.
13 *Op. cit.,* p. 146.
14 Antonio S. Pedreira, *Insularismo,* 2nd ed. (San Juan: Biblioteca de Autores Puertorriqueños, 1942), p. 15.

were the stages during which preparations for the future of our nation were made. The very nature of the works published on our island—like the *Historia* of Abbad—testify to the fact that something called Puerto Rico was taking shape. Actually, Abbad himself tells us that by then "they give the name of creole indistinctly to everyone born on the island, no matter what race or mixture he comes from. The Europeans are called whites or, to use their own expression, *men of the other band.*"[15] Here is the distinction between the creole and the European, the native son and the foreigner, the Puerto Rican and the "man of the other band." The Puerto Rican is already taking his first steps.

[15] *Op. cit.,* p. 181.

2 | Reform or Revolution: The Nineteenth Century

The autonomist program can be refuted by one simple
sentence: "Spain cannot give what she does not have."
BETANCES

The nineteenth century marks the decisive period in our
formation as a people, a nationality. Literature, music,
painting—in short, all the cultural expressions—offer evidence that in this century a culture we can call Puerto
Rican came together.[1] Pedreira calls this period—which
concludes with the North American occupation of 1898—
one of "awakening and beginning," for if "in the first
moment we were nothing but a faithful extension of Hispanic culture, in the second we began to reveal an independent manner within that culture."[2] This awakening of a
national consciousness is evident in many ways but especially in the increasingly sharp distinction made between
the peninsular Spaniard and the native-born creole. This
distinction—which under the prevailing regime of privilege
placed the well-to-do Spaniard against the Puerto Rican—

[1] See F. Manrique Cabrera, *Historia de la literatura puertorriqueña*
(1965) and María Teresa Babín, *Panorama de la cultura puertorriqueña* (1958).
[2] Pedreira, *Insularismo*, p. 15.

soon took on the character of a social struggle translated into political terms. As Cruz Monclova says in his monumental *Historia de Puerto Rico en el siglo XIX,* by the beginning of the century the liberals and the conservatives had already arisen in Puerto Rico—as a reflection, to be sure, of the same groups in the colonial power, but more or less clearly defined on the basis of their economic and social situation. "In the heart of the conservative sector," says Cruz Monclova, "were the civil and military leaders of the colony: the great shop owners and merchants, generally Spanish, who had control over relations with peninsular Spain's exporters and the means to finance and buy the island's products; their agents and associates; and some landlords and professionals who, in conjunction with the shop owners and merchants, formed the demographic element of greatest economic importance in the colony. In the liberal reformist sector were grouped the majority of the professionals, small farmers, cattlemen, native industrialists, and merchants . . . and the great mass of the middle and lower classes, all of whom as a unit constituted the demographic element of greatest social importance in the island."[3]

As a basic consequence of Spanish-American independence, in Puerto Rico we have the presence of the *independentista* or separatist sector, determined from the very beginning to liberate Puerto Rico and also Cuba from the colonial condition of which each was a victim. Thus extreme unconditionalists or assimilationists, reformists or autonomists, and revolutionaries or *independentistas* were

[3] Lidio Cruz Monclova, *Historia de Puerto Rico en el siglo XIX,* three volumes (Río Piedras: Editorial Universitaria, 1957–1964). Vol. 1, pp. 42–43. From now on, I will refer to this work as Cruz Monclova, *Historia.*

the three basic political forces in the nineteenth century. Nevertheless, it is important to underline the fact that Puerto Rican–creole opinion was divided basically between the liberal-reformist and the radical-independent bands. Although there were Puerto Ricans involved in it, the conservative-unconditionalist sector was the representative of the extreme right and, as its name clearly indicates, was unconditionally loyal to Spain in the face of any attempt— whether reformist or radical—to alter the status quo of the colony.

It is truly interesting to see how these same tendencies are evident even today, although the colonial power has changed. It is of particular interest to the student to see how little the arguments of the unconditionalists (now annexationists) as well as those of the autonomists (now "commonwealthers") have changed. But we will take this up later. I emphasize this fact now so that the reader will later see how appropriate to our situation is the philosopher's observation that he who does not know his history is forced to repeat it.

The issue raised above enables us to see with total clarity the effects of our eternal problem—the colonial situation.⁴ This situation is manifest more or less clearly through the hegemony⁵ which the mother country held over the politics

---

⁴ See in this regard the interesting article by George Balandier, "The Colonial Situation—A Theoretical Approach" (1951), in Immanuel Wallerstein (editor), *Social Change: The Colonial Situation* (New York: John Wiley, 1966), pp. 35–61. The typology of Balandier is applicable essentially in the case of the African experience, although it does have relevance with respect to other countries in a similar situation.

⁵ In this instance I follow the concept of *hegemony* offered by Gramsci, as succinctly explained by Genovese: "the apparently spontaneous loyalty which a ruling class evokes in the masses through its cultural position and its capacity to promote its cosmic vision as the general will."

of the period through various political groups whether unconditionalist or autonomist—whose needs she satisfied in return for support. From this observation, a general political axiom can be stated: those groups possessing a monopoly on the material and spiritual resources of a society to a great extent manage it so that those conceptions which best coincide with their interests prevail. In the case of a colony—which by its very nature is the object of exploitation by the colonial power—the purpose of every colonial administration is and always has been to overcome by all possible means the resistance of the subjugated people. To accomplish this goal requires the active control by those in power of the cultural and educational systems, but also requires the use of a more or less flexible practice of concessions, that serve as palliatives in the maintenance of the colonial condition. The policy of assimilating the colony—accepted by unconditionalists and autonomists alike up until the last moment, when a defeated Spain conceded autonomy as a last recourse—is nothing but politics predicated on the most perfect colonialization (the term as used by Fanon) of the inhabitants of the colony. The achievement of assimilation—i.e., the loss of identity of a people on fusing with a subjugating nation—is not just the beginning of every colonialist policy but also its goal or purpose, not just its point of departure but also its point of arrival.

Let us analyze, by the way, the colonial policy of Spain with respect to Cuba and Puerto Rico. First, extermination of the indigenous race. Then, enslavement of the black race. Finally, oppression of the creole, or, with his consent,

---

Eugene D. Genovese, "Marxian Interpretations of the Slave South," in Barton J. Bernstein, *op. cit.,* p. 123.

use of the creole in the governing process—as long as he served the interests of the colonial power faithfully, that is.

In this sense, during the nineteenth century many profound historical events occurred, the lessons of which are still important. We have said that up until the last moment, until the eleventh hour of the North American intervention and the triumph of the Cuban rebels, the reformist autonomism represented by Baldorioty and Muñoz Rivera (its two great leaders) did not receive anything from the Spanish government except perhaps ratification of the policy— enunciated with the restoration of the absolutism of Ferdinand VII—of governing at all times through the aid of the unconditionalists. In this sense, it was of little consequence whether the regime in power in Spain was liberal or conservative, republican or monarchist. Like all imperialists imbued with that elementary principle of politics—do not voluntarily give up power—the Spanish governments of the period strove uselessly to preserve at all costs an empire whose decadence was clearly evident. This preservation involved nothing but perpetuation of the regime of privilege and oppression that Bolívar had banished from the continent, but that continued to be put into effect in the two Antilles as one more anachronism linked to the colonial power.

Unconditionalism, as representative of the hard line, is but an echo of those elements within the Spanish political scene that most benefited from the continuation of a system where any reform, any concession, presaged imminent disaster. In *El Boletín Mercantil,* the news organ of the Spanish Unconditionalist party, Pérez Moris continually declares himself in support of clerical, authoritarian, militarist, monarchic Spain, although that does not keep him from lending his conditional support to any government holding power in the mother country. As Cruz Monclova says, influenced by the reactionary ideas of Bonald and De Maistre, unconditionalism tries to do nothing other than to say *No* to the principles of the bourgeois revolution set forth in France in 1789. As the standard-bearers of extreme conservatism, the unconditionalists subscribed to the thesis of Burke that tradition and custom represent the distillation of the wisdom of a people and that consequently they should not be altered or changed except very slowly. Like their namesakes of today, the conservative unconditionalists saw separatists everywhere: they accused the autonomists of being *independentistas* in disguise, and they were bitter enemies of any attempts to liberalize relations between the colony and the colonial power. Like the radical right of our times, they were continually sounding the alarm, motivated by imagined or real conspiracies against the general order; they supported without hesitation the Civil Guard and the Institute of Volunteers*; and they insisted that the free diffusion of ideas was a constant threat to the established system. Perhaps no other document of that epoch illustrates so well as the book by Pérez Moris y Cueto, *Historia de la insurrección de Lares* (Barcelona, 1872) the characteristic traits of unconditionalism: its perennial lack of confidence in everything Puerto Rican, its irreducible hostility toward social and political reforms, its insidious alarmist oratory, its continual use of innuendo and calumny to diminish the prestige of the opposition. This book—whose main thesis is that our great insurrection of the nineteenth century was insignificant; worse, of criminal character—will be rewritten with the necessary historical reservations by those who have the dubious honor of dar-

---

* A kind of militia created by the Spanish authorities for purposes of repression of Puerto Rican liberals and radicals. (Author's note to the English edition)

ing, in the twentieth century, to insult the still-inconclusive struggle of our people for independence.

Perhaps of even greater interest than the theory and actions of the conservatives of the period—a faithful reflection, as we have said, of their namesakes in Spain, although at times in their Hispanizing zeal they exceeded the very Spaniards of peninsular Spain—are the theory and actions of the Puerto Rican autonomists of the nineteenth century. I say this because in the twentieth century the autonomists finally came to power through an alliance with the North American colonial regime, a taking of power which had already been initiated under the Spanish government in the frustrated Autonomist Charter of 1897. Then, as now, reformist autonomism developed within the restricted framework of the prevailing colonial system in order to try to reform it "from within." In accord with the liberalism that served as its guide, its purpose was to achieve certain changes of a quantitative rather than qualitative nature— changes that might result in a greater dose of self-government for the oppressed side of the equation without, however, fundamentally changing the colonial power/colony relationship. Or, to use a phrase of Ortega y Gasset, autonomist groups attempted merely to alleviate some of the most flagrant abuses of the colonial system without attacking the uses of the system at their root.

As for ideology, Puerto Rican autonomism took its present form as early as 1812, in the famous instructions of the municipal government of San Germán to the Congress of Cádiz[6] to "inform the government about the social, economic and political problems of the islands and to propose *special laws appropriate for their happiness.*"[7] This philos-

[6] In the Plan of Instruction for the Economic and Political Government of the Overseas Provinces presented by the departing deputy to the

ophy became a political platform with the creation of the Liberal Reformist party. (Later, in 1887, the party changed its name to the Puerto Rican Autonomist party.) Its most distinguished spokesmen were Baldorioty de Castro, Rafael María de Labra, and, once Baldorioty was dead, Luis Muñoz Rivera and José Celso Barbosa. As I already indicated above, it was not until 1897, on the eve of the North American occupation and concurrent with the triumph of the Cuban revolution, that the colonial power decided at last to grant autonomy to Puerto Rico. Throughout the long period from 1812 to the end of the century the autonomists faced defeat after defeat. The continued struggle testified to their strong ability to withstand, in the name of reformism, the worst criticisms from the colonial power and her unconditionalists in Puerto Rico. Each time a change in the government of the colonial power brought with it the hope for a more liberal regime, the Puerto Rican autonomists showed their joy—only to discover soon after that as far as colonial policy went, there was no difference between the attitudes of the liberals and the conservatives, nor was there an appreciable difference between the two Spanish politicians who were to take turns in power from 1885 on: Antonio Cánovas del Castillo and Práxedes Mateo Sagasta.

In reality, a superficial analysis of Spanish politics during the nineteenth century demonstrates the accuracy of Betances' observation to the autonomists that "Spain cannot give what she does not have." Bled by civil wars and

---

Congress, José María Quiñones, in 1823, and in the conclusions of the famous Committee on Information of 1867, composed by Segundo Ruiz Belvis, Francisco Mariano Quiñones, and José Julián Acosta.

7 Cruz Monclova, *Historia,* Vol. I, p. 486.

class struggles, the Spain of that period could not, in fact, grant her colonies a more open, generous regime. The truth is that there was nothing to hope for from Spanish liberalism because this liberalism was already occupied with the process of consolidating the achievements of the bourgeois revolution, which had reached Spain relatively late (around 1868), and it was operating against a vigorous push from peasants and the proletariat.[8] Moreover, it is not particularly bold to make the general observation that historical experience offers evidence to the fact that there is nothing to hope for from liberals when it is a matter of the colonial power/colony relationship. The reason for this is clear: liberalism is the ideology of the bourgeoisie or the ruling class in the capitalist system of production. And this system needs colonies—or neo-colonies—for the perpetuation of its world hegemony. Hence imperialism has always been the Achilles' heel of liberalism, even in the cases of its most advanced exponents. Thus, for example, the most celebrated English liberal of that period, John Stuart Mill, a spirit tuned to the intellectual currents of his time, still believed that colonial peoples were in need of "tutelage" by the industrially more advanced nations. In his famous *Essay on Liberty* he wrote:

It is, perhaps, hardly necessary to say that this doctrine is meant to apply only to human beings in the maturity of their faculties. We are not speaking of children, or of young persons below the age which the law may fix as that of manhood or

[8] See in this regard Ignacio Fernández de Castro, *De las Cortes de Cádiz al Plan de Desarrollo, 1808–1966* (Paris: Ediciones Ruedo Ibérico, 1968), chapters 1–5. Also Gerald Brenan, *El laberinto español* (Paris: Ediciones Ruedo Ibérico, 1962), and Melchor Fernández Almagro, *Historia política de la España contemporánea*, Vol. 1, 1868–1885; Vol. 2, 1885–1897; Vol. 3, 1897–1902 (Madrid: Alianza Editorial, 1968).

womanhood . . . For the same reason, we may leave out of
consideration those backward states of society in which the race
itself may be considered in its nonage . . . Despotism is a
legitimate mode of government in dealing with barbarians,
provided the end be their improvement, and the means justified
by actually effecting that end. Liberty, as a principle, has no
application to any state of things anterior to the time when man-
kind have become capable of being improved by free and equal
discussion.[9]

It is clear that for the colonial power and her interests the
maturation of the society of the colony takes a long time,
perhaps centuries. In this sense, the liberalism prevailing in
the colonial power is, by its own nature, given to operating
with a double standard: one for the colony and another for
the dominating force in the relationship. Thence its inveter-
ate hypocrisy . . .

The matter becomes even more serious when it is a question of liberalism in the colony. Colonial liberalism is above
all an intellectual current that not only reaches the colony
late, but is in itself a paradox in a regime which is antiliberal out of necessity and by tradition. Since the conditions which nurture the growth of liberalism in a colonial
power are almost totally absent, liberal attitudes toward the
governing of colonies have absolutely no political support
within the colonial power. Thus though these ideas manifest
themselves in the writings of political philosophers, they
often die there. (In a way, one can say that colonial liberalism is seeking to reform the unreformable, that it moves in
a phantom-ridden world where the most insignificant lib-

[9] *On Liberty,* in Marshall Cohen, ed., *The Philosophy of John Stuart
Mill* (New York: Modern Library, 1961), pp. 197–98. This essay was
originally published in 1859.

eralizing concession of the colonial power serves as a source of hope for future political demands, only to crash repeatedly against the barricade of an invincible system predicated on its antithesis.) The liberal creole, who still believes that the colonial power can liberalize its thinking, is therefore one of the most imaginative forgers of illusions, illusions which day after day are encouraged rather than exposed by the crumbs granted by the regime. Puerto Rican liberal reformism, in the nineteenth as well as in the twentieth century, provides substantial proof of this.[10]

Two historical examples will illustrate the foregoing: the creation of the Committee on Information in 1867, and the events which led to the repression of the autonomists in 1887.

One of the most glorious pages in nineteenth-century Puerto Rican liberalism was written in defense of the abolition of slavery, "with or without indemnification,"[11] and in support of the rights of the Puerto Rican people to self-government[12] by Ruiz Belvis, Acosta, and Quiñones of the

[10] See José A. Gautier Dapena, *Trayectoria del pensamiento liberal puertorriqueño en el siglo XIX* (San Juan: Instituto de Cultura Puertorriqueña, 1963).

[11] See Ruiz Belvis, Acosta, and Quiñones, *Proyecto para la abolición de la esclavitud en Puerto Rico,* with an introduction and notes by Luis M. Díaz Soler (San Juan: Instituto de Cultura Puertorriqueña, 1959). Also, Luis M. Díaz Soler, *Historia de la esclavitud negra en Puerto Rico* (Río Piedras: Editorial Universitaria, 1965).

[12] The demands of the commissioners of Cuba and Puerto Rico were summarized in the following general program: 1) decentralized municipalities with their own governments elected by direct popular vote; 2) provincial districts with delegations and councils organized similarly to those of peninsular Spain and with the extension of powers demanded by the special circumstances of the islands; 3) provincial district governors in whose election (which involved the civil governor alone) the people have some influence; 4) island-run corporations with sufficient

famous Committee on Information. Here is the reply of the Spanish government as Cruz Monclova describes it to us:

Against the recommendations of the liberal as well as the conservative and governmental commission members, a decree was promulgated by which 6 percent on the net product of real and industrial property was fixed as the standard contribution; the governor was authorized to set additional taxes which he considered necessary to cover the needs of the municipal governments; and the municipal governments were also empowered to arrange the levy of new tributes up to 12 percent if the ones set were not sufficient to cover expenses. And all without their recommending the suppression of the indirect customs tax.[13]

---

power to deliberate on and propose solutions to everything which directly and particularly interests the islands; 5) representation in the National Congress for all matters which in conjunction with the other provinces may affect the former; 6) the administration of justice organized in such a way that it adequately services the needs of those countries' inhabitants and keeps them from having to go to the mother country for aid; 7) finances, bookkeeping, statistics, civil and property registration, taxes, and public archives organized, regulated, and watched over by competent employees; 8) instead of being detrimental, naturalization, settlement, and continuous residence in those countries be considered a reason for preference in obtaining jobs there and a guarantee of better performance in the fulfillment of pledges; 9) absolute separation of the civil government and the military command; 10) representation of the executive power of a civil governor; 11) power of the government to station in the Antilles at the expense of the national budget the sea and land forces that it considers suitable, and to name higher officers with all powers necessary for command but with no authority conflictions with that of the government or allowing them to take precedent over the representative of the executive, who will always be considered the highest authority of the respective island; 12) inviolability of constitutional freedoms, rights and guarantees and predetermination of those cases in which they will be able to "suspend some, the best defense of liberties and rights." Cruz Monclova, *Historia*, Vol. 1, pp. 553–54. These demands fell on deaf ears. Spain did nothing with respect to them.

[13] Cruz Monclova, *Historia*, Vol. 1, pp. 557–58.

In the colony, Governor Marchesi responded to the appeal of the liberals with generally repressive measures and finally exiled many of those involved under multiple sentences. (It was at that moment when, finally convinced of the futility of reform, Ruiz Belvis and Betances fully committed themselves to the revolutionary path.) Nonetheless, the liberals continued to support a program of reform, incapable as they were of seeing that a system corrupted at its roots would never accede to true reform without outside pressure.

The autonomists withstood arbitrary acts of abuse during the period from 1865 to 1887, with the exception of the ephemeral flirtation with real power which carried Baldorioty de Castro to the Spanish Cortes* in 1870 and terminated with the fall of the Spanish Republic in 1874.[14] Eighteen hundred eighty-seven has been justly called "the terrible year of '87."[15] Due to the usurious practices of the Spaniards, the Puerto Ricans developed a secret organization known as The Boycotter, the purpose of which was to boycott Spanish firms. The Spaniards retaliated in turn with measures restricting credit. Faced with this situation, the unconditionalists spurred the governor, Romualdo Palacios, to use his powers to repress those responsible for this uprising. As a consequence, the fiercest repressive measures were directed against the autonomists. Among many other forms of torture, the colonial government instituted componente† as well as arbitrary imprisonment, and placed

---

* The Cortes is the Spanish Parliament. (Translator's note)

[14] See Lidio Cruz Monclova, *Baldorioty de Castro* (San Juan: Instituto de Cultura Puertorriqueña, 1966).

[15] See Antonio S. Pedreira, *El año terrible del 87* (San Juan: Biblioteca de Autores Puertorriqueños, 1935).

† Various types of torture used by the Spaniards to force "good behavior" on the part of the Puerto Ricans. (Translator's note)

obstacles of every kind before the autonomist flock in 1887. Palacios attempted to finish the task by imprisoning the entire autonomist leadership—starting with Baldorioty—and would have had them executed if his dismissal had not been decreed by the government of Spain before the deed was done. But instead of rebelling against the injustices of the system, the autonomists attributed its misdeeds solely to Palacios, and once Palacios was gone, hastened to declare their loyalty to Spain and to the new governor, Contreras Martínez. Julián Blanco Sosa, the spokesman of the autonomist commission sent to interview the governor, said:

In the solemn and special circumstances in which Your Excellency has just taken charge of the government of the island, the Autonomist party believed it to be its duty, which it gladly fulfilled, to present itself to reiterate once again testimony of its profound loyalty to the mother country, to the institutions which govern her, and to the high powers of the State, of its consideration and respect for Your Excellency, who so worthily represents those powers in this Antille, and of its definite, considered love of peace and order, without which progress and all social welfare are impossible.[16]

Celebrated and published by the unconditionalist organ, *El Boletín Mercantil*, this obsequious declaration indicates to what point the liberals of that time—like their contemporaries—saw in the Spanish regime not the basic evil of colonialism but the passing evil of a benign sickness capable of being cured by an effective palliative.

Nevertheless, whatever the philosophical differences between liberals and conservatives, unconditionalists and autonomists, they were to be forgotten as soon as revolu-

[16] Cruz Monclova, *Historia*, Vol. 3, p. 177. The quote is from *El Boletín Mercantil*.

tionary action placed the colonial system in danger. Whenever that happened—as, for example, in 1868 with the Cry of Lares, and the 1896 Yauco uprising—the autonomists closed ranks with the conservatives to roundly condemn attempts at emancipation. Moreover, when it was a matter of defending the continuation of a system which they themselves recognized as unjust, the autonomists rivaled the conservatives in the harshness of their invective and the length of their prison terms. Although accused by the unconditionalists of being separatists in disguise, the liberals—Muñoz Rivera offers a good example of this—outdid each other in pledging their unconditional love of Spain. In the crucial moments when the ruling regime found itself threatened, there was no essential difference between Tyrians and Trojans. It appeared to be of little importance that the colonial power perpetuated "cunerism,"[17] allowed widespread electoral fraud, bossism, authoritarianism, administrative arbitrariness, police and military brutality. It was essential to show unconditional loyalty to the colonial power. A palpable sign of this is how efficient even then was the "colonization" of the Puerto Rican—the destruction of his self-confidence and the squelching of his rebelliousness, even in the cases of those liberals who were spokesmen of the most advanced ideas of their time.

After abolition of slavery by the Cortes had been obtained in 1873—the maximum achievement of Puerto Rican liberalism in the nineteenth century—autonomism continued its patient, slow fight for colonial reform. Tomás

---

[17] "Cunerism," Cruz Monclova tells us, was "the evil practice of the Ministry of designating from Madrid as candidates for deputies for Puerto Rico people who—even though they may have felt well disposed toward the island—not only had not been born there, but were not familiar with her problems." *Historia,* Vol. 2, p. 199.

Blanco says: "While Cuba was taking up arms for the defense of colonial interests and the cause of freedom, Puerto Rico, unable to imitate her, carried the fight to Parliament, defending not only the freedoms of the island, but also those of the nation and of the other colonies."[18]

In fact, once continental Spanish America had been freed, the role of vanguard in the struggle for freedom in the Antilles was relegated to Cuba. From the Ten Years' War (1868–1878) through the "Little War" and culminating with the War for Independence (which began in 1895), Cuba was the center of the resistance to colonialism that finally ended Spanish domination in the hemisphere.

Puerto Rico, however, did not remain outside the struggle for freedom. If the Cuban revolutionary spirit was personified in the brilliant figure of Martí, the Puerto Rican had its fullest expression in that most remarkable of nineteenth-century Puerto Ricans: Dr. Ramón Emeterio Betances. And if Cuba had her Cry of Yara, Puerto Rico also had her rebel yell, the Cry of Lares. In the rebellious struggle of Ruiz Belvis, Betances, Hostos, Rius Rivera lay the true, authentic spirit of opposition to colonialism and its continuation in our country. Opposed to the compromising spirit of unconditionalism and autonomism, the nineteenth-century Puerto Rican *independentistas* forced a reluctant Spain to grant the ephemeral autonomist government of 1897. But we will return to this subject.

From the very first, Simón Bolívar, the liberator of a continent, intended to free Puerto Rico and Cuba from the Spanish yoke. He demonstrated this intention at the Congress of Panama (1826), and on January 25, 1827, he

---

[18] Tomás Blanco, *Prontuario histórico de Puerto Rico* (San Juan: Biblioteca de Autores Puertorriqueños, 1935), p. 77.

resolved to send an expedition to Puerto Rico and Cuba, hoping to take advantage of the war he felt to be imminent between Spain and England.[19] But the United States declared its determined opposition to any alteration of the status quo in Puerto Rico and Cuba,[20] a position she would maintain throughout the nineteenth century. Bolívar's action provoked the Spanish government in Puerto Rico to invoke "all-embracing powers," which powers continued in force throughout practically all of the remainder of the century. The frustrated expedition of Luis Guillermo Doucoudray Holstein in 1822, which culminated in the execution of Doucoudray's agent, Pedro DuBois, can be said to have had the same effect. By creating alarm in the colonial government, each of these actions stimulated the repressive elements that are the very essence of the colonial nature and made their application more intense.

As we have already pointed out, when General Marchesi ordered the exile of Ruiz Belvis and Betances, they escaped to Saint Thomas and then to New York, where they soon found themselves working as brothers in the cause of the Puerto Rican revolution. In New York, both of them— through Dr. José Francisco Basora—came into contact with the Republican Society of Cuba and Puerto Rico, an association created in 1865, the constitution of which read in part: "only by the force of arms can we wrest from the government and the Spanish nation the right to manage our own affairs, enjoy our liberty, insure and defend our interests, and occupy the position that is due us among the nations of the earth.[21]

[19] See Simón Bolívar, *Documentos* (La Habana: Casa de las Américas, 1964), pp. 317–23.
[20] Antonio Gómez Robledo, *Idea y experiencia de América* (México: Fondo de Cultura Económica, 1958), p. 136.
[21] Quoted in Cruz Monclova, *Historia*, Vol. 1, p. 566.

Sworn to defend until death the independence of Puerto Rico, Ruiz Belvis went off to Chile, where he died mysteriously on November 4, 1967, while Betances began his plotting in Saint Thomas and Santo Domingo.

Like Martí, Betances was convinced that nothing could be won from Spain through appeals for internal reform. As a revolutionary, he saw revolution as the only method of altering the status quo. Like Martí, like Juarez, like Maceo, Betances was what Martinez Estrada calls a "revolutionary by conviction," since these extraordinary men were convinced that "the prevailing legal system in subjugated countries is injustice plainly legalized and sanctified. It is a system of established, canonic violence; and violence represents the only viable way of placing it (the system) in a normal equilibrium, eliminating by the only functioning means the obstacles which make the status quo unchangeable."[22] Betances symbolized the Antillean revolutionary creed. For him the revolution was "the only anchor of salvation," being "that alone which forms men and strengthens nations."[23] His incessant conspiratorial activities resulted in many attempts by others to persecute him. He was continually having to move: Saint Thomas, Santo Domingo (where, when Báez tried to turn him over to the Spanish authorities, he was forced to seek asylum in the

[22] I have used the term to refer to other great revolutionaries of this century: Ernesto "Che" Guevara, Camilo Torres Restrepo, and Pedro Albizu Campos. I refer the reader to my essays, "Pedro Albizu Campos, o el sacrificio del valor y el valor del sacrificio," *Cuadernos Americanos* (January–February, 1966), and "Ernesto Guevara y Camilo Torres: revolucionarios por convicción," in *Casa de las Américas,* no. 47 (1968).

[23] Luis Bonafoux, *Betances* (Barcelona: Imprenta Modelo, 1901), p. 439. See also Carlos N. Carreras, *Betances, el antillano proscrito* (San Juan: Editorial Club de la Prensa, 1961), and Ada Suárez Díaz, *El doctor Ramón Emeterio Betances: su vida y su obra* (San Juan: Ateneo Puertorriqueño, 1968).

North American consulate), Curaçao, Haiti. Betances was the chief organizer and the intellectual and tangible inspiration of the Cry of Lares. On July 16, 1867, he circulated in Puerto Rico the following proclamation, which, although signed by "The Revolutionary Committee," seems to be the work of Betances:

> Puerto Ricans . . . Your brothers who have left have conspired—and they should conspire—because one day the colonial regime on our island must end; because Puerto Rico must finally be free—like the continent, like Santo Domingo.
>
> They should conspire without any letup, and we with them, because we suffer from lack of action and intervention in public affairs; because, overwhelmed by the weight of taxes which we do not vote for, we see them distributed among a number of inept Spanish employees and the so-called National Treasury, while the natives of the land, more deserving, work only at subordinate or unpaid jobs, and while the island lacks roads, schools, and other means of intellectual and material development.
>
> We ought to conspire, because in exchange for these certain evils—the insults we suffer daily, the obstacles which everywhere fence us in, the immorality which slavery sows in its path—the material order does not gain and increase in proportion to effort expended, but rather stagnates or drags along sluggishly. Finally, we should conspire because there is nothing to hope for from Spain nor from her government. They cannot give us what they do not have.[24]

Here is a masterful exposition of the complaints against Spain, joined with a no less vehement justification of the conspiratorial or revolutionary path. Faced with such a

[24] The proclamation in question is reproduced in Pérez Moris y Cueto's book, *Historia de la insurrección de Lares* (Barcelona, 1872), pp. 282–83.

regime, compromise, accommodation, optimism, and conciliation were not appropriate. On this issue, Betances—like every other revolutionary—was intransigent. He did not permit bungling compromises. Like Martí, he considered that "in her present state and with her current problems," Puerto Rico, like Cuba, had reached "the point of understanding again the inadequacy of a conciliatory policy" and that consequently there existed, as the Apostle (Martí) expressed it years later in a letter he wrote to Máximo Gómez, on July 20, 1882, "the necessity of a violent revolution."

In Puerto Rico Betances conspired with several societies whose abolitionist and emancipative orientation had necessarily to remain secret. The period from the moment of his exile (July 1867) to the insurrection of Lares (September 1868) was one of intense activity, devoted to collecting funds, purchasing military stores and weapons, editing proclamations, etc. Like Martí, Betances did not let up in his revolutionary activity; like the Apostle, he wanted to die with his boots on.

The insurrection of Lares was meant to explode on September 29, 1868, the day on which the slaves celebrated their festival of Saint Michael. The secret societies agreed to work together to strike the blow at an agreed-upon time. But an indiscretion caused the plans of the conspirators to be discovered and they were obliged to move up the date of the insurrection to September 23. The Spanish government went into action, preventing Betances and his expeditionary force from getting to Puerto Rico. His ship *El Telégrafo* was detained at Saint Thomas, and he was personally prevented from going to San Juan with his liberating army of three thousand men. The unconditionalist chief Pérez Moris also informs us that "one of the reasons why Betances did not come to Mayaguez with men, arms, and munitions at the end of September 1858 was because Báez* seized the armaments and prevented the departure of the revolutionaries."[25]

The insurrection was then primarily in the hands of the Venezuelan, Manuel Rojas, and the North American, Matías Brugman. On September 23, 1868, the revolutionaries marched from Rojas' estate in the Pezuela de Lares quarter to the town of Lares and under the motto *Viva Puerto Rico Libre* they declared the Republic of Puerto Rico. The rebels filed by with a flag designed by Mariana Bracetti. They also carried a white flag with the inscription *Muerto o Libertad; Viva Puerto Rico Libre, Año 1868,* and a red flag symbolizing the social nature of the struggle. The revolutionaries took the town hall and forced the parish priest to celebrate a *Te Deum* for the establishment of the republic. Used as a kind of manifesto at this time was a proclamation by Betances entitled "The Ten Commandments of Free Men," in which the immediate abolition of slavery was decreed as well as the end of Spanish despotism in all its forms. In addition, they adopted a "Provisional Constitution of the Puerto Rican Revolution," in which a Revolutionary Committee of Puerto Rico was constituted as the government of the Puerto Rican revolution. Article 2 of the provisional constitution explicitly stated that "the Committee has as its object the independence of Puerto Rico under a democratic republican form of government."[26] After having duly constituted the government of the Republic of Puerto Rico in Lares, the rebels went toward San

---

* Burnaventura Báez, a Dominican traitor to his own people and a bitter enemy of the Puerto Rican liberation struggle in the nineteenth century. (Author's note to the English edition)

[25] *Ibid.,* p. 52.

[26] Cruz Monclova, *Historia,* Appendix 9 to Vol. 1, p. 707.

Sebastián del Pepino, but there were driven back by Spanish troops. When the Spanish finally succeeded in strangling the insurrection, they immediately instituted harsh retributive measures against the revolutionaries and those suspected of being sympathizers.

The Republic of Puerto Rico, founded that twenty-third of September, 1868, lived only for a short time, but there remains for posterity the example of Borinquén, who had men no longer willing to tolerate the regime of iniquity and exploitation imposed by Spain. A short time later—on October 10, 1868—the Cry of Yara burst forth in Cuba, the Greater Antilles thus setting the tone of the West Indian revolutionary movement during the nineteenth century. The fires lit in the rising of Céspedes from his estate in La Demajagua, Cuba, could not be extinguished. The truce imposed in the Peace of Zanjón, ten years later, was a mere interlude in the armed struggle that culminated in the War for Independence in 1895.

Lares and Yara. Aborted revolution and war to the death. Sharp contrasts. Why the difference? Here is a specu-lation on that matter.

First let us formulate a question. Puerto Rico, no less than Cuba, lived with a situation that carried within it the germ of revolution. The prevailing slave system, the condi-tion of day laborers* forced to perform acts of odious servi-tude to fulfill the demands of the work books[27] (one of the

* *jornaleros* in Spanish. (Author's note to the English edition)

[27] The day laborers' work books (*libretas*) originated with the infamous Police and Good Government Edicts of Governor López Baños (1838) and the Regulation of Pezuela (1849). Cruz Monclova says about these dispositions (*Historia*, Vol. 1, pp. 307, 377: On the Edict of López Baños):

. . . day laborers were obliged to work personally on repair of the roads in their respective towns, a measure which involved an enormous first acts of the rebels was the destruction of these books), the arbitrary increase in taxes which provoked the revolutionary slogan, "Down with taxes"—in short, all the complaints which Betances echoed in his proclamations could have been written by Céspedes, and vice versa. Nevertheless, in Puerto Rico the revolutionary movement did not catch on as it did in Cuba. Why? Putting aside as frivolous

injustice, for it relieved of responsibility the proprietors, landlords, and merchants, who were precisely those who most benefited from said ways of communication . . . every individual who lacked an income or a profession was declared a vagrant; it [the edict] provided that said individual be condemned to labor on public works if in the period of twenty days he did not provide proof by means of a paper filled out by a proprietor or head of a firm that he had a job; it prohibited all claims to the contrary; and it waived the competency of the high court and other tribunals in cases of vagrancy, which it left to the exclusive control of the municipal administrations.

On the Regulation of Pezuela Cruz Monclova says:

A day laborer was declared to be a person sixteen years or older who, lacking capital or a business, was engaged in someone else's service— be it in field labor or the mechanical arts, for all or part of the year —working for a salary. The condition of the day laborer was determined by the town judges. Every day laborer was required to enter himself in the registry of the judge in his place of residence; and to provide himself with a work book, renewable each year, which he obtained free from the judge and was replaceable without charge in case of loss. The day laborer was also obliged to carry the work book with him, and if he was caught without it he had to work eight days on any public work, receiving only a half-day's pay. He was likewise required to be constantly employed. When he wasn't, the judge of his town was to provide work for him on private or public works, in which case he would be paid a full day's pay, according to the custom of the place. Finally, he was required to go live in his respective town before June 11, 1850 (the regulation was dated June 11, 1849), and to build there a shanty or dwelling, except in the case where, before said date, he should present the judge with a paper signed by some estate-owner, farmer or cattleman of the district, declaring that he had con-the supposed docility of the Puerto Rican as compared to the Cuban, by way of an hypothesis let us take the following factors into consideration.

In the first place, for a simple numerical reason the echo of Céspedes' proclamation abolishing slavery had to be louder in Cuba than that of Betances' in Puerto Rico. When the Ten Years' War began, the population of Cuba was divided in the following way: whites, 797,596; free colored, 238,927; colored slaves, 363,288 (including men and women).[28] In Puerto Rico circa 1863 there were 13,440 slaves, representing a fourth of the free day laborers employed in the countryside. According to Díaz Soler, by 1865 "the class of free workers exceeded the slave class by 56,554 men." And the previously mentioned Committee on Information made the following count (1865): Free population (white), 300,406; free population (colored), 241,037; slave population, 41,738.[29] Even taking into account the difference in number of inhabitants between Cuba and Puerto Rico, the reader can get an idea of the preponderance of blacks in Cuba—especially black slaves.

tracted to receive the worker on his property as a laborer or subordinate.

Although the work books were abolished by Primo de Rivera in 1874, when the Spanish Republic fell, his successor, General Sanz Posse, reinstituted the custom in his infamous Edict of Vagos (1874).

See Cruz Monclova, *Historia*, Vol. 2, pp. 388–89. Also the essay by Salvador Brau, "Las clases jornaleras en Puerto Rico" (1888), in the book edited by Eugenio Fernández Méndez, *Salvador Brau: Disquisiciones sociológicas* (Río Piedras: Universidad de Puerto Rico, 1956). Consult also the opinion of Baldorioty de Castro on the problem of day laborers in Cruz Monclova, *Baldorioty de Castro*.

[28] I take the figures from the "Cuadro sinóptico de los principales censos de la isla de Cuba desde 1768 hasta 1879," as they appear quoted in Fernández Almagro, *op. cit.*, Vol. 1, p. 453.

[29] Díaz Soler, *op. cit.*, pp. 137, 141, 259.

This factor was very important in the whole Cuban revolutionary movement. For despite its decree abolishing slavery, the Puerto Rican revolution did not draw to it the already-freed black masses, as the Cuban revolution would. This was in spite of the fact that there had been brutally repressed slave uprisings during the nineteenth century. Perhaps what was missing was a leader like Maceo or at least a few black rebel generals who—being black—could serve as figures with whom the black population could identify and stand. Very few slaves participated in the Puerto Rican rebellion. Lacking the numerical preponderance of their brothers in Cuba, they did not commit themselves to the liberating step.

In the second place, the revolution of Lares did not sustain itself in the days following the initial uprising, but was snuffed out immediately. Generally the experience of revolution imparts to those in rebellion a clearer, more accentuated revolutionary conscience. That is to say, revolution breaks the vicious circle of oppression, and in the process of seeking their own liberation men discover their own capacity for struggle. Or, in other words, the vicious circle is broken which has determined that there is no revolutionary consciousness because there is no revolution and that there is no revolution because there is no revolutionary consciousness. Unfortunately, the uprising of Lares was aborted at so early a stage in its development that the new consciousness had insufficient time to take root in the masses.

In the third place, there was missing what was so generously present in Cuba: skill in battle. Maceo, Máximo Gómez, and Calixto García were generals in their own right, experienced in the art of war. In Lares the revolt was led by leaders unskilled in military matters and was readily crushed by Spanish military power.

Finally, the greater territorial expanse of Cuba made a struggle in the jungle more propitious. This factor should not be underestimated, although one need not thereby be led to accepting a thesis of geographic determinism.

After the revolt at Lares failed, Betances did not desist in his efforts to liberate his people. Likewise, disillusioned by the achievements of the reformists, Eugenio María de Hostos followed the path of Betances and embraced the revolutionary cause in the Antilles. Hostos—a profound thinker, a teacher of teachers, a pilgrim of liberty—left evidence wherever he went in America that the struggle for freedom in Puerto Rico was not dead.[30] Betances, stubborn revolutionary that he was, decided to wait for better days in Puerto Rico and dedicated himself body and soul to helping rebel Cuba. Both had a long wait. But when Martí founded the Cuban Revolutionary party, he stated in the party's fundamental principles, written up on January 5, 1892, that the purpose of the party was to achieve independence in Cuba and "to encourage and help Puerto Rico in her struggle." As a consequence, the Puerto Rican section of the Cuban Revolutionary party was created in New York.[31] When the war for Cuban independence broke out in 1895, Cuban revolutionaries made preparations to send an expedition to Puerto Rico. It was even suggested that General Juan Rius Rivera direct it. He was a Puerto Rican who had distinguished himself in the Ten Years' War with General Antonio Maceo. But none of these proposals developed into concrete action. Nevertheless, on March 24,

[30] See Antonio S. Pedreira, *Hostos, ciudadano de América* (San Juan: Instituto de Cultura Puertorriqueña, 1964).

[31] *Memoria de los trabajos realizados por la Sección Puerto Rico del Partido Revolucionario Cubano, 1895–1898* (New York: Imprenta de A. W. Howes, 1898).

1897, a rebellion, promptly put down by the Spaniards, was attempted in Yauco.[32] The time of the North American invasion was drawing nigh.

Muñoz Rivera, the most sagacious and opportunistic of the autonomist politicians, made a pact with Prime Minister Sagasta through which he obtained a promise of an autonomist charter in exchange for fusion with and support of the party of Sagasta in Spain. When Prime Minister Cánovas was assassinated, Sagasta formed a government and in the first council of ministers (October 6, 1897) conceded autonomy to Puerto Rico. By the Royal Decree of November 25, 1897, Spain conceded to Puerto Rico a regime which, with the passing of time, turned out to be much more concessive in matters of self-government than the government set up under the first organic laws approved under United States domination. Guaranteed to Puerto Rico by this royal decree were universal suffrage, representation in the Cortes, power to ratify commercial treaties and to set tariffs, provisions guaranteeing the consulting of the colony in all those matters in which it was affected by legislation, and other rights.[33] The first autonomist cabinet, presided over by Muñoz Rivera in the role of colonial prime minister, hardly got a chance to function at all, because in May 1898 the colonial governor suspended the constitutional guarantees in response to Admiral Sampson's bombardment of the Bay of San Juan. And on July 25, 1898, North American troops disembarked at the port of Guánica, thus bringing to a close the newborn autonomist regime.

The autonomist charter was actually the swan song of the Spanish Empire in the Antilles. Threatened on the one hand by the Cuban revolution and on the other by the United

[32] Cruz Monclova, *Historia,* Vol. 3, pp. 47 ff.
[33] See the document in Manuel Fraga Iribarne, *Las constituciones de Puerto Rico* (Madrid: Ediciones Cultura Hispánica, 1953).

States, Spain granted—after it was already too late—what she had not been willing to grant throughout almost a century of struggle. But the autonomy that came to Puerto Rico came not because of the strength of Puerto Rican autonomists in relation to Spain but because of Spain's weakness in relation to the United States. Captained by Muñoz Rivera, the colonial creole elite came into power as a result of this charter, but in no sense did autonomy result in true self-government for Puerto Ricans. By means of the Autonomist Charter, Spain attempted to hold on to her last bulwarks, to defend herself against the inevitable. And the joy of Muñoz Rivera and the autonomists was interrupted shortly thereafter. With the North American occupation the autonomists hastened to serve a new master.

With that sibylline vision that also characterized Martí, Betances knew that nothing could be expected from autonomy because it neglected to deal with the fundamental problem of Puerto Rico: colonialism. Until the end, Betances rejected the autonomist solution. When he was asked to write an article honoring the memory of the Puerto Rican autonomist leader Baldorioty de Castro, he wrote to Antonio Vélez Alvarado, on February 16, 1892:

You know that in our country the separatists have been cursed for some time; and I don't feel up to doing an article that will justfy either today's autonomists or yesterday's. I know that I am among the defeated, but I have the hope that some day our countrymen will say that if any party in Puerto Rico has given proof of virility it has been the party of Lares, the separatists. The Spanish government has been able to put to sleep the majority of those who were with us by granting them the insignificant concessions they now possess; but it is good to remember that all despotic governments have at all times followed the same policy when they have believed a nation to be capable of demanding its rights with arms in hand. Let us not forget, then, that Lares means something in the Hispanic-Puerto Rican battle for liberty; and I—who have been, am, and will die a separatist —imagine that without revolution and without independence we will never be anything but the *eternal colony of Spain.*[34]

This is a forceful refusal, for Betances was unwilling to concede that the autonomists' "achievements" (which at that time were still remote) were due to their actions. He chose instead to point to the increasingly important role of revolutionary action, attributing even to those attempts at revolution that failed their influence in speeding up govern-mental reform. With brilliant foresight, he expressed this idea all his life. Back in 1868 he was telling us clearly that independence and only independence was "capable of sav-ing us from the American minotaur; I believe in the nearby future independence of my country . . . I believe in the equality of our rights with all civilized peoples. The great are only great because we are on our knees. Let us arise."[35]

On September 16, 1898, Dr. Ramón Emeterio Betances, father of his country, died in Paris. The act of the "Ameri-can minotaur" was already consummated. The reformists, like Muñoz Rivera, hastened to serve him. But Betances wrote, "I don't want a colony either of Spain or of the United States. What do Puerto Ricans do that they do not rebel?" And he said to Bonafoux, "It is the same being a Yankee colony as being a Spanish one." Nothing quite equaled in prophetic force the letter which he wrote to José Julio Henna more or less at the time the North American flag was being raised over the castles of San Juan:

What are the Puerto Ricans doing? Why don't they take ad-vantage of the blockade to rise up as a mass? It is essential that

[34] Bonafoux, *Betances,* p. 433.
[35] *Ibid.,* p. 129.

when the vanguards of the American Army land they be received by Puerto Rican forces waving the flag of independence, and that it be the latter who give them their welcome.

Despite the liberating actions of Betances and the *independentistas* who fought beside him, in the nineteenth century reformist autonomism finally prevailed as a political force. The fight for colonial power was, as we have seen, between unconditionalists and autonomists. The autonomists won. The system was changed very slowly and, as we have noted, too late for the change to have any real value. The anticolonialist spirit of Puerto Rican separatism remained perforce on the periphery of the events we today euphemistically call "the change of sovereignty." The next chapter will briefly examine this change.

3 | "Booty of War": The Spanish-American War and the Treaty of Paris

> To change owners is not to be free, above all when there
> is one nation which begins to look on liberty as a per-
> sonal privilege—when it is a universal, perennial aspi-
> ration of man—and to invoke it in order to deprive
> other nations of it.
>
> MARTÍ

In one part of his analysis of Spanish society from the Cortes of Cádiz to our times, Ignacio Fernández de Castro examines the topic of the decadence of the Spanish Empire:

In a schematic way, we can accept the hypothesis that the commerce in precious metals with America—in truth, the primary colonial exploitation of American territory, the systematic spoilation of the Indian—had been artificially maintaining in Spain a paralyzed structure, preserving it—in spite of the demographic and economic dynamism of the eighteenth century in Europe—from the revolutionary changes which had been imposed on other European countries. In the first years of the nineteenth century the wars with England, by affecting the shipment of metals, produced an explosive disorder, a state of acute crisis which affected absolute power, the political superstructure of a system of production incapable of providing for the necessities of a population that under those artificial conditions had experienced a strong growth during the last one hundred years . . .

What was in its death agony at the end of the nineteenth century was not the people—who were increasing at a rather high rate and who were acquiring a consciousness of their existence and their interests—but the parasitical class, with its worn-out concepts of honor and country. Conquered and defeated by the bourgeois revolution, the aristocratic class nevertheless outlived its economic and political death by incrusting itself onto the conquering bourgeoisie, whose revolution lacked the destructive strength necessary to completely bury it, and who, little by little, has become infected wth some of the old, paralyzing attitudes.[1]

The Spanish-American War dealt the final blow to an empire existing only in name, one whose internal and external weaknesses led her to an ignominious and quick defeat. The "last rosettes" of the Spanish crown in America thus passed from the hands of a Spain incapable of preserving them to the hands of a country whose industrial and military power marked her as the most powerful in the hemisphere: the United States of America. The pathetic defeat of the fleet of Admiral Cervera in the Bay of Santiago showed plainly the true relationship between the naval power of the United States and that of Spain. The rest was merely the culmination of the process of disintegration that had begun years earlier. Spain had no chance of coming out ahead in that unequal conflict.

Even more demeaning than the military defeat were the negotiations which led to the Treaty of Paris (1898). In his

---

[1] Ignacio Fernández de Castro, *De Las Cortes de Cádiz al Plan de Desarrollo* (Paris: Editions Ruedo ibérico, 1968), pp. 30, 125–26.

book, *Historia política de la España contemporánea*—a zealous and well-documented study of the period which concerns us—Melchor Fernández Almagro shows us, step by step, the process by which Spain capitulated totally.[2]

In a note written on August 1, 1898, Jules Martin Cambon, a representative of Spain, took exception to the request for Puerto Rico made to him by the U.S. government:

His Majesty's government hopes that since it is a simple question of a concessive payment, the United States will not insist on imposing on the party reputed to be obligated the harsh law of taking away that which, without ever having been in litigation, has a very special sentimental value. I should like to know, then, if the President of the Republic would accept the proposal of substituting some other form of territorial compensation for Puerto Rico.

To which note President McKinley replied that "if the cabinet of Madrid did not resign itself immediately to making certain sacrifices, such as that of Puerto Rico, the conditions to be demanded later on would be more onerous and would increase in proportion to the delay in the discussions." The government of Madrid was consequently obliged to accept the conditions imposed by the United States, and Puerto Rico came to form part of the North American empire.[3]

The interest of the United States in Cuba and Puerto Rico was certainly not of recent origin. From the declaration by Adams that Cuba was like an apple which inexo-

[2] Melchor Fernández Almagro, *Historia política de la España contemporánea* (Madrid: Alianza Editorial, 1968), Vol. 3.

[3] The quotes appear in Cruz Monclova, *Historia,* Vol. 2, pp. 266, 267.

rably, by the force of gravity, would fall into the United States' lap, to the instructions of Clay to the North American plenipotentiaries to the 1826 Congress of Panama, one can observe the early and steady formation of U.S. imperialist designs. In fact, as we discussed in the previous chapter, the United States—working with England—prevented the revolutionary activities of Simon Bolívar from including the liberation of Cuba and Puerto Rico. As Henry Clay said in 1825, the United States "is satisfied with the present condition of Cuba and Puerto Rico, as belonging to Spain and keeping their doors open, as they presently do, to our commerce: this government does not, therefore, desire any political change in their system of administration."[4]

Throughout the nineteenth century U.S. interest in having Cuba and Puerto Rico fall within the direct influence of the North American empire—whether by purchase or by conquest—manifests itself. Reiterating U.S. support of the status quo in Cuba and Puerto Rico—that is, U.S. support of Spanish colonialism—Secretary Seward stated in 1867: "The United States has constantly cherished the belief that someday she can acquire these islands by just and legal means and with the consent of Spain." And in 1876 Blaine—more explicit even than Seward—said: "I believe there are three non-continental places of enough value to be taken by the United States. One is Hawaii; the others are Cuba and Puerto Rico." The Spanish-American War fulfilled these expansionist prophecies. In 1891, Blaine announced that "the United States ought to annex the islands of Cuba and Puerto Rico." Without any embarrassment, Senator Henry Cabot Lodge stated (1898) that

---

[4] Quoted in Cruz Monclova, *Historia,* Vol. 1, p. 273.

"with its population and advantageous strategic position, the island of Puerto Rico, the easternmost and most beautiful of the Antilles, had constantly been on the minds of the Army and Navy from the very moment the war had begun; and this war was to constitute the last step in an inexorable movement begun by the United States a century ago to expel Spain from the Antilles."[5]

U.S. interest in Puerto Rico at that moment was twofold: as a market (in fact, from a commercial point of view, our colonial power by that time was the United States) and as an area of vital strategic and military importance. From the very first, North Americans justified their interest in the annexation of Puerto Rico by viewing it as an integral part of an empire that would extend from the Atlantic to the Pacific in fulfillment of U.S. manifest destiny as standard-bearer of the Anglo-Saxon virtues and race. Professor Richard Hofstadter offers a perfect example of the imperialist rhetoric of this period:

"We will not renounce our part in the mission of our race, trustees under God, of the civilization of the world," said Senator Albert J. Beveridge. "God has not been preparing the English-speaking and Teutonic peoples for a thousand years for nothing but vain and idle self-contemplation and self-admiration. No! He has made us the master organizers of the world to establish system where chaos reigns. He has made us adept in government that we may administer government among savages and senile peoples."[6]

[5] The quotes are all from Cruz Monclova, *Historia*. Vol. 1, p. 668; Vol. 2, p. 941; Vol. 3, p. 224.

[6] Quoted in Richard Hofstadter, *The Paranoid Style in American Politics and Other Essays* (New York: Knopf, 1965), p. 176. See also, by the same author, *Social Darwinism in American Thought* (Boston: Beacon Press, 1944).

To fulfill this "sacred mission," on July 25, 1898, North American troops disembarked in Guánica under the orders of General Nelson W. Miles. Spanish resistance toppled rapidly. It is sufficient to read the work of Rivero, *Crónica de la guerra hispañoamericana en Puerto Rico,*[7] to understand the ridiculousness of the Spanish war effort when faced with the Yankee occupation army. The civilian population of the island was hardly disturbed by the event. Furthermore, among certain segments of the Puerto Rican population there were signs of jubilation over the end of the Spanish regime. The mayor of Yauco, for example, received the invaders with a proclamation full of praise for the new masters. The overall reaction of the civilian population to the North Americans was not hostile. Likewise, confronted with the U.S. invasion of Cuba, the Puerto Rican section of the Cuban Revolutionary party, which had fallen under the domination of annexationists such as Dr. José Julio Henna, Roberto H. Todd, and others of a similar orientation, responded with as positive a reaction as did the general Puerto Rican population. How far those Puerto Rican elements had separated themselves from the ideas of Martí became apparent when one of its members was able to write that Puerto Ricans "will spill their last drop of blood and will sacrifice everything to obtain the separation of our small island from the barbarous colonial power and her annexation to the Great American Republic"![8]

Faced with the reality of an invasion—it is bitter to say so—the colonial elite, who had faithfully served Spain,

[7] Madrid, 1922. The author was a participant and observer in the war.

[8] Letter from Dr. J. J. Henna to the Honorable John Morgan (March 14, 1898) in *Memoria de los trabajos realizados por la Sección Puerto Rico del Partido Revolucionario Cubano 1895–1898* (New York: Imprenta de A. W. Howes, 1898), p. 130.

immediately prepared itself to serve the new colonial power in a similar manner. All the old protestations of loyalty to Spain changed as if by magic into protestations of loyalty to the United States. (The majority of the population—the peasants and workers—of course remained on the periphery, accepting the change of sovereignty with the same fatalism with which they accepted hookworm, hurricanes and tuberculosis.) The colonial elite, composed of professionals and businessmen, stood to lose nothing from the change if they could get themselves incorporated into the new colonial government; all the North Americans had to do was offer the colonial elite a share of the power—they had never had more than that—and the elite would hurry to place themselves at the North Americans' service. This was accomplished by the two most established political leaders of that time: Luis Muñoz Rivera and José Celso Barbosa. Of the two, the latter became, as time went by, the Puerto Rican politician most loyal to the North American empire.[9]

Muñoz Rivera, on the other hand, once again showed himself to be an opportunistic and accommodating politician. Muñoz Rivera himself had said on one occasion (1891), foreseeing what would one day happen: "In that intermeddling of the foreigner which offends our national dignity, we stand by our Iberian origin, our Latin blood, with the popular masses rising up and protesting in Seville and Madrid. The United States is richer and more populous than Spain; but in cases of honor, force cannot be measured nor harm calculated. The people who knew how to die in Genoa and Zaragoza will know how to put their foot down on North American pride."[10] On September 7, 1899—

---

[9] See the eulogistic biography of Barbosa done by Antonio S. Pedreira in his book *Un hombre del pueblo: José Celso Barbosa* (San Juan: Instituto de Cultura Puertorriqueña, 1965).

[10] Quoted in Cruz Monclova, Vol. I, p. 217.

eight years later, a year after Spanish pride had suffered its rude defeat—he commented on his return from the United States as a member of a commission: "The Liberal [Autonomist] party desires and requests that Puerto Rico become a kind of California or Nebraska. Our native sons must demand their identity. By serving the national cause we serve the island's cause . . . and for us to be good, loyal Puerto Ricans, we cannot be, we must not be, we do not want to be, absolutely and without reservations, anything but good and loyal Americans."[11] Later on we will examine opportunism as it manifests itself as a trait of Muñoz Rivera. It is sufficient to note here that this ardent defender of the Spanish colonial government now became an ardent defender of the North American, without a doubt ignoring the statement of Martí that "to change owners is not to be free." The vision of North America as a rapacious and expansionist power gave way to a new vision in which appeared a "generous, republican America," a vision more appropriate—as the Apostle Martí said—to those who live "by the illusion of taking nations for their word and accepting as the realities of a nation what Sunday sermons and books say about them."

Blows, however, teach lessons. With the passing of time an unrestrained optimism—the fruit, no doubt, of an insufficient knowledge of true North American designs or of the functioning of the U.S. constitutional system—received a rude awakening.

Under the peace treaty between Spain and the United States of America (December 1, 1898), Spain ceded Puerto Rico to the United States (Article 2), providing that "the civil rights and political condition of the territories here ceded to the United States will be determined by Con-

[11] Luis Muñoz Rivera, *Campañas políticas,* Vol. 1, pp. 236–37.

gress." Upon the signing of this treaty—in regard to the contents of which we were never consulted—the United States Congress became obliged to determine the political status of Puerto Rico. Those who saw in General Miles' proclamation (July 28, 1898) signs that Puerto Rico would be given U.S. statehood would not be vindicated. For in spite of Miles' encouraging phrases—"The principal objective of the North American military forces would be the overthrow of the armed authority of Spain"; the people of the island would be able to have "the greatest possible measure of liberty *compatible with this military occupation* (author's emphasis)"; later on they would go about "procuring for us the privileges and blessings of the liberal institutions of our government"—it was evident from the context in which they were written that these words of General Miles contained only a very vague promise of self-government and that in any case this promise would have to be honored by the political body given by the Treaty of Paris the power to determine the political status of the Puerto Ricans: the Congress of the United States. The Puerto Rican politicians pondered this fact while the North American colonial government established itself on the island.

Nevertheless, the exchange of Puerto Rico as war booty had implications for the country's future which would not pass unobserved by some of the most alert men of the period.

On September 13, 1898, our great Eugenio María de Hostos, for example, wrote in his *Diary* while looking at Puerto Rico from the deck of the steamship *Philadelphia:*

Yesterday I spent the whole day with my binoculars in my hands: from El Desecheo to El Ataúd and from Borinquén

Point to Point Ponce, I saw everything; I looked and looked again; I admired it, blessed it, and felt it. I felt it: I mean what the literary dialect expresses in that phrase, not what it says in itself. I felt for her and with her her beauty and her misfortune. I thought how noble it would have been to see her free by her own effort, and how sad and overwhelming and shameful it is to see her go from owner to owner without ever being her own master, and to see her pass from sovereignty to sovereignty without ever ruling herself.

A sad premonition by one who succeeded in glimpsing the future! But it is Muñoz Rivera's colleague on *La Democracia,* Mariano Abril Ostaló, who had some thoughts that, owing to their prophetic value we transcribe as follows:

To think that the Yankees are going to give us all their freedoms and all their progress for our pretty face is to think blindfolded. Yes, they could give us those freedoms which they judge adequate to our culture—in exchange for a broad and certain exploitation.

We could indeed have elevated trains crossing our streets; large, beautiful ports with docks and wharves; an unheard-of manufacturing and business activity; but all this would be in their hands, monopolized and exploited by them. These things are only created with great amounts of capital—which would have to be Yankee capital because there is not enough capital in our country for such enterprises. And after a few years, industry, commerce, and even agriculture would be monopolized by Yankees, and the West Indian would be reduced to the condition of a wretched colonist, without country, home, or fortune . . .

And we would have, as far as freedoms go, a Yankee army, a Yankee navy, Yankee police, and Yankee courts, because they would need all this to protect their interests. And the beautiful and rich Castilian tongue would disappear from our lips, to be replaced by the cold, impoverished English language.[12]

But with the Treaty of Paris and the North American military occupation our fate seemed cast. As we have seen, in the development of events the old autonomists became the elite that served as an intermediary between the colonial power and her recently acquired colony. As such, they were only demonstrating an old principle of colonialist politics: that power is exercised with less friction when it is exercised by the natives of the colonized country. There not being in Puerto Rico—as there was in Cuba and the Philippines—an independence movement firmly established among the native population, the work of the North Americans was relatively easy: to find those Puerto Ricans who were willing to collaborate with the new regime—under conditions imposed by the regime, of course. Thus annexationism sent down its first roots in Puerto Rico. Only later, as North American imperialism showed its true face, would the Puerto Rican independence movement rise again. But this is a subject to be dealt with in the following chapters.

[12] Quoted in Cruz Monclova, *Historia*, Vol. 3, p. 386. The article quoted dates from 1892.

Part II | *The First Four Decades of North American Domination (1898–1940)*

4 | "Designs on Us as a Factory and Strategic Pontoon": Economy and Society Under the North American Empire

> There are those who in good faith believe in our incapacity for self-government, although they believe in that capacity as soon as we make ties with a nation different from our own which has designs on our country as a factory and a strategic pontoon.
>
> MARTÍ

Among the many attempts to disguise the true past and present of Puerto Rico were those based on the theory of "benevolent imperialism," as advanced by the apologists of colonialism under North American domination. The new mythology, created by Jaime Benítez, Muñoz Marín, Arturo Morales Carrión, Teodoro Moscoso, Rafael Picó, and others unnecessary to name, portrayed the United States at the time of the Spanish-American War as a forgetful, kindly giant who by a trick of fate found itself unexpectedly with an empire on its hands. If each generation truly writes history with one eye on its present necessities and interests, the generation composed of the above-mentioned men took on the immense task of writing the history of Puerto Rico—even further, that of the United States—starting from the watchwords that were currently in favor with the cold-war ideologists in the capitalist world. Suffice it to say here that from their positions of power and leadership the proponents of the theory of "benevolent imperialism" were and still are determining factors in the perpetuation of the colonial mentality in vast segments of our population. But we will return to this subject later.

The theory of "benevolent imperialism"—as expressed in its many forms—suffers from a very serious weakness. Given its use to absolve the United States of all imperialist designs, the theory has become a product of fiction rather than a historical interpretation based on irrefutable evidence. In the previous chapter, we quoted statements by U.S. officials showing that the United States had coveted Cuba and Puerto Rico right from the early stages of its development. More recent studies of this subject confirm this observation. For example, in comparing England's imperial experience with that of the United States, Professor Richard W. Van Alstyne tells us:

Both empires were the creatures of natural forces—of emigration and colonization, of commerce and religion, and of the desire to extend political influence. But in neither case was expansion unintentional, unplanned or "absent-minded." Each empire followed a strategic pattern, and the history of each shows the influence of much conscious planning and direction.[1]

[1] *The Rising American Empire* (Chicago: Quadrangle Books, 1965), p. 100.

Professor Van Alstyne thinks that the imperialist designs of the United States were present in the very inception of her assumption of power as an independent country.

In his important contribution to the study of U.S. imperialism, Professor Walter La Feber comes to much the same conclusion. Examining U.S. expansion from 1860 to 1898, La Feber reaches these conclusions:

First, the United States did not set out on an expansionist path in the late 1890's in a sudden, spur-of-the-moment fashion. The overseas empire that Americans controlled in 1900 was not a break in their history, but a natural culmination. Second, Americans neither acquired this empire during a temporary absence of mind nor had the empire forced upon them.[2]

The expansion of the United States must therefore be seen in its proper perspective as a movement destined to gain commercial, industrial, and financial hegemony in the Western Hemisphere, and, as a necessary corollary to that, naval and military bases indispensable to maintaining this hegemony. Nor can this expansionist movement to the south be seen apart from U.S. expansion to the Orient—in search of new markets in the Philippines, Hawaii, China, and other countries for its surplus products. Acquiring influence in all of these geographical areas fell within the great master plan of this empire which, according to its most fervent apologists, sought to extend to "savage and backward" people the immense benefits of its civilization.[3] The rhetoric of the period—stripped of all pretense about

[2] *The New Empire, An Interpretation of American Expansion 1860–1898* (Ithaca: Cornell University Press, 1963), p. viii.

[3] See in this regard chapter 5 of La Feber, *ibid.* For a study about the influence of the ideologists of imperialism in Europe on their namesakes in North America, see the interesting book by Ernest F. May, *American Imperialism, a Speculative Essay* (New York: Atheneum, 1968).

the sensibilities and rights of colonized peoples—reveals that in its monopolistic phase, North American capitalism had as its motivating force the pressing need to expand its influence beyond its borders or face crises of overproduction—as, for example, the depression of 1893—which shook the system at its roots.

Imperialism is inherently a global system of domination. Therefore, with successful North American expansion at the end of the nineteenth century there arose a curious mixture of colonialism in the classic sense (Puerto Rico, Hawaii, the Philippines) and what we today know of as neocolonialism (as, for example, in the case of Cuba, and later Santo Domingo, Haiti, etc.). Viewed in perspective, neocolonialism did not first develop in the postwar period; at the time of the War of 1898 it was already germinating in North American foreign policy. The Monroe Doctrine, with its particular corollaries (Olney, T. Roosevelt), and "manifest destiny" are more or less comprehensive examples of the phenomenon referred to.[4] When Olney, because of the dispute between England and Venezuela over British Guiana, issued his famous corollary—"The United States is today practically sovereign in America, and her fiat is the law in those matters in which she intervenes"—he unabashedly admitted that the North American hegemony was already so deeply entrenched that no other power had sufficient strength to oppose its will. When England bowed to Olney's claim, his assertion proved to be correct. And the stage was also set for what John Hay called at one time "the splendid little war." William Appleman Williams, a zealous historian, tells us that with the

[4] On this matter, see Albert K. Weinberg, *Manifest Destiny* (Chicago: Quadrangle Books, 1963); Samuel Flagg Bemis, *The Latin American Policy of the United States* (New York: Harcourt Brace, 1943).

development of a corporate economy—i.e., capitalism in its monopolistic phase—the United States "emphasized increasingly the role of foreign policy in solving domestic troubles and consciously initiated a broad program of sophisticated imperialism . . . Underlying that expansion, and sustaining it on into the twentieth century, was the central idea that overseas economic expansion provided the *sine qua non* of domestic prosperity and social peace."[5]

Seen from this point of view, U.S. interest in Puerto Rico can be more clearly understood. First of all, about 1898 the United States was considered the "commercial metropolis" of Puerto Rico.[6] For a system that, as we have seen, needed markets for its surplus products, the smallest of the Antilles could not be unimportant. In the second place, once the United States became a great naval power, it found it necessary to construct coaling stations, provision centers, and so forth, to enable the U.S. Navy to cross the seas with as few stops as possible. In 1891 Blaine wrote to Benjamin Harrison, "I believe that there are only three places of sufficient value to be taken: one is Hawaii and the others are Puerto Rico and Cuba."[7] In addition, Harrison's administration considered acquiring the Dutch West Indies, the Bay of Samaná in Santo Domingo, and the St. Nicholas Mole in Haiti. This preoccupation with the acquisition of strategic areas continued to manifest itself as a major characteristic

[5] William Appleman Williams, *The Contours of American History* (Chicago: Quadrangle Books, 1966), p. 355. See also Ramiro Guerra y Sánchez, *La expansión territorial de los Estados Unidos a expensas de España y los países hispañoamericanos* (La Habana, 1964). On the concept of monopoly capital I follow Paul Baran and Paul Sweezy, *El capital monopolista* (México: Siglo XXI Editores, 1968).

[6] Eugenio Fernández Méndez, "Introducción" to *Salvador Brau, Disquiciones sociológicas* (Universidad de Puerto Rico, 1956), p. 25.

[7] Quoted in La Feber, *op. cit.*, p. 110.

of U.S. foreign policy with the opening of the Panama Canal some years later. Let us read La Feber's evaluation of the expansionist policy of the United States in 1890:

> To Mahan, William McKinley, Theodore Roosevelt, and Henry Cabot Lodge, colonial possessions, as these men defined such possessions, served as stepping stones to the two great prizes: the Latin-American and Asian markets. This policy much less resembled traditional colonialism than it did the new financial and industrial expansion of the 1850–1914 period. These men did not envision "colonizing" either Latin America or Asia. They did want both to exploit these areas economically and give them (especially Asia) the benefits of Western, Christian civilization. To do this, these expansionists needed strategic bases from which shipping lanes and interior interests in Asia and Latin America could be protected.[8]

Therefore, to convert the Caribbean into a "North American Mediterranean" was not something alien to the concerns of the ruling North Americans. Because of her strategic position, Puerto Rico had her importance to the new empire. The same could be said for Cuba, Hawaii, and the Philippines.[9]

---

[8] *Ibid*, p. 91.

[9] In this sense the theories of Admiral Mahan on naval power are extremely influential. Referring to them, Guerra y Sánchez tells us:

> In regard to the Caribbean, the security of the United States and of communications with the future canal through the Isthmus of Panama —which necessarily would have to be a North American canal— required a North American naval station in the most favorable strategic spot. The strategic importance of the Caribbean was no less than that of the Mediterranean—the center of naval power, as Mahan called it. Without control over the Caribbean, absolute control over the canal and the isthmus, and the possession of naval stations in the

On annexing Puerto Rico (a consequence of the Treaty of Paris) the United States embarked upon an action which had no precedent in its previous expansionist history. For the first time, the United States acquired colonies overseas.¹ In October 1898, the raising of the United States flag over all the public buildings in Puerto Rico began the first North American experience in governing a country of almost a million inhabitants with a different culture and language. And from that moment on—without ever having been consulted—Puerto Rico passed under the cover of the wings of the imperial eagle. This historic event marks what Pedreira has called "the period of indecision and transition" in our country's history and what Manrique Cabrera in his turn has called "the trauma of 1898." From this point on the annexation of Puerto Rico became a reality that had to be dealt with. The process of colonizing Puerto Rico under the aegis of the North American empire began immediately. As Professor Fernández Méndez says, "After the War of 1898, Puerto Rico would again rehearse—now under the aegis of U.S. industrial expansionism and basing her measures on less active and resistant social levels: a debilitated creole bourgeoisie and a *jíbaro** peasantry in rapid transition to the proletariat—all the old drama of validation and recognition of her national identity."¹⁰

This struggle for our own national and cultural identity would shape the course of our country's history up to the

---

Pacific, including the China Sea, to protect North American commerce and interests in Asia, the United States could not guarantee the security of its position at that time, nor continue the future development of the nation. [*Op. cit.*, p. 376]

* *Jíbaro* is a Puerto Rican term for "peasant," in the most ethnic sense. (Translator's note)

¹⁰ *Op. cit.*, p. 11.

present. This history would outline the process by which the island became the object of an economic, political, military, and intellectual colonization. The profound lessons we have learned from this experience should serve as a warning to those who still cannot see the essentially immoral character of every form of colonialism.

The first four decades of imperialist domination in Puerto Rico (1898–1940) mark a period during which inch by inch our country gradually fell into the hands of U.S. industrial and financial capitalists. Consequently, all of the elements indicating the exploitation of a colony occurred here during this period: the captive market; an increase in the value of goods due to an abundant work force and the payment of subsistence-level salaries; the exploitation of native natural resources by a handful of foreign investors; the predominance of finance capital from the colonial power; latifundism and monoculture; the military occupation of the territory; the superimposition of an administrative structure responsible only to the colonial power; the systematic attempt to bring about the cultural assimilation of the colony. Present from the beginning of North American domination, all these elements crystallized during the first three decades of the twentieth century and were subsequently placed in jeopardy during the period in which world capitalism suffered its most serious crisis: the decade of the thirties. As a result of this financial crisis, the thirties would become a crucial period in our history—I would almost dare to say the most crucial decade of the twentieth century. This, however, will serve as impetus for later discussion. Let us return to the previous discussion.

In 1898 the most important products in the Puerto Rican economy were coffee, tobacco, and sugar cane. At that time, coffee was the most common export. North American tariff barriers deprived Puerto Rican coffee of its principal markets in Europe; Puerto Rico found it could not meet the competition of other coffee-producing countries (like Brazil) and did not receive any protection from the North American tariff system. Add to this the effects of the devastating hurricane of 1899 and the devaluation of money by the North American authorities, and it will be understood why coffee cultivation never became important again after its decline under U.S. domination.

The effects of the tariff were, of course, much more comprehensive. Prevented from negotiating commercial agreements with other countries, Puerto Ricans were forced to buy in the most expensive markets without being able to modify in the least the rigors of a tariff which was actually created for the benefit of the manufacturing interests of the United States. Puerto Rico was therefore a captive market at the mercy of the economic fluctuations of world capitalism. This situation persists to the present day. An indisputable sign of a colonial economy is the colony becoming a passive receptacle for the commodities manufactured in the colonial power.

Formed in Puerto Rico by North American industrialists, the sugar, tobacco, and fruit trusts got protection for their interests under the cloak of the tariff. American industrialists counted on an abundant labor supply: a reserve army of workers obliged to work for subsistence-level salaries. The agricultural worker gradually shifted from the mountain coffee plantations to the sugar plantations. Thus developed a vast rural proletariat that worked for a few months during the sugar harvest and then was laid off during the period known as the "dead time." In a study sponsored by The Brookings Institution (1930), the information above is verified. The study notes that Puerto Rico is "a community of agricultural laborers" and that of every five persons who live in the country four are not landowners. The salaries for that period (1926) were 75¢ a day (sugar cane); 50¢ a day (coffee); 8¢ an hour (fruit); 80¢ a day (tobacco), while the average income per family was from $250 to $275 a year. The study concludes: "In general, births, illnesses, accidents, and death are borne without much effort being made to alleviate them. In the mountain houses of the *jíbaro,* one too often finds that illness and suffering are accepted with helpless fatalism.[11] A pathetic picture of all colonial exploitation. While the abundance of labor depressed workers' salaries, the essentially fluctuating nature of the world market placed the workers at its mercy. Unemployment, sporadic work, and the rapaciousness of foreign investors contributed to the accentuation of class differences and consequently of the class struggle.

In one of the best studies made of this period, Bailey and Justine Diffie calculated the percentage of the Puerto Rican economy absorbed by North American capital. According to the Diffies, at the beginning of the thirties, 60 per cent of the sugar production was controlled by four large absentee corporations, and the same could be said of tobacco (80 per cent), public services and banks (60 per cent), and maritime lines (100 per cent).[12] During the first three decades of North American government in Puerto Rico, absentee investment reached $120,000,000.[13] The grab-

---

[11] Victor S. Clark (editor), *Porto Rico and Its Problems* (Washington, D.C.: The Brookings Institution, 1930), pp. 13, 21, 27, 37.

[12] Bailey W. and Justine Whitfield Diffie, *Porto Rico: A Broken Pledge* (New York: The Vanguard Press, 1931), p. 150.

[13] Harvey S. Perloff, *Puerto Rico's Economic Future* (Chicago: University of Chicago Press, 1950), p. 28.

bing of goodies did not pass unobserved by local leaders, for by 1912 Muñoz Rivera could say, "Puerto Rico sells almost everything she produces to the United States. And by virtue of the new tariffs [referring to a plan then pending before the U.S. Congress] all of her products except tobacco and fruit will continue to lack any protection at all: the tobacco monopolized by an American trust named the Porto Rico American Tobacco Company; the fruit nearly monopolized by American capital."[14] The effects of colonial exploitation became more marked with the passing of time, as we have already observed.

In his aforementioned essay, Professor Fernández Méndez stresses that cultivation of sugar cane by the great sugar companies contributed to a gradual but persistent process of concentration of landholdings during the nineteenth century. The Diffies, however, inform us that around 1899 Puerto Rican agriculturists owned 93 per cent of the existing farms and estates in Puerto Rico, so that on the island "a great number of people from the rural population were homeowners and permanent residents of the island."[15] At that time the land was divided for use among the following areas of production: of the total arable area of Puerto Rico (total area: 3,435 square miles or 2,198,400 acres), 41 per cent was used for the cultivation of coffee, 15 per cent for sugar cane, 32 per cent for edible foods, and only 1 per cent for tobacco. Great sugar latifundia con-

---

[14] Quoted in Sebastián Dalmau Canet, *Luis Muñoz Rivera, su vida, su obra, su carácter* (San Juan: Tipografía Boletín Mercantil, 1917), pp. 332–33.

[15] *Op. cit.,* pp. 21–22. See also in this regard Henry K. Carroll, Special Commissioner for the United States to Puerto Rico, in his *Report on the Island of Puerto Rico* (Washington, D.C.: Government Printing Office, 1899).

trolled by North American stockholders were established on the island. Moreover, the Puerto Rican economy began to revolve around one product: sugar cane. The changes pointed out above had a definite influence on the development of our social classes. Obviously, the rise and development of a national bourgeoisie having relatively autonomous sources of wealth barely managed to get started. In Puerto Rico, therefore, we have an example of a typical colonial economy that consumes what it does not produce and produces what it does not consume.

A classic colonial system such as that which the United States imposed on Puerto Rico cannot get along without the repressive apparatus set up to preserve the structures which best respond to the interests of the colonial power. The primary, elemental act of force consisted of the bombardment and invasion of Puerto Rico in 1898. Thus, the military's part in the determination of Puerto Rican politics was clearly established. The U.S. Army came to dictate, to establish without ambiguity the "right of force." The fate of Puerto Rico was decided during the period in which the military served as an interim government between the Spanish and the U.S. civil governments.[16] Puerto Rico was considered—as we have already seen—to be of great strategic value because of her proximity to the Panama Canal. The U.S. military presence was felt more strongly during World Wars I and II. During World War I, the precedent was established for compulsory military service for Puerto Ricans. During World War II, our function as a "strategic pontoon" in the Caribbean was definitively established.

That the U.S. military felt an increasing interest in

[16] See Edward J. Berbusse, S.J., *The United States in Puerto Rico 1898–1900* (Chapel Hill: The University of North Carolina Press, 1966), for the most concise study made of this period in our colonial history.

Puerto Rico can be verified by the statements of General George Marshall on his visit to Puerto Rico and by the U.S. government's appointment of Admiral William D. Leahy as governor. On May 15, 1939, *The New York Times* quoted General Marshall as saying that "in recent years the importance of Puerto Rico to national defense has been restudied by all the government departments, resulting in an announcement by the Department of War that Puerto Rico will become a military department similar to that of the Canal Zone, Hawaii, and the Philippines." Marshall's statement stimulated the Washington *Post* (May 28, 1939) to comment editorially that the designation of Leahy could be traced to "the plans to establish an enormous naval and air base there, in order to make Puerto Rico the Gibraltar of the Caribbean." It is not necessary to say that this decision has been implemented during the last three decades.

The superimposition of an administrative structure responsible only to the colonial power unloaded on Puerto Rico a whole avalanche of carpetbaggers—to such an extreme that Matienzo Cintrón once called us the southerners of Latin America. The criterion used by the President of the United States to choose the colonial governor and his cabinet was, with very few exceptions, one of compensation for political favors received. Many of these men came to Puerto Rico without knowing the language or, at times, even the location of the island. They would then begin to govern—or misgovern—a country which could surely give lessons in civilization to the states from which these men came. The same can be said of many of the bureaucrats sent to Puerto Rico in the colonial free-for-all: they were ignorant and prejudiced, with the feeling of superiority common to all colonizers. They came to our shores to dictate to us the course of our collective life. In truth, the matter was so irritating that Roberto H. Todd—whose record of unquestioning service to the North American empire is above dispute—wrote a book from which the reader emerges convinced that the colonial governors who filed through Puerto Rico during the first four decades of this century were with very few exceptions a living illustration of ineptitude, insolence, and lack of respect for our people.[17]

Nothing illustrates this better than the absurd attempt—going back to the beginning of North American domination—to culturally assimilate the Puerto Rican people and to make us, like it or not, good and loyal North Americans. In itself disastrous, a policy like this was even more dreadful when implemented by remote bureaucrats totally ignorant of the Puerto Rican situation. Since we will take up this topic in the next chapter, we will drop the subject here for the moment.

If we examine the period which we have herein attempted to superficially sketch, we can observe in its general features the class character of Puerto Rican society during this time. The social structure cannot help but reflect the already strained economic structure, for the material conditions determining the lives of the individuals making up a society always leave a powerful imprint on the composition of the social classes. When we are dealing with the economy of a capitalist country with a high technological development—the United States, for example—the horizontal and vertical mobility of many sectors of its population makes it more difficult to describe clearly the exact or approximate position of each social sector. Nevertheless, if

[17] Roberto H. Todd, *Desfile de governadores de Puerto Rico,* 2nd ed. (Madrid: Ediciones Iberoamericanas, 1966).

we select as criteria the distribution of income and the relative access of different groups to the material and spiritual goods of a society, we can draw certain conclusions which support the existence of a well-defined class structure in the United States. Actually, an event in the sixties—the struggle of North American blacks for their dignity—has forced a reexamination of the already frequently discredited thesis that in the United States the abolition of social classes was near at hand. Two books published during the last five years have contributed to the demystification of the subject: Michael Harrington's *The Culture of Poverty in the United States* and Gabriel Kolko's *Wealth and Power in the United States*.

I mention these facts because one should never lose sight of the essentially colonial character of the Puerto Rican economy and society. We should see the problem in its proper perspective, taking care not to impose the criteria of a superdeveloped society (Marcuse) on a superexploited society—or underdeveloped, if you want to use the polite euphemism.

The social structure of a colonial society is a reflection of the dependence of that society on the colonial power. We can say the same thing, of course, about its economic structure. In the case of Puerto Rican society, therefore, we must point out an important characteristic of its basic social structure—the absence, for all practical purposes, of a well-defined national bourgeoisie. Consequently, I prefer to use the term *colonial elite* or *creole elite* to designate that group of people in Puerto Rican society who have more access to the material and spiritual goods of our society than other Puerto Ricans. With an economy dominated by a handful of corporations responsible to stockholders in the United States, the principal task of the creole elite has been to serve as intermediary between the hegemony of the colonial power and Puerto Rican society. This elite adjusts to the new order of things because its economic interests require it. Pressured from below by the mass of workers demanding their social rights, the colonial elite receives from the colonial power the protection necessary to continue its economic activity in the shadow of the great interests which threaten to devour it. The life style (in the Weberian sense of the term) of this elite is the life style of those who have as a point of reference and support the upper-middle class of the colonial power.

At the base of the social pyramid, we find the rural and urban proletariat, who live practically at a subsistence level and make up the largest group in the population. According to the previously cited study made by The Brookings Institution, in 1930 only 27 per cent of the population could be considered urban. According to the U.S. census of 1960, in 1940, of a total population of 1,869,255 inhabitants, only 566,357 lived in urban areas. The bulk of the labor force, therefore, was the contingent of workers involved with the fruit, sugar cane, tobacco, and coffee crops. I do not think it necessary to stress the extremely poor condition of the general population during these four decades. According to the criterion set up earlier, these were the ones cut off from access to the material and spiritual goods of Puerto Rican society.

Between these two groups was the middle class, made up of professionals, small businessmen, small farmers, government employees, and teachers in the public schools and universities. The most distinguished intellectual figures of this period came from the middle class. Their life chances were defined by powerful alien forces keeping the economy of the country in constant danger.

All groups, the elite as well as the workers and the middle class, for their very life chances had to depend on decisions made outside Puerto Rico—without their being consulted—and had to live with the possibility that at any moment a fluctuation in the price of sugar in the world market might throw thousands into unemployment and desperation.

When the great capitalist crisis of the thirties occurred, Puerto Rico also felt its tremendous impact. In that crucial decade world capitalism was in crisis and so, therefore, was the prevailing colonial system in Puerto Rico. Worker and student agitation, nationalism, the class struggle, anti-imperialist consciousness, strikes, the struggle for independence—all crystallized in that historic moment. In reaction to these events, unconditionalists took a tougher stand and the colonial government tightened its control over the population. Matters became so serious that Franklin D. Roosevelt—elected President in 1932—extended some of the New Deal programs to Puerto Rico.[18]

During the decade from 1930 to 1940 the gradual breaking down of the prevailing colonial system in Puerto Rico became apparent. The Depression revealed the vulnerability of the capitalist system. In Puerto Rico the labor movement decided to follow more radical paths than those set by the founder of the labor movement in Puerto Rico, Santiago Iglesias Pantín, who now belongs to one of the most re-

[18] See the definitive account of this period, written by Dr. Thomas Mathews and entitled *Puerto Rican Politics and the New Deal* (Gainesville: University of Florida Press, 1969). Also of interest for the understanding of this period is the autobiographical account of Governor Rexford Guy Tugwell, appointed proconsul in Puerto Rico by Roosevelt at the beginning of the era of Muñoz Marín. See R. G. Tugwell, *The Stricken Land, the Story of Puerto Rico* (New York: Doubleday, 1947). The subtitle is deceptive. It should read "The Story of Tugwell."

actionary sectors of Puerto Rican society. The cause of independence gathered strength as never before. There were indisputable advances in the Puerto Rican people's consciousness of the colonial condition as well as in their resistance to the attempts at cultural assimilation that emanated from the colonial power. For the first time in the twentieth century, Albizu Campos spoke out on the struggle for independence from a revolutionary standpoint. Muñoz Marín, on the other hand, proclaimed that independence "is just around the corner." The ground was fertile for nationalist and anti-imperialist preachings, for demands for social justice and for the achievement of our independence. With this panorama in mind, let us now turn our attention to the political parties within the colonial system.

5 | Political Parties Within the Colonial System

Independence, sovereignty is the chief and primary liberty of nations. Sovereignty is the source of all rights: collective independence can, in fact, generate all despotisms—but also all freedoms—while all the secondary freedoms cannot generate the superior unity of national sovereignty, which is creative; and all the other freedoms are like creatures emanating from national sovereignty and are incapable of supreme creation.

JOSÉ DE DIEGO (1916)

The supreme definition is on the boards: Yankees or Puerto Ricans.

ALBIZU CAMPOS (1926)

One cannot observe Puerto Rican life close up without reaching the conclusion that every form of tutelage is morally degrading. As long as sovereignty does not reside in us, there will be genuflections and degradations before those in whom it does reside. This is the political illness of colonial Puerto Rico and its only cure is a dose of unadulterated sovereignty.

LUIS MUÑOZ MARÍN (1932)

When what some people today euphemistically call the transfer of sovereignty from Spain to the United States took place in 1898, the autonomous government Spain had granted Puerto Rico was abruptly cut short. Our country was barely able to enjoy the presumed victory won by Muñoz Rivera in his pact with Sagasta. As we have already seen, however, both the autonomists who followed Muñoz Rivera and those who followed Barbosa offered to serve the new regime. So a little more than a year after Admiral Sampson's bombardment, two political parties were founded in Puerto Rico: the Puerto Rican Republican party, founded July 1, 1899, and presided over by Dr. José Celso Barbosa; and the Federal party, founded October 11, 1899, and presided over by Muñoz Rivera. Both presidents supported U.S. statehood for Puerto Rico.[1] Recalling this bit of historical information we cannot help but note that of the three Spanish-speaking Antilles, Puerto Rico was the exception to the strong annexationist tendencies which caused such a stir in Cuba as well as in Santo Domingo in the nineteenth century. (In fact, these tendencies were so strong in Cuba that Martí had to devote a great deal of his energies to combating them.) Perhaps the issue had lain latent in the autonomist leaders and they had not dared express it while Spanish hegemony lasted. Perhaps in the

[1] In the manifesto of the Puerto Rican Republican party two substantive principles are stated: "A definitive and sincere annexation of Puerto Rico to the United States and a declaration of Puerto Rico as an organized territory as a means of then becoming a state of the Federal Union." The Federal party stated: "North America is a state and a republic of republics. In the future, Puerto Rico must be one of these states, one of these republics. And the Federal Party will direct its efforts towards it being one as soon as possible." Quoted in José A. Gautier Dapena, "Nacimiento de los partidos políticos bajo la soberanía de los Estados Unidos: programas y tendencias," *Historia,* Vol. III, no. 2 (October, 1953), pp. 153–78. See also Bolívar Pagán, *Historia de los partidos políticos puertorriqueños,* two volumes (San Juan: Librería Campos, 1959), Vol. I, and Robert W. Anderson, *Party Politics in Puerto Rico* (Stanford: Stanford University Press, 1965).

case of Barbosa, these latent feelings were influenced by the impression produced by his medical studies in the north. Or finally, the lure of power under the new American symbol—along with a lack of perspective in regard to the true intentions of the recently arrived invader—made them embrace the flag of the country which had defeated in war the nation that scarcely a year before had brought forth their fervent protests of enthusiasm and loyalty. It is difficult to judge motivations, but less so when those motivations are revealed in concrete deeds. And the evidence shows that with only an ambiguous proclamation by a recently arrived military chief and a poorly hidden eagerness to serve the new master, Muñoz Rivera and Barbosa began from that early date the struggle for a watered-down, ridiculous, and degrading power, while true power—the ultimate power of decision—rested on the desk of some North American legislator. Thus the principle of collaboration with the colonial regime, of participation in a system which was itself based on the principle of legal and political inequality, was established. Like the liberal reformists of the nineteenth century, the political parties mentioned above fought from then on to obtain concessions and reforms while awaiting the final solution of our political status. Only it became necessary to choose new points on the compass and to undertake the pilgrimage to Washington instead of to Madrid, to return from there with many promises and empty hands. When Barbosa and Muñoz Rivera began to walk that treadmill in 1899, perhaps they did not conceive of the possibility that in 1968 we would be in an equal or similar position. But little doubt remains that they were the precursors of that policy which for seven decades has kept us in the state of political inferiority from which we suffer now.

Nevertheless, difficulties in the relationship with the new

imperial power developed very quickly. First, under the military government (1898–1900) and then under the first civil government, Muñoz Rivera soon saw that he was being disregarded by the North American colonialists; he therefore supported Puerto Rican withdrawal from participation in the colonial elections. Barbosa, on the other hand, now took the position the unconditionalists had taken under the Spanish government. He supported total North Americanization; in his faithful support of the new colonial administration, this Puerto Rican leader has been surpassed by very few men in our history.

It is in this context that we should examine the Foraker Law, the first organic law,* approved by the United States Congress and signed by President McKinley on April 12, 1900. This was the first of two organic laws passed to provide a civil government for Puerto Rico. Under its provisions, the first colonial governor of Puerto Rico took office on May 1, 1900. Allen was appointed to the position by the President of the United States.

When this law was approved, there was a Republican administration in power in Washington. When the "splendid little war" was over, the United States was faced with the necessity of administering the empire her founding fathers had visualized long before. Although lacking much experience in governing overseas territories, the rulers of the newly acquired empire nevertheless manifested the classical mentality of all imperialists: divide the peoples of the world into the powerful and the weak, the civilized and the backward, those capable of governing themselves and those who for their own welfare must be governed. William

---

* An organic law is a charter passed by Congress that sets down the basic legal framework for the organization of a colonial government. (Author's note to the English edition)

McKinley, Mark Hanna, John F. Foraker—all shared a belief in the hegemony of the Anglo-Saxon peoples over the "inferior" races, a thesis which received its intellectual formulation in the writings of the Adams brothers, Josiah Strong, John W. Burgess, and John Fiske, among others. For example, Theodore Roosevelt's teacher at Columbia Law School, John W. Burgess, assigned a special role to the Teutonic peoples because they showed a very high "capacity for political organization." "The Teutonic peoples," said Burgess, "can never consider that the exercise of political power is a right of man. For them this power is based on the capacity to fulfill political duty, and they themselves are the best entities that so far have appeared to determine when and where this capacity exists." For his disciple, the drama of the racial expansion of the English-speaking people— which he, like his teacher, traces back to the moment of the rise and spread of the Germanic tribes—culminated in the imperialistic development of the North American people.[2] In that period this tie between imperialism and racism flourished in the rhetoric of those who dominated North American policy-making, since in those days it was not necessary, as it is now, to hide the iron fist of designs for world domination behind a veneer of equivocal language. The issue transcended the alignment of political parties. In the most complete study that has been made of the Foraker Law, William Jay Gould tells us that although the Democrats posed as anti-imperialists, they were still capitalists and as such were concerned about the entrance of foreign goods into the U.S. market and competition from "coolie"

[2] The quote from Burgess and the reference to T. Roosevelt are from Richard Hofstadter's book, *Social Darwinism in America* (Boston, 1944), p. 175. In this respect, see also Walter La Feber, *The New Empire* (Ithaca, N.Y.: Cornell University Press, 1963), chapter 2.

labor.[3] And in the Southern wing of the Democratic party the racist theme came up often in the discussion of the plan. Thus on the floor of the U.S. Senate, Senator Bate (Tennessee) said:

Under this new order of expansion, what is to become of the Philippines and Puerto Rico? Are they to become States with representation here from those countries, from that heterogeneous mass of mongrels that make up their citizenship? That is objectionable to the people of this country, as it ought to be, and they will call a halt to it before it is done.

[Jefferson was the greatest expansionist] But neither his example nor his precedent affords any justification for expansion over territory in distant seas, over peoples incapable of self-government, over religions hostile to Christianity, and over savages addicted to head-hunting and cannibalism, as some of these islanders are.[4]

It is evident that for this Southern legislator the mere thought of the incorporation of "inferior" races into the Union entailed a serious danger to the guardians of Western Christian civilization. (One wonders if Dr. Barbosa—black, and the son of artisans—knew of this outburst against his race, or if he was conscious of the Caucasian chauvinism of the men who controlled affairs in Washington. His political career shows that even if he were conscious of it, it never made much of an impression on his spotless record of support for North Americanism.)

[3] Lyman Jay Gould, *The Foraker Act: The Roots of American Colonial Policy* (University of Michigan, Ph.D. dissertation, 1958), p. 117. Also see Edward J. Berbusse, S.J., *The United States in Puerto Rico 1898–1900* (Chapel Hill: University of North Carolina Press, 1966), chapters 4 and 5.

[4] *Congressional Record* (Senate), April 2, 1900, p. 3612.

The Republicans were the ones who dominated both Congress and the Presidency of the United States in 1900. Senator Foraker (Ohio) was in charge of steering the Foraker plan through Congress. Public hearings were held and the testimony of people with an interest in Puerto Rico was heard. President McKinley, on the other hand, had designated Dr. Henry K. Carroll to make a report on the prevailing social and economic conditions in Puerto Rico.[5] In addition, Dr. Victor S. Clark made a report on education in Puerto Rico, in which he expressed the opinion that "the social, industrial, moral, and intellectual condition of Puerto Rico is such that it seems to me to demand, before they are given local self-government, that they pass through a probationary period."[6] The question of the capacity of our people to govern themselves reappears frequently in the congressional debates on our political condition. Legislators agreed that the military government should end, but could not conceive of our people as being ready for self-government.

The very congressman who produced the plan lets us know this on repeated occasions. The Puerto Ricans, Foraker tells us, "have not been prepared for any kind of experience for participation in government."[7] The United States has won a war and has annexed several territories. These territories are indispensable to the welfare of the United States:

We have reached the point in the development of our resources and the multiplication of our industries where we are

[5] See Henry K. Carroll, *Report on the Island of Porto Rico* (Washington, D.C.: Government Printing Office, 1899).

[6] Senate Document No. 363, 56th Congress, 1st Session, p. 8.

[7] *Congressional Record* (Senate), March 2, 1900, p. 2475.

not only supplying our home demands, but are producing a large surplus, constantly growing larger. Our greatest present and prospective commercial need is for markets abroad. We cannot find them in the countries of Europe. Their demand upon us is limited. They strive to supply themselves and to compete with us in the markets of the world.[8]

For this reason—thought Foraker out loud—the recently acquired territories ought to have a *sui generis* political status within the North American union. They could not be states because they were not prepared for statehood: nor could they be territories, because that would be a step toward federated statehood. They should therefore have the character of mere "possessions" or parts of the United States, without this being taken as an indication of congressional intent to convert them into incorporated territories or states of the Union.[9]

As a consequence of what was said, paternalism was imposed—tutelage for Puerto Rico until she should come of age in political matters. Foraker used the worn-out argument of imperialists of all ages when he said on March 8, 1900, in his speech on the Senate floor:

The people of Puerto Rico differ radically from any other people for whom we have legislated previously. Above all, they have had a different experience in matters of government. They have had no experience which would qualify them—in the light

[8] *Congressional Record* (Senate), April 30, 1900, p. 4856.

[9] See, with regard to North American policy toward its territories and the granting of statehood to them, the doctoral thesis of Whitney Trow Perkins (Fletcher School of Law and Diplomacy, 1948), entitled *American Policy in the Government of its Dependent Areas. A Study of the Policy of the U.S. Toward the Inhabitants of its Territories and Insular Possessions.*

of testimony made before our committee in the hearings which were held—for the great work of government with all the bureaus and departments needed by the people of Puerto Rico.[10]

The Foraker Act—which until 1917 provided the legal framework for the political development of Puerto Rico— faithfully reflected the thinking of men like Foraker and McKinley.

Much has been written about whether the Autonomist Charter granted by Spain was or was not superior, from the point of view of self-government, to the Foraker Act. The members of the Federal party, among them Muñoz Rivera, considered the latter retrogressive in comparison with the Autonomist Charter granted by Spain. Cayetano Coll y Cuchí expressed this sentiment, saying "if the Foraker Act had been imposed on Puerto Rico before autonomy, it would undoubtedly have been a retrogression in our political makeup; after autonomy it has been a black page in our history."[11]

One simply has to read the text of the new law to see that this statement by the autonomist leader was more than justified. The most important provisions are the following: "the laws of the United States that are not locally inapplicable, unless before now or later on something in particular should be arranged, should have the same strength and vigor in Puerto Rico as in the United States, with the exception of those of internal revenue" (Section 14); "all laws approved by the Legislative Assembly of Puerto Rico should be remitted to the United States Congress, which by the

[10] *Speech of Hon. J. B. Foraker of Ohio in the Senate of the United States* (Washington: Government Printing Office, 1900), p. 6.

[11] Cayetano Coll y Cuchí, *La Ley Foraker* (San Juan: Tipografía del Boletín Mercantil, 1904), p. 70.

present law reserves the power and the authority to annul them, if it considers that action suitable" (Section 32); in the elections for the Chamber of Deputies, only those men who knew how to read and write and who have also paid a certain quantity as a contribution to the public treasury would be allowed to vote. As a consequence, the great majority of Puerto Ricans did not have access to the polls. The governor and all the eleven members of the Executive Council—of which only five would be Puerto Ricans—were to be named by the President of the United States. The governor would have an absolute veto over any legislation approved by the only elective body provided for in the law, the Chamber of Deputies, even though the Chamber was required to pass approved legislation through the sieve of the Executive Council, which acted both as a Cabinet for the governor and as the upper chamber of the Legislative Assembly (which was composed of the Executive Council and the Chamber of Deputies).[12]

I have described here the most salient characteristics of the organic statute by which Puerto Rico was governed from 1900 to 1917. As can be observed, the U.S. Congress possessed the power—which it still keeps today—to approve laws and make them applicable to the island at its own discretion. In addition, Congress itself could annul any legislation passed by the Legislative Assembly if it considered it appropriate to do so. With the passing of time, the Chamber of Deputies became the only body to more or less faithfully represent Puerto Ricans, for from its inception the Executive Council became the lackey of the colonial administration.

---

[12] The complete text of this law translated into Spanish appears in the book by Manuel Fraga Iribarne, *Las constituciones de Puerto Rico* (Madrid: Ediciones Cultura Hispánica, 1958).

This being the state of affairs, the Republicans now took the place of the old unconditionalists and appeared in the 1900 elections. The Federal party withdrew from participation in the elections. With the dissolution of the Federal party, until the Union party of Puerto Rico was created in 1904, the Republicans were alone at the helm of colonial power.

The situation changed after 1904 with the founding of the Union party of Puerto Rico. From that date on the Union party won all the elections held under the Foraker Act and became the most powerful party in Puerto Rico. Throughout this period the Republican party assumed the role of vigorous proponent of North Americanization and of the final annexation of Puerto Rico to the North American union. The Unionists defended both autonomy and independence—and even, on occasion, statehood for Puerto Rico—seeking a political grouping that might suit all Puerto Ricans, regardless of their opinions concerning the final resolution of our status.

In his decision to adopt independence as the political base of the Union party, the Puerto Rican orator, José de Diego, stands out singularly. In the assembly of Miramar on the eighteenth and nineteenth of February, 1904, he convinced the assembly to revoke a previous agreement and announce itself in favor of independence as one of the possible solutions to the Puerto Rican problem.[13] At that

[13] The fifth point of the Union party's platform said: "We declare that we understand it to be feasible that the island of Puerto Rico be confederated with the United States of North America, a means by which we can be granted the self-government which we need and request; and we also declare that the island of Puerto Rico can be declared an independent nation under the protectorate of the United States, a means by which we also can be granted the self-government which we need and request." Quoted in Bolívar Pagán, *op. cit.*, p. 112. See the article of

moment began the persistent struggle of this great man from Aguadilla for the independence of Puerto Rico. This struggle would grow more fierce in time, and with the passing of the second organic law (1917), would put him in opposition to Muñoz Rivera when the latter assumed his habitual posture of the political opportunist.

As a solution to the colonial problem of Puerto Rico, independence was thus made a part of the program of the most powerful political force at the beginning of this century. This fact is of great historical significance. We have seen previously that the two parties created at the beginning of the military occupation came out in favor of annexation to the United States. To Puerto Ricans the Foraker Act was a slap in the face. All illusions in this respect came tumbling down: independence became a refuge for Puerto Rican dignity. But the other two solutions—autonomy and statehood—were not abandoned.

A *modus vivendi* with the colonial regime was then sought. There was talk of a transitional status, and our politicians once more set out upon the road of reform just as they had under the previous rule. The traffic of commissions to Washington began. Republicans and Unionists became lobbyists before the U.S. government, with each group pushing its own special project. History repeated itself. Changes in the Washington administration were carefully observed by Puerto Rican leaders. The Republicans rejoiced when their namesakes in the United States won

---

Professor Ramón Meléndez, "La base quinta del Partido Unión de Puerto Rico," in the *Revista del Instituto de Cultura Puertorriqueña,* fifth year, no. 14 (1962). On De Diego as a fighter for independence, I refer the reader to my article, "La idea de la independencia de Puerto Rico en el pensamiento de José de Diego," *Asomante,* Vol. XXII, no. 4 (October–December, 1966), pp. 16–32.

anything; the Unionists preferred the Democrats. The only difference from the nineteenth century—when it was discussed whether Cánovas would be better than Sagasta—was the pronunciation of the names: Taft versus Wilson. The problem was similar to the one that existed under Spanish colonialism: Puerto Ricans could not make the basic decisions governing our collective life. Nevertheless, the commissions to Washington multiplied; brilliant, impassioned speeches were made while the situation remained as static as ever.

Increasingly frustrated by the failure of the U.S. to respond to their appeals for reform, Unionist party members turned more strongly to *independentista* thinking. Relations between the colonial governor and the Chamber of Deputies reached a critical impasse in 1909 when the Chamber recessed without having approved the budget for the current fiscal year. At the suggestion of President Taft, the U.S. Congress passed the Olmstead Act, amending the Foraker Act to the effect that when the Chamber did not approve the budget, the one from the previous year would remain in force. Thus a well-aimed blow was struck at the power of our only representative body, and at the same time the colonial regime then in power revealed itself with absolute crudity. To the insult of the passage of the Olmstead Act, President Taft added the injury of the following message:

"As we face, with the consent of the Puerto Rican people, the tutelage and direction of their destiny, we must keep in mind that it was not to be expected that a people who had been given so few opportunities to become educated would be able to exercise with confidence the full power of self-government, and the present contingency is only an indication that we have pro-

ceeded too rapidly in the concession to the Puerto Ricans, for
their own convenience, of self-government."[14]

All these factors contributed to the gradual drift of militant members of the Union party away from the belief in
statehood as the solution to the problem of Puerto Rico's
political status, while the Republicans stubbornly maintained their position favoring annexation.

One of the most seriously debated issues during this
period was North American citizenship for Puerto Ricans.
The Foraker Act had created a body called "The People of
Puerto Rico" and had declared the inhabitants of this island
to be "citizens of Puerto Rico," although from a legal
standpoint the island lacked identity in international law.
At this time the majority of Puerto Rican leaders considered North American citizenship to be a step toward the
achievement of greater equality between Puerto Rico and
the colonial power, but they found an unreceptive atmosphere in Washington. The same can be said of the aspiration toward federal statehood, petitions for which were
received in a cool manner in the United States Congress
and were rejected outright as a solution for Puerto Rico by
Secretary of State Elihu Root from the first moment the
issue was raised.

In that moment of uncertainty and collective humiliation
for the Puerto Rican people, Rosendo Matienzo Cintrón's
voice was raised. Together with De Diego, Zeno Gandía
and Llorens Torres, he brought independence before the
public as the only solution worthy of the Puerto Rican
colonial problem. When during a trip around the island on
November 21, 1906, President Theodore Roosevelt said he

[14] House Document No. 48 (May 10, 1909), 61st Congress, 1st
Session.

saw no defect in the Foraker Act, Matienzo Cintrón, a man of honor and strength, replied to Roosevelt: "You can deny us citizenship—it is within your rights—but in that case, you cannot deny us independence, because that is ours." Although an autonomist under the Spanish regime and an annexationist during the early part of the new domination, Matienzo gradually became convinced that the United States intended to keep Puerto Rico in a state of political inferiority.

In his judgment, "colonial life is indecorous; to accept it is a humiliation which can only be tolerated in the half-conscious state of peoples who are just beginning to live. Only an invincible force must serve as a base to such a depressing situation."[15] Therefore, all Puerto Ricans should unite and put aside sterile quarrels and conflicts of personality. Matienzo was one of the first to criticize the system of political parties established to gain power within the colony. For this criticism, Muñoz Rivera—who controlled the central committee of the Union party—without ceremony removed Matienzo from the presidency of the Chamber of Deputies, declaring that "the Union Party is pro-government, a friend of the governor, and in favor of so continuing." This action set the precedent for the action Muñoz Rivera later took to silence the independent voice of De Diego, and which subsequently led him, moreover, to remove all *independentistas* from the lists of candidates for the Chamber in the elections of 1911–12. Matienzo carried

[15] Quoted in Luis M. Díaz Soler, *Rosendo Matienzo Cintrón, orientador y guardián de una cultura,* two volumes (Universidad de Puerto Rico: Ediciones del Instituto de Cultura Puertorriqueña, 1960), Vol. 1, 340, 329. This biography of the patrician from Luquillo is, moreover, indispensable as a source of information and analysis with regard to the first twelve years of U.S. domination in Puerto Rico.

his preaching further, abandoned the Union party, and in 1912 formed the Independence party.

In a manifesto made public on February 8, 1912, Matienzo and his co-signing companions stated that the moment had arrived for Congress to define the political status of Puerto Rico as either statehood or independence. Among other considerations, the following was stated:

From a detailed and prudent examination of this problem, it is evident that an alliance under the same nationality in order to establish a sovereign state of the United States on the island of Puerto Rico does not suit the interests of the people of the United States nor those of the people of Puerto Rico . . . it is unjust for the United States to keep in its power for an indefinite period of time the sovereignty of a people proud of its culture, loving its liberties, master before God and reason of a country prodigious in wealth . . . and gifted with . . . the necessary energy to govern its own destiny; nor is it just to keep that people in servitude and not to recognize it after having accepted by virtue of a treaty the duty to define its rights. Therefore we have agreed to associate together in order to defend the right of our country to be constituted as an independent nation; to consult the will of the Puerto Rican people by means of plebiscite, agreeing to propose to Congress . . . that it postpone all legislation referring to our status . . . until we inform it what the will of our people is.[16]

Although the Independence party did not succeed in maintaining the electoral franchise in the elections of 1912, for the first time in Puerto Rican history Matienzo Cintrón and his comrades created a pro-independence political party. Unlike the Union party, in which political oppor-

[16] Quoted in Díaz Soler, *op. cit.*, Vol. I, pp. 526–27. See also Bolívar Pagán, *op. cit.*, Vol. I, pp. 146 ff.

tunists alternatively supported the three formulas of statehood, independence, and autonomy, the Independence
party held firm in its support of Puerto Rican independence. This set a precedent of great importance to the
struggle for independence. The liberation of Puerto Rico
was finally presented as something desirable in itself. Without mincing words, Matienzo and his supporters defended
independence as the only total and worthy solution to the
problem of liquidating colonialism on the island. Matienzo
Cintrón died on December 27, 1913. With his death,
Borinquén lost a man who had the courage to go against
the annexationist current at a time when the assimilationism
of Barbosa and the opportunism of Muñoz Rivera com-
peted for illusory power in a country of which Puerto
Ricans could not call themselves masters.

But Matienzo Cintrón's gesture was not isolated. Within
the Union party, De Diego continued preaching for independence. In fact, the *independentista* force in the Union
party was so strong that even Muñoz Rivera was obliged to
defend it. It was, however, a tepid, weak defense. For
Muñoz Rivera, independence was the "last recourse of the
dignity" of the Puerto Rican people; and in his determination to continue on good terms with the regime, he played
with independence, statehood, and autonomy like a circus
juggler. Typical of Muñoz Rivera's wavering is the following statement, made at the Mohonk Lake conference in
1910: "Our problem has three solutions: the proclamation
of statehood, which would intermingle us with you in
national life; the concession of self-government (home
rule), which would unite us with you in a sentimental bond
of gratitude and which would be the true nexus for the
interchange of commercial products; and the concession of
independence, by law of Congress, which would make us

the only masters of our destiny. Of these three solutions we would prefer the first; we propose the second, and we reserve the third as the last refuge of our rights and honor."[17] This compromising and ambiguous position taken by Muñoz Rivera forms a sharp contrast with the unequivocal one of De Diego in the same conference: "To think of an ambiguous, intermediate formula of a self-government for Puerto Rico—under the sovereignty of the United States but without a definite position as a state, in a regime like that of Canada or Australia—would be to attempt to introduce into the American constitution an exotic element contrary to its spirit. Therefore, two possible arrangements remain: Puerto Rico, State of the Union; Puerto Rico, independent state. The entrance of our island into your brotherhood of states—let us speak frankly and loyally—is something neither you nor we desire, nor do we believe in it. With the road toward your federation closed, the only solution to the problem seems to be the explicit recognition of the Republic of Puerto Rico, under the protectorate of the United States." Placing independence, as the ultimate recourse of the Puerto Rican people, on the Greek calends,* Muñoz Rivera was simply bypassing the colonial problem of Puerto Rico, using equivocal expressions that served only to confuse public opinion.

In his patriotic rhetoric Muñoz Rivera always had one eye on the seat of power, and he was not seeking to antagonize the colonial power that ruled Puerto Rico. Throughout his political career until his death in 1913, Matienzo Cintrón's opinion of Muñoz Rivera as a politician could not be more accurate: "Muñoz," said the great man of Luquillo,

---

[17] Quoted in Bolívar Pagán, *op. cit.,* Vol. I, p. 154.

* As there were no Greek calends, this is a time that will never come. (Translator's note)

"was the exponent of the easy success, of traditional double-talk, which has such enormous roots in our national laziness . . ." In a devastating criticism of Muñoz, Matienzo said, "Muñoz . . . is prepared to place himself at the front of any majority. Here are his words: 'We are certainly partisans of autonomy, backed up by independence, as long as we are not given statehood, which after all would be the best.' "[18] It is of no great consequence that in his political testament Muñoz spoke of independence as his preferred solution to the problem of status or that he opposed the imposition of North American citizenship on Puerto Ricans.[19] Political opportunism was always behind his anti-imperialist pronouncements. Once Matienzo Cintrón was dead, De Diego—and not Muñoz Rivera—became the champion of the Puerto Rican people's right to independence. In fact, from 1904 until the passing of the Jones Act in 1917, the Union party was dominated by these two historic figures: De Diego, *independentista,* President of the Chamber of Deputies, and Muñoz Rivera, autonomist(?), Resident Commissioner of Puerto Rico in Washington. Muñoz appears to have finally won the battle with De Diego when the U.S. Congress passed the Jones Act, another political crumb his maneuvers obtained from the colonial power. Let us see.

The Union party of Puerto Rico dominated the Puerto Rican political scene from 1904 on, controlling the only really representative body of the Puerto Ricans provided for by the Foraker Act: the Chamber of Deputies. Agitation within the Union party for a more generous helping of

18 Quoted in Díaz Soler, *op. cit.,* Vol. I, p. 475.
19 See the biography of Muñoz Rivera by Sebastián Dalmau Canet, *Luis Muñoz Rivera, su vida, su política, su carácter* (San Juan: Tip. *Boletín Mercantil,* 1917).

self-government brought the issue to Washington. Under this pressure, the Jones Act was presented to Congress in 1912. Its purpose was to modify the Foraker Act, liberalizing some of its more onerous aspects. It was not until 1917 that the U.S. Congress passed the Jones Act and it was signed by President Wilson. Then the work of lobbying in Washington began. In his first speech defending the Jones Act, Muñoz Rivera, in his typical role of the equivocal politician, said in Washington in 1912: "Puerto Ricans, like all human beings in the world, love their national independence. Of all the possible solutions, they would prefer the one which leads them to being a free and sovereign nation; but they are intelligent [*sic*], they know the obstacles that prevent the triumph of their supreme ideal, and they know that at the present moment, *patriotism consists of fighting for practical reforms, which will assure the preponderance of local control in local affairs.*"[20]

Not so De Diego. On November 22, 1913, he drew up and had approved (without amendments) in the General Assembly of the Union party the programmatic statements listed below:

I. The people of Puerto Rico are subject to a regime of government decreed by the Congress of the United States, as a consequence of an international treaty and by the force of a law, in which the people of Puerto Rico were unjustly kept from participation in matters that have to do with their lives, their dignity, and their liberty. Such a regime—which imposes on the people of Puerto Rico legislators named by the President of the United States and places in the hands of persons foreign to the country all the executive departments, which excludes islanders from the management of public funds, and which at-

[20] *Ibid.*, pp. 318–19. The emphasis is the author's.

tributes to the dominators an all-embracing power in all branches of the administration—is unworthy of the institutions of the American people and of the capacity and honor of the Puerto Rican people. The Union party of Puerto Rico states its loudest, most vigorous protest against the ruling system and energetically demands action and justice from the people of the United States, to free us from an oligarchy which acts in their name and rejects their spirit.

II. We declare that the supreme ideal of the Union party, like that of every strong group and all free men throughout the world, is the founding of a free country, absolute mistress of her sovereignty, for the present and for the future. Within this ultimate goal, the Union party of Puerto Rico proclaims the constitution of Puerto Rico as a completely independent Republic, or one with the protectorate and friendship of the Anglo-American Republic.

III. Reaffirming this ideal with profound energy, we consider that until circumstances permit the country to attain the desired goal of her own complete sovereignty, the Union party would be untrue to its highest patriotic duties if, dedicating itself exclusively to the defense of that sovereignty, it should neglect or abandon the struggle for other transitory solutions which recognize the island as a system of autonomous government with full power to govern her domestic legal relationships, by means of a concurrent intervention by the government of the United States.

Muñoz Rivera replied by instituting the "rule of the padlock." Under this rule all Unionist legislators were prohibited from spreading pro-independence propaganda both in and out of Puerto Rico. The Assembly adopted this rule in October 1915. Once more Muñoz imposed his will on the *independentistas,* this time to secure the passage of the Jones Act, which was at that time being considered by the Congress of the colonial power. Even though the bill imposed North American citizenship on Puerto Ricans

—against the expressed will of the Union party and even against Muñoz' will (he opposed it in Congress)—Muñoz Rivera accepted the bill as a transitory but necessary reform. The Jones Act, he wrote, should be accepted "as a step forward on the right road and as a reform that will prepare the way for another, more satisfactory one, which will come a little later, provided that my fellow countrymen can demonstrate their ability to govern themselves."[21]

Finally, the second organic law, or the Jones Act, was passed by Congress over the objections to certain provisions by Muñoz himself and the Union party. This was one more indication of how little the opinion of the Puerto Rican majority party counted in Washington.

The Jones Act made its appearance in the United States Congress in 1912 and it was not until 1917 that it was passed. Five years of incessant lobbying and countless commissions to Washington—all to finally achieve only a slight liberalization of the organic statute in force. We will discuss this further on. We would first, however, like to enlarge a little on the discussion of the origins of the Jones Act and the forces that fought for its approval.

Since 1912 a Democratic administration under the Presidency of Woodrow Wilson had been in power in Washington. World War I broke out, and in their greedy scramble for markets and colonies the capitalist countries prepared to divide up the world. Corporate capitalism had arrived to stay in the United States. President Wilson proclaimed the "New Freedom" and described World War I as the way to "make the world safe for democracy." At the same time, he defended the right of the United States to intervene in any Latin American country straying from the path of what he meant by "democracy." A contemporary historian defines

21 Quoted in *Ibid.*, p. 366.

the foreign policy of President Wilson in regard to "backward" countries:

United States leaders identified colonial and undeveloped areas as neo-frontier wastelands—wasted in the sense that their resources were not being developed and used by the industrial nations for the benefit of the whole world economy. There would continue to be international conflict among the industrial powers until that situation was corrected. America's mission, or new manifest destiny, was to bring to "waste areas" political democracy (as much as such peoples could absorb) and stability. In this view, selfish exploitation (such as colonial monopoly systems), which did not contribute to the overall system, was almost as bad as not making use of the area at all. Though very often covered with the thick rhetoric of morality (especially in the Wilson years), this was the foreign policy reflection of the Gospel of Efficiency, or of a Darwinian Constitution.[22]

Haiti, Santo Domingo, Mexico—all have firsthand knowledge of this "Gospel of Efficiency." Only the rhetoric has changed since the time of Taft and Roosevelt; the reality continues to be the same.

In the context of Wilsonian politics, Puerto Rico continued to have great strategic importance in the broader framework of North American control of the Panama Canal. In congressional hearings on the Jones Act, Congressman Cooper (Wisconsin) hit the nail on the head when he said:

We are never to give up Puerto Rico for, now that we have completed the Panama Canal, the retention of the island be-

[22] Lloyd C. Gardner, "American Foreign Policy 1900–1921," in Barton J. Bernstein, ed., *Towards a New Past: Dissenting Essays in American History* (New York: Pantheon, 1968), pp. 214–15. See also in this respect Gabriel Kolko, *The Triumph of Conservatism: A Reinterpretation of American History 1900–1916* (New York: Free Press, 1968).

comes very important to the safety of the Canal, and in that way to the safety of the nation itself. It helps to make the Gulf of Mexico an American lake. I again express my pleasure that this bill grants this people citizenship.[23]

That is to say, the extension of North American citizenship to the Puerto Ricans was meant to be the final checkmate to any move for Puerto Rican independence. There is no doubt that this assumption weighed considerably in the decision to grant citizenship to Puerto Ricans. At that moment, the North American authorities granted the concession of U.S. citizenship with the unspoken but mutual knowledge that on their own they would never concede independence. Thus the Secretary of War, Lindley M. Garrison, gave the following testimony before a congressional committee:

As I understand the situation, there is no sentiment whatever in the United States that the island of Puerto Rico should be an independent sovereignty. There is no suggestion that it should not be connected with the United States government for all time and that we should not in the fullest measure be responsible for it as we are for any other thing under our flag.[24]

Even more eloquent is the following testimony of Muñoz Rivera before the same committee:

Chairman: The position of your party is this, as I understand it: you want this question of citizenship left in abeyance, because you think that if you are declared citizens now it will prejudice your case and will preclude your obtaining complete independence or independence with an American protectorate in the fu-

---

[23] *Congressional Record* (House of Representatives), February 24, 1917, p. 4171.

[24] *Hearings before the Committee on Insular Affairs, House of Representatives,* 63rd Congress, 2nd Session on H. R. 138118, p. 49.

ture. That is a correct statement of the idea you want to present to the committee, is it not?

Muñoz Rivera: That is my position, exactly.

Chairman: Now it seems to me, on the other hand, that the people of the United States desire that Puerto Rico shall remain a permanent possession of the United States but that it should be given the most liberal form of territorial government that its people are capable of directing . . . This bill is framed upon the idea that Puerto Rico is to remain a permanent possession of the United States. It proposes to settle this question and thus remove it from Puerto Rican politics. What do you say about that, Mr. Rivera?

Muñoz Rivera: That is a very difficult thing for me to solve, because, as you know, the final aspiration of my party is nationalism with or without an American protectorate, and as the Puerto Rican people understand it, the granting of citizenship will interfere with their aspirations for independence.

Chairman: I do not think that that would change the sentiment in the United States, and I think, speaking for myself, this talk of independence is an idle dream of the Unionist party, and that it would be much better to have the matter settled now, better for the Puerto Rican people themselves.[25]

I have quoted this exchange between Muñoz Rivera and the President of the Committee on Insular Affairs of the U.S. House of Representatives so that the reader can hear the imperative tone in Congress at that time. As can be seen, the object of the exchange was to resolve the question of our destiny; however, the decision would be made unilaterally in Washington—for our own benefit, of course . . .

In Puerto Rico, the annexationists recognized—correctly, in my opinion—the transcendental character of the decision concerning citizenship. And they did not hide their

[25] *Ibid.,* p. 61.

joy over what they considered to be the final blow to all hope for independence. De Diego himself sees it in this light when he writes prophetically: "If we are to proclaim the redeeming solution in our political program, and if we are to lead our people in the holy undertaking, it would be better and more opportune to do so before the suggested reforms, so that no one will be deceived, to prevent, in the new reform bill as in all the previous ones, the declaration of American citizenship from destroying the basic element of our aspiration to independence, which is our own citizenship."[26] But the die was already cast. Once more it was obvious how little majority representation in the colony was worth. Muñoz Rivera compromised because his vision of politics as a process of gradual change always inclined him toward the compromise solution. The protests of the Union party were to no avail. The Jones Act imposed North American citizenship collectively on the Puerto Rican people. And from that very instant the road was open for the recruitment of Puerto Rican youths into the United States armed forces. On June 27, 1917, President Wilson issued a proclamation ordering the registration and recruitment of inhabitants of the territory of Puerto Rico between the ages of twenty-one and thirty-one. In accordance with a cable from Secretary MacIntyre to Governor Yager, dated October 18, 1918,[27] this provision applied both to the new North American citizens and to those who chose to retain their Puerto Rican citizenship.

[26] José de Diego, *Nuevas campañas* (Barcelona: Sociedad General de Publicaciones, 1916), p. 69.

[27] See the interesting book, *Report of the Adjutant General to the Governor of Puerto Rico on the Operation of the Military Registration and Selective Draft in Puerto Rico* (San Juan, P. R.: Bureau of Supplies, Printing and Transportation, 1924).

Puerto Ricans who chose to retain their Puerto Rican citizenship were divested of all their political rights, thus becoming pariahs in their own country. Only two hundred and eighty-eight citizens renounced North American citizenship at that time. De Diego considered that he ought to continue fighting for independence with the instruments which destiny had provided him and so he pronounced his famous postulate of the struggle of the *independentistas:* "against the regime from within the regime." But not without first rising to denounce the outrage in energetic terms:

Never was anything like this seen before, in private international law, in the democratic nations of the world: one million, two hundred thousand human beings, who by law of the Congress of a Republic—which seems more like an order from the times of the Low Empire—are deprived of their natural citizenship, but under the threat and coercion of losing their right as electors and of being eligible for all public offices, in a country where they are obliged to carry all the burdens of the state and to render military tribute to the dominating nation, in the country of their birth and their life, where they long to be buried, Puerto Ricans, who for a crime unknown as yet in universal law —love of their own citizenship—are reduced to the condition of foreigners in their own country, are exiled from their land; and so, through terror, and because of the harshness of the punishment, only a very small number of Puerto Ricans have renounced the imposed citizenship, for almost all of them accept it, to present afterwards to the world with this unheard-of deed the fictitious demonstration that the Puerto Ricans voluntarily and joyfully accepted United States citizenship and with it they abandoned the ideal of constituting their country among the free and sovereign nations of America.[28]

[28] José de Diego, *El plebiscito puertorriqueño* (San Juan: Tipografía Boletín Mercantil, 1917), pp. 75–76.

The Jones Act differed from the Foraker Act in that it provided for a bill of rights and a popularly elected legislature. In every other respect the previous law remained practically unaltered. Above all, the plenary authority of the United States Congress to legislate for Puerto Rico on those matters "not locally inapplicable" remained in force; the absolute veto of the governor was retained, but if the legislature overrode the veto, the President of the United States had the final veto. In addition, Congress reserved the right to annul any legislation passed by the Legislative Assembly of Puerto Rico. Given this situation, the protest of De Diego is not surprising, when he said that the plan really ought to be entitled, "For the one and only purpose of assuring a despotic government for Puerto Rico and for no other reason." But neither Muñoz Rivera nor De Diego would live long enough to see the Jones Act functioning. Muñoz Rivera died in 1916, on his return from Washington; De Diego died in 1918.

Muñoz Rivera and De Diego. The two men who by their magnetic personalities dominated the Puerto Rican political scene during the first two decades of North American domination. Both defended independence for Puerto Rico. But while the former skillfully used the cause of independence for political purposes, the latter became consistently stronger in his nationalist preaching. Muñoz Rivera believed in autonomy under a constitutional system, but that category did not exist. In one sense, one can say about autonomy under United States domination what Betances said about it under Spanish domination. To paraphrase, "The United States cannot give what it does not have." In this case what it did not have was sufficient flexibility within its constitutional system to grant an autonomy similar to the one Spain belatedly granted to the Puerto Ricans. Muñoz Rivera went on, however, speaking of home rule and self-government in a vacuum which the United States could not fill. De Diego did perceive this reality and he saw only two solutions: statehood or independence. After 1912 he showed himself to be unequivocally behind independence as the only solution to the political status of Puerto Rico.

Poet, brilliant orator, legislator, lawyer, patriot, De Diego kept alive the idea of independence at a crucial moment in our nation's history. Defender of our Hispanic cultural heritage, he defended Puerto Rican culture tenaciously and he fought resolutely against cultural assimilation to the United States. Anti-imperialist and anticolonialist, he helped to create the foundation for a consciousness of our real dilemma. An internationalist, he actively defended the cause of Antillean and Spanish-American solidarity.

With Matienzo Cintrón, he was one of the men who taught our people to resist colonialism, to say *No* to the empire: "From the almost prehistoric uprisings of savage tribes against the leaders of Asiatic empires, the refusal to submit, the protest against tyranny, the *No* of the oppressed has been the word, the genesis of the liberation of peoples; and even when the impotence of the means and the virtuality of the ends, as in our country, remove the revolutionary fire for the vision of the ideal, *No* must be and is the only word which will preserve the liberty and dignity of the peoples in servitude."[20] Against autonomy because it seemed to him a transitory state and a disguised form of colonialism, he put things in their right perspective by placing independence and sovereignty before any other temporary consideration. For him, "independence, sovereignty is the chief and primary liberty of the people: sovereignty is

[29] De Diego, *Nuevas campañas,* p. 17.

the source of all rights; collective independence can, in fact, generate all despotisms, but also all freedoms; while all the secondary freedoms cannot generate the superior unity of national sovereignty which is creative, and all the other freedoms are like creatures which have emanated from it and are incapable of supreme creation."[30] With his death, Puerto Rican independence did not have another champion of his category until the great figure of Pedro Albizu Campos appeared on the Puerto Rican horizon. But for him we had to wait until 1930. What happened in the period from the death of De Diego to the moment Albizu Campos consented to accept the presidency of the Nationalist party? Let us see.

In the first place, the Socialist party had reappeared, headed by Santiago Iglesias Pantín—founder of the labor movement in Puerto Rico at the end of the nineteenth century. As one of his fellow socialists pointed out, "in their speaking, Santiago Iglesias and the press and other socialist orators defended Americanization and the permanent association of Puerto Rico with the United States, as a supreme guarantee of the protection of individual rights and of the hopes for democracy and civilization in Puerto Rico."[31] Socialist in name only, this party managed to draw into its fold a large part of the labor sector of Puerto Rico. Like the North American reform labor movement—headed by Samuel Gompers—with which it maintained close ties, the Socialist party supported the development of labor unions in Puerto Rico similar to those beginning to appear in the United States at that time. From its beginning, the Socialist

---

[30] *Ibid.,* p. 360.

[31] Bolívar Pagán, *op. cit.,* Vol. 1, p. 171. In respect to Santiago Iglesias Pantín, see also his *Luchas emancipadoras (Crónicas de Puerto Rico),* Vol. 1 (San Juan: Cantero Fernandez y Co., 1929).

party supported annexation and emerged as a political force marked with the sign of colonialism. Its historical development led it, in the course of time, to align itself with the most reactionary elements in Puerto Rican society, in order to fulfill its aspirations for public power. However, one cannot deny its important role in the struggle for the most urgent social needs of the Puerto Rican people. Faced with the obvious hostility of the political bosses and the government, Iglesias and his supporters created an instrument of social struggle which—if it had not been for the contradiction implicit in a so-called Socialist party operating within the framework of a colonialist system or for the dependence its close ties to the labor movement of the colonial power created—might have been more fruitful than it was in exposing the exploitation to which the island was being subjected by North American interests. Dedicated to the cause of annexation, Iglesias never resolves the fundamental problem with annexation for many: namely, that annexation to the United States, should it take place, was based on the previous deed of an act of force, and was part of a program designed to destroy Puerto Rican national identity. To a great extent the divorce which has existed in Puerto Rico between the *independentistas* and the masses of workers and peasants can be explained, at least in part, by the fact that our labor movement came of age under the leadership of a man who had no qualms about defending imperialism as a North American policy, reaching the point, on occasion, of suggesting the sacrifice of the island whenever it served North American interests. The testimony of Iglesias with respect to the Jones Act is instructive on this point, since it reflects faithfully the vision which he sustained to the end of his days of the political status of Puerto Rico:

Puerto Rico is now, and always will be, of much value to the United States because of the island's large business interests and possibilities, and its important and rapidly increasing trade with this country . . .

Aside from these considerations, we are firmly of the opinion that with the completion of the Panama Canal, Puerto Rico will become of such great strategic importance as to preclude all doubt concerning its permanent retention by the Government of the United States.[32]

For the record, the man speaking is none other than the highest leader of the organized labor movement in Puerto Rico.

In the second place, under the presidency of Antonio R. Barceló—successor to Muñoz Rivera at the helm of the Union party—independence was eliminated from Point Five of the party's platform. The party declared itself in favor of the Commonwealth of Puerto Rico.[33] This alteration was made at precisely the moment that a new Republican administration had installed one of the most inept colonial governors of our history: E. Mont Reilly, whom the people nicknamed "Moncho Reyes." A stalwart enemy of independence, vulgar and insolent, Reilly purged the *independ-*

[32] *A People Without a Country. Appeal for U.S. Citizenship for the People of Puerto Rico* (Washington, D.C.: American Federation of Labor, 1912). Senate Document No. 509, 62nd Congress, 2nd Session.

[33] Contrary to what some people believe, it was not Muñoz Marín who invented the Commonwealth but Barceló and Guerra Mondragón. The text of the Unionist resolution, passed in their assembly on February 11, 1922, says: "The creation in Puerto Rico of a People's State or Community, which is free and associated to the United States, is the desideratum of the aspirations of Puerto Ricans, and it will solve in an honorable, satisfactory and final manner the problem—still awaiting a solution—of what the relations are to be between the two peoples." Bolívar Pagán, *op. cit.,* Vol. I, pp. 212–13.

entistas from all political posts. Confronted with this insult, the Union party responded weakly, ratifying "the expression of our loyalty to the United States of America and her flag" in an assembly held on August 21, 1921. These two decisions—to eliminate independence from Point Five and to knuckle under to Reilly's arbitrary acts—were really the prelude to the agreement that would later be forged in the United States by Barceló and Tous Soto (president at the time of the Republicans) when the Puerto Rican Alliance was formed for the 1924 elections. From the point of view of the struggle for independence, these two decisions constituted an historical retrogression. Sacrificing independence at that time, Barceló was following the opportunistic pathway bequeathed to him by Muñoz Rivera.

As a consequence of what had been allowed to happen, the most radical element in the Union party conceived the idea of founding a party specifically dedicated to the struggle for independence. This is how the Nationalist party of Puerto Rico was born. It was founded on September 17, 1922; its declaration of principles included the following statement: "The Nationalist party aspires to make of Puerto Rico a free republic, sovereign and independent, in accordance with the principle of nationalities." A young lawyer from Ponce, a recent graduate of Harvard University, was one of those who finally abandoned the Union party and entered the ranks of the Nationalist party. In an interview held years later by the magazine *Los Quijotes,* Pedro Albizu Campos explained how he came to enter the Nationalist party: "When, a short time after I entered it, the leadership of the Union party resolved to bow to the will of the North American government, so that there would be no more separatist campaigns in the country, I immediately

withdrew and contributed to the formation of the Nationalist party, made up by the breaking away of the few patriots
that were in the Unionist ranks."[34] Nine years later—in
1930—Albizu Campos was elected president of the Nationalist party in Puerto Rico.

The Nationalist party thus followed the pattern set by
Matienzo Cintrón with the creation of the Independence
party in 1912: that is to say, the pattern of a party that did
not think of independence as one among many political
formulas—as had been the case with the Union party in
1922—but that declared firmly that its essential, primary
purpose was to liberate Puerto Rico. Although the Nationalist party had in its origins a markedly cultural orientation, it responded so well to the real needs of Puerto Ricans
that its imprint was firmly based in the Puerto Rican
ambience. For when independence had no defenders and
was confronted with a hostile administration, the nationalists raised it again from where it had fallen with the death of
De Diego, and placed it at the vanguard of the concerns of
our people.

During the period from 1924 to 1932, the political scene
was dominated by the Puerto Rican Alliance, composed of
the Unionists, led by Antonio R. Barceló, and the Republicans, presided over by José Tous Soto. Opposing the Alliance at that time was a group who had broken off from the
Republicans and called themselves "pure," presided over by
Martínez Nadal, and the Socialist party of Santiago Iglesias,
who also subsequently formed an alliance to constitute
what would be known in time as the Coalition.

A little after the Puerto Rican Alliance came to power in

---

[34] This interview appears in Paulino Castro, *Historia sinóptica del
Partido Nacionalista de Puerto Rico* (San Juan: 1947), p. 61.

1924, Pedro Albizu Campos was commissioned by the Nationalist party to undertake a pilgrimage through the Latin American countries in order to elicit their support of the cause of Puerto Rican independence. That is how the great Puerto Rican leader set off on a second pilgrimage, one similar to that of Bayoán.* This pilgrimage began in 1925 and concluded in 1930, when Albizu Campos returned to Puerto Rico. During this period he visited Cuba, Santo Domingo, Haiti, Mexico, and Peru. There he met the great leaders of Antillean nationalism of that period. Juan Marinello evokes the memory of Albizu Campos when he spoke before the Havana public:

Before the masses that small and fragile man grew large as a giant, and in a few moments all were spellbound by his oratory. His powerful and original reasoning—in which he revealed much reading, much meditation, and many long vigils—was supported by his impassioned speech. Among friends his voice was calm and suggestive; before the public it acquired a vibrant, metallic tone which reached the most remote listener, like a bugle calling orders which could not be evaded. And no matter how long the speech was, the tone stayed the same—vigorous and bright, deep and distinct, like a clamorous cry that came from beyond the body that gave birth to it.

On his return to Puerto Rico, Albizu Campos gave to the Nationalist party the radical tone which characterized it from then on. Placing himself in Betances' tradition of revolutionary independence, the nationalist leader opened a new page in colonial Puerto Rican history of the twentieth century.

* *La peregrinación de Bayoán* is a Puerto Rican classic of the nineteenth century written by our great Eugenio María de Hostos. (Author's note to the English edition)

On May 11, 1930, the general assembly of the Nationalist party met in the Puerto Rican Atheneum. The oath
sworn at the conclusion of the assembly made clear its new
orientation, "We hereby solemnly swear that we will defend
the Nationalist ideal and that we will sacrifice our property
and our lives if that is necessary for the independence of
our country." The assembly thereafter declared: "We cannot postpone the immediate suppression of North American
colonialism, and we agree to hold a constituent convention
which will establish in Puerto Rico the government of a
free, sovereign and independent republic as soon as it receives the vote of the majority." Its position was clearly anti-
imperialist, and as part of its platform it declared that
"Under the harsh yoke of North American colonialism,
from a nation of proprietors we have changed into a mass
of peons, a rich economic mine for exploitation by the
capitalist invader." As its economic platform, the Nationalist party drew up the following statements:

1) It will organize the workers so that they can demand from
foreign interests participation in the earnings which they have a
right to: assuming control of them immediately, placing men of
stature, responsibility and patriotism in the positions of control.
2) It will seek through all means for the tax burden to fall on
those who are not residents, in order to destroy latifundism and
absenteeism, and to divide real property among the greatest possible number of landholders. 3) Using every means within its
reach it will attempt to revoke the effect of free coastal trading
between the United States and Puerto Rico, which today benefits the invader exclusively. 4) It will favor the exclusive con-
sumption of local fruits and the patronage of Puerto Rican industries, attempting with all means to satisfy the country's needs.
5) It will encourage exportation and the establishment of a
maritime transportation industry. 6) It will favor exclusively

native banks; where there are none, it will seek to organize them. 7) It will try to organize finances in such a form of native banking respectability that national deposits are made only in those banks; and it will try to free the country from foreign loans, public or private, so that a strong resurgence of agriculture, commerce, and industry in the hands of Puerto Ricans may occur.[35]

As the reader will notice, both the economic and political platforms of the party were nationalistic. The truth is that Albizu Campos fits into that current of Latin American thought which we might call anti-imperialist nationalism. The intellectual roots of this posture may be found in Martí, Rodó, Darío, and Vasconcelos. The maximum political expression of this ideology is found in the brilliant figure of Augusto César Sandino. Moreover, it is worth noting that the nationalists decided to take part in the 1932 elections—influenced, as Albizu Campos himself phrased it, by the example of Republican Spain.

By the time of the elections of 1932, the Puerto Rican Alliance had been dissolved (in 1929) and Barceló, together with the *independentistas* who were militant in the Union party, founded a new party, the Puerto Rican Liberal party, on March 12, 1932. Thus the old Union party ceased to exist, and a new group was created, one whose political platform favored independence. Antonio R. Barceló presided over it. Also founded that year was the Republican Union party, under the presidency of Martínez Nadal.

At the previously mentioned assembly, the Liberal party pronounced itself in support of independence as the only solution to the colonial problem of Puerto Rico, declaring its purpose of "demanding immediate recognition of Puerto

[35] Pagán, *op. cit.*, pp. 331–34.

Rican sovereignty—to be made effective by the swiftest, most practical and most direct means, thus establishing the absolute independence of Puerto Rico in the brotherhood of nations—as well as dedicating her strength, by exercising the functions and prerogatives of government, to creating economic independence for Puerto Rico, adapting it to the moment when, the colony having disappeared, Puerto Rico assumes her full functions as a sovereign and independent nation."

One of the most outstanding leaders of the Liberal party —but above all, of its leftist or radical independent wing— was at that moment Luis Muñoz Marín, the son of Muñoz Rivera. A socialist during his years of residence in the United States, upon his return Muñoz Marín rejoined the struggle in Puerto Rico and proclaimed independence as the only solution to the Puerto Rican problem. Furthermore, he addressed himself to the most urgent social problems of the island. Declaring himself to be anticolonialist and anti-imperialist, he made the following pronouncements during 1932. "I am," he wrote to Governor Roosevelt, "a radical nationalist, for moral and spiritual reasons that are undebatable, and for economic reasons that I am always ready to debate." Affirming that autonomy was only freedom "with a long chain," Muñoz Marín stated: "One cannot observe Puerto Rican life close up without reaching the conclusion that every form of tutelage is morally degrading. As long as sovereignty does not reside in us, there will be genuflections and degradations before those in whom it does reside. This is the political illness of colonial Puerto Rico, and its only cure is a dose of unadulterated sovereignty." Muñoz even declared that independence was "just around the corner," and he stood up for his defense of the cause in Puerto Rico as well as abroad. No one who listened to him advocating independence in those days would have thought that this man would, in the end, desert the *independentista* camp and, with time, become one of the most tenacious enemies of independence.

The colonial elections of 1932 brought the coalition of Republicans and socialists into power. The Liberal party, although it got more votes than the Republicans and socialists taken separately, succumbed, however, before the combined force of the two. The Nationalist party won some 5,000 votes and disappeared as an official party. Faced with this situation and the fact that the colonial elections did not solve the colonial problem of Puerto Rico but simply helped to perpetuate it, Albizu Campos categorically declared his resistance to colonialism and to the regime in power, at the same time proclaiming the need for armed struggle to achieve independence. In fact, the concept of an armed struggle against colonialism had been developed years before. In the previously mentioned interview for *Los Quijotes,* we already (1926) find the nationalist leader adopting the following tone:

Puerto Rico must present a serious crisis to the colonial administration in order to have her demands attended to. Until now the colonialist has formulated requests for things of little value. In Washington, they have failed to recognize the members of her commissions and the latter have resigned themselves to returning to make more genuflections. A nation like the United States, with enormous national and international problems, does not have time to attend to servile, submissive men. What is required is the formation of a rebel organization which represents all the people of Puerto Rico, which will break definitively with the regime of the colony, and which will solicit from the free nations recognition of our independence. Thus we will achieve the concentration of the North American mind on our situation.

On evaluating the consequences of colonialism on Puerto Rico, Albizu Campos issued the following declaration when he learned of the final results of the 1932 elections: "Puerto Rico presents a picture of a shipwreck of the most prized human values: honor, patriotism, sacrifice. In moral matters, Yankee imperialism has led us to scorn ourselves; in material affairs, it has converted us from proprietors into peons, and from peons into beggars sentenced to death. Nationalism is the only salvation because it causes to be reborn in each one of us the conscience of a free man, for whom human dignity has no price and who cannot conceive why he does not have the right to rule the destinies of his children or of his country."[36] Later he stated his opinion of the electoral process: "The electoral struggle is a periodic farce to keep the Puerto Rican family divided."[37] To him is also attributed this famous sentence: "The triumph of Puerto Ricans over Puerto Ricans is the defeat of the fatherland."

It is suitable at this moment to turn our attention to the colonial power. After the Republican interlude of Harding, Coolidge, and Hoover, Franklin Delano Roosevelt came into power as President of the United States. If previous Presidents had designated inept colonial governors for Puerto Rico, the champion of the New Deal did no less in his appointment of two of the worst governors in our colonial history, Robert H. Gore (from July 1, 1933, to June 10, 1934) and Blanton D. Winship (from February 5, 1934 to August 31, 1939). In fact, imperialism, the Achilles' heel of the liberals, was never so clearly vulnerable to attack as it was under Roosevelt. With Roosevelt,

---

36 *El Mundo,* November 16, 1933.
37 *El Mundo,* June 28, 1933.

however, a new phase in the colonial policy of the United States was initiated, a phase in which programs of federal aid were extended to the island. While they relieved the worst evils of colonial exploitation, these programs became effective political weapons for the perpetuation of colonialism. Other Democratic Presidents after Roosevelt have essentially maintained this policy: filing down the roughest edges of the prevailing system, yet leaving intact its substance and repressing without qualms all those who were not prepared to obey the rules of the game fixed by the rulemakers. In this sense there was no essential difference in the policy of the Republicans and the Democrats, except perhaps in their rhetoric.

A colonial regime such as the one we are describing could not tolerate a movement like the one led by Albizu Campos, which sought to go to the root of our problems. Repression of the nationalists began with Gore but reached its most complete expression under Winship. Colonel E. Frances Riggs was chief of the insular police at the time. The hostilities began on October 24, 1935, the day the nationalists have designated as the day of the "Massacre of Río Piedras." On this occasion, there was an encounter between the police and the nationalists outside the university; four nationalists and one insular policeman were killed, and about forty people were wounded. It was clear by that time that the colonial regime and the Winship–Riggs twosome had decided—doubtlessly following orders from Washington—to destroy the Nationalist party by force.

On February 23, 1936, two young nationalists, Hiram Rosado and Elías Beauchamp, executed Colonel Riggs on the streets of San Juan. Brought to general police headquarters, they were vilely assassinated there, it being alleged later that they had tried to escape. Governor Winship took an important part in the persecution of the nationalists, personally supervising the accumulation of evidence against them.[38]

As a consequence of the death of Riggs, Senator Millard Tydings presented in Washington a basically punitive plan for granting independence to Puerto Rico. Albizu Campos of course accepted independence but rejected the demand for a plebiscite of the Puerto Rican people on the matter, because he considered that a plebiscite held in an occupied country like ours would never reflect our people's authentic desire for freedom. Barceló—after exclaiming, "Let independence come even if we die of hunger!"—retracted and chose to parley with Washington. Muñoz Marín did the same, foreshadowing the course he would take during the following years. It is interesting to observe that through the actions of Beauchamp and Rosado, Puerto Rican independence—which merited only scorn and flat negation from the members of the U.S. Congress and from U.S. Presidents—gained an unheard-of strength in national and international opinion. An heroic act of two Puerto Rican youths ready to sacrifice everything for the liberation of their country did more to put the colonial government in check than all the commissions sent to Washington for three decades and all the declarations and pronouncements of all the politicians who during that period had perorated on the subject. Far from cowering at the challenge, however, the government responded with a substantial increase in its repressive activity.

Following instructions from President Roosevelt, Secre-

[38] See in this regard Thomas G. Mathews, *Puerto Rican Politics and the New Deal* (Gainesville: University of Florida Press, 1960), p. 251.

tary of the Interior Harold Ickes made the next logical decision: the nationalists and Albizu Campos should be put in jail. Albizu Campos and many of the nationalists were consequently indicted by a grand jury in a U.S. Federal Court presided over by Judge Cooper. Federal prosecutor J. Cecil Snyder accused them of sedition and of "conspiracy to overthrow the government of the United States by force and violence." As Dr. Mathews demonstrates in his previously cited book, the charges against Albizu Campos had an eminently political character. Lawyers from the U.S. Department of Justice prosecuted the case. Even though two additional lawyers were sent from Washington to aid the prosecution, the trial ended in a hung jury. The court then proceeded to retry the defendants and picked a new jury, *composed of ten North Americans and only two Puerto Ricans.* This time a conviction was obtained; Albizu Campos and his companions were each sentenced to a prison term of up to fifteen years, to be served in a prison in Atlanta, Georgia. The director of PRERA,* Dr. Ernest Gruening, was overjoyed and cabled Governor Winship that "those satisfactory results . . . would go far in the restoration of order and tranquility."[39] Thus the ways in which justice was administered in the colony when someone threatened the existing order were clearly apparent.

The trial, conviction, and imprisonment of Albizu Campos are only a part of the harassment perpetrated against the nationalists. On March 21, 1937—Palm Sunday—a second event occurred, one which plainly showed how far the regime would go to attack the patriots. In Ponce, the nationalists had received a license from the

* Puerto Rico Emergency Reconstruction Administration. (Translator's note)

[39] *Ibid.,* p. 268–69.

mayor of the city to hold a peaceful demonstration. At the last minute, the license was revoked. Under orders from Colonel Orbeta, the police mobilized in force with rifles, carbines, and hand machine guns. In a show of force some one hundred and fifty policemen placed themselves in front of the parade. The marchers—including women and children—decided to go ahead with the march. The men were wearing the black shirts of the movement and the women were dressed in white. When the moment to march came, the *Borinqueña* was played, and at a signal from their leader the nationalists—totally unarmed—began to march. The police opened fire against them, wounding some one hundred persons—among these, some innocent bystanders —and killing nineteen. Thus the Ponce Massacre was perpetrated that Palm Sunday. Years later, in a lecture at the Puerto Rican Atheneum, the prosecutor who investigated the event, Rafael V. Pérez Marchand, revealed the heavy involvement of Winship in the fatal denouement. From the investigation carried out by the American Civil Liberties Union it was concluded that "the police had been responsible" for this act of brutality.[40] But Winship, Ickes, and Roosevelt remained unperturbed at the magnitude of the deed. The colonial legislature, dominated by the Republican-Socialist Coalition, declared Winship an "adopted son of Puerto Rico" and blamed the nationalists for the massacre, while as far as the police force was concerned, the crime remained unpunished.

In view of these two actions, it is difficult not to conclude that the government of the United States had decided to break the Nationalist party of Puerto Rico once and for all.

[40] Textual quote from the letter of Arthur Garfield Hayes to Governor Winship, quoted in *ibid.,* p. 315.

At the same time the road remained open for Luis Muñoz Marín—struggling against Barceló—to found in 1938 the Popular Democratic party (PPD). The motto of the party was "Bread, Land, and Freedom," but the party immediately agreed to postpone the achievement of independence until economic conditions in Puerto Rico improved. Or, to put it in the words of Muñoz himself, the political status of Puerto Rico was not to be an issue for the PPD in the 1940 elections. It is a good idea to take a look at the close relationship that developed between Muñoz Marín and Roosevelt's New Deal administration—a relationship the existence of which is fully documented in the basic study by Dr. Thomas Mathews—and to examine Muñoz Marín's actions with this relationship in mind. Likewise, it can be said that programs of North American aid such as the PRRA* and the PRERA were administered with an eye on Senator Muñoz Marín. In 1938 the United States was feverishly preparing for the approaching war. Without a doubt, this oncoming war must have been presented as a factor contributing to Muñoz Marín's "conviction" that all talk about independence should remain in abeyance until after the war. Whatever his motives were, the fact is that upon the founding of the Popular Democratic party, Muñoz Marín attracted to his movement the great mass of the Liberal party—a party originally oriented toward independence.

The very fact that at that crucial moment the PPD abandoned the cause of independence marks an historical retrogression in the independence struggle which is only comparable to the loss inflicted by the death of De Diego and the adoption in 1922 of the Commonwealth as the

* Puerto Rico Reconstruction Administration. (Translator's note)

political platform of the Union party. We have seen that in the decade of the thirties—with the preachings and example of Albizu Campos, but also of Barceló and Muñoz Marín himself—sentiment for independence in Puerto Rico had reached its highest point. The thirties constitute the decade in which we were closest to achieving independence. But the movement in question did not use its potential power in an effective way. The Nationalist party finally was brutally removed from power and its highest leader was imprisoned. And the desertion of Muñoz Marín—as events would show—was to set back an entire generation's struggle for independence. This struggle—the advance of which in this crucial decade is unquestioned—thus suffered an historical retrogression the consequences of which we are still feeling today, three decades after Muñoz Marín's fateful decision.

A few last observations about Albizu Campos and the Nationalist party must be made. If we take into consideration the fact that after returning to Puerto Rico in 1930, the nationalist leader was free for only six years before he was imprisoned, it cannot be denied that his influence in the creation of a national anti-imperialist consciousness among Puerto Ricans bore fruit. Six years—from 1930 to 1936—is an extremely short period of time in the history of a nation. And yet Albizu Campos managed to personify the spirit of resistance to colonialism, the fight against cultural assimilation, the termination of our handing-over of our national patrimony, the respect for our traditional values, the revolutionary tradition of Betances and Martí, the spirit of sacrifice reflected so perfectly in his sentence, "The fatherland is courage and sacrifice." At the moment when the cause of independence fell—with the death of De Diego— he raised it to the place where it belonged in the eyes of our people. It fell to him, however, to face the most powerful empire in the world. Once more, let us remember the fate of Sandino . . .

That he made mistakes is indisputable. The Nationalist party needed a firmer relationship with the masses; it suffered from the weakness of the cult of personality and from its inability to institutionalize power and guarantee the succession of command; it did not succeed in developing into a movement capable of incorporating the masses into the struggle. But none of this takes away from its very important role as the vanguard of the Puerto Rican pro-independence struggle during the crucial decade of the thirties. Awakeners of consciousness, Spartans in the defense of all that is ours, essential creators of an international consciousness concerning our colonial situation—no one could deny the disinterestedness, the abnegation, and the patriotism of these men who knew how to sacrifice themselves for the achievement of our liberation. In the history of the unfinished struggle for our independence, Albizu Campos and his comrades merit the veneration and respect which our people, at the right time, will confer upon them.

6 | Cultural Assimilation vs. National Consciousness: The Essential Dilemma

And Puerto Rico? My ardent island,
for you everything has ended.
In the wasteland of a continent
Puerto Rico lugubriously bleats like
    a stewed goat.
      LUIS PALÉS MATOS (1937)

Gentlement of the marvelous, fertile North, the center
is also part of the ball of the world.
      JOSÉ DE DIEGO (1916)

Pity, Lord, pity on my poor nation where my poor people
will die of nothing.
      LUIS PALÉS MATOS

The tradition of past generations weighs like an incubus
on the mind of the living.
      KARL MARX

In a famous passage from *The German Ideology,* Marx tells
us the following:

    The ideas of the ruling class are in every epoch the ruling
ideas: i.e., the class, which is the ruling material force of society,

is at the same time its ruling intellectual force. The class which has the means of material production at its disposal, has control at the same time over the means of mental production, so that thereby, generally speaking, the ideas of those who lack the means of mental production are subject to it. The ruling ideas are nothing more than the ideal expression of the dominant material relationships, the dominant material relationships grasped as ideas; hence of the relationships which make the one class the ruling one, therefore the ideas of its dominance. The individuals composing the ruling class possess among other things consciousness, and therefore think. In so far, therefore, as they rule as a class and determine the extent and compass of an epoch, it is self-evident that they do this in their whole range, hence among other things rule also as thinkers, as producers of ideas, and regulate the production and distribution of the ideas of their age: thus their ideas are the ruling ideas of the epoch.[1]

In the case of a colonial society, the Marxist thesis of the hegemony of the dominant class just expounded presents an element which Marx could not have foreseen, having concentrated his attention on the experience of the more developed capitalist countries: the development of a social class whose purpose is to serve as an intermediary between the society of the colonial power and that of the colony—what I here call the colonial elite. The experience we have had up until now with colonialism as a system of domination indicates that one of the basic purposes of colonizers is to make the colonized subject a kind of carbon copy of the colonizer, for upon accepting the values and the behavior patterns of the colonizer, the colonized subject loses one of the elements basic to his struggle against the dominator: his identity and his pride in belonging to a group whose interests—divergent from those of the colonial power—will lead

[1] Karl Marx and Friedrich Engels, *The German Ideology* (New York: International Publishers, 1947), p. 39.

him unfailingly to the process which will liberate him from material and spiritual tyranny. In his classic work, *The Wretched of the Earth,* the most brilliant, perceptive student of the contemporary colonial phenomenon, Frantz Fanon, has pointed out in a masterly fashion how this process of intellectual colonization is carried out through a colonial elite that collaborates with and serves the best interests of the colonial power.[2]

As is natural, a process of this kind must penetrate to the roots of the culture, for cultural resistance to the social and political changes imposed by the colonizers generally involves an affirmation by the masses of their own life style. Because domination is not only the material but also the spiritual suppression of one nation by another, in colonialism, soldiers, capitalists, priests, and teachers march hand in hand. The cultural assimilation of a colony by the colonial power is nothing but the culmination of the process by which the nationality of the occupied country is destroyed or dissolved, or by which the occupied country's culture is so hybridized that it becomes difficult to distinguish between what is indigenous and what is foreign.

In a society whose culture is threatened, the examination of the national consciousness of a people faced with attempts to denationalize them has generally been the essential task of the most alert intellectuals. This happens because they are the ones most capable of articulating their protests and they can see with greatest clarity the true nature of the process of cultural assimilation. To the extent that the colonial power and the colonial elite serving it attempt to veil the true problems of the country, the intel-

[2] On Fanon's thought, I refer the reader to my article "Frantz Fanon and contemporary anti-colonialist thinking," *Revista de Ciencias Sociales,* Vol. XI, no. 1 (March, 1967), pp. 179–92.

lectuals who defend their besieged national identity contribute to the lifting of the veil, to the demystification of matters which the former try to keep hidden. Nevertheless, when this critical thought fails to channel itself into social action capable of giving institutional concreteness to its predicament, the result generally is a state of frustration or alienation which can lead to a fatalistic or defeatist interpretation of reality. Utopian solutions, escapism, and "bad consciences" are the logical results.

The cultural history of Puerto Rico during the first forty years of North American domination offers us the opportunity to test these hypotheses. Let us see.

From the beginning of North American occupation of Puerto Rico, the goal of the colonial power to culturally assimilate Puerto Ricans and to make "good North Americans" of them was clear. The recommendation of Commissioner Henry K. Carroll to President McKinley leaves no doubt that English was to be the language in which classes were to be taught in our public schools.[3] This disastrously unpedagogical educational policy was implemented—with only a brief interval of teaching in Spanish during the decade of the thirties—and the directive issued by Franklin D. Roosevelt to his subordinate, Commissioner Gallardo, illustrates the policy in all its crudity: the task of the commissioner should be to make Puerto Ricans good North American citizens; for this it will be necessary to intensify the teaching of English in the public schools.[4] This practice was continued without interruption until 1948, thus provid-

[3] Henry K. Carroll, *Report on the Island of Porto Rico* (Washington, D.C.: Government Printing Office, 1899), p. 63.

[4] Thomas G. Mathews, *Puerto Rican Politics and the New Deal*, pp. 318 ff. Roosevelt directive came a little more than a month after the death of Riggs.

ing the absurd case of a country which by ukase of an occupying power, could not allow its public school students to be taught in their native language.

The same thing happened with all the symbols of Puerto Rican nationality: the flag, the national anthem, etc. As part of the process of cultural assimilation, Puerto Rican students had to daily swear loyalty to the North American flag *in English*. Thus did they attempt to rob us of every source of identification with all that is Puerto Rican. Songs in English composed to inspire patriotism in North American children were brought to Puerto Rico and sung by Puerto Rican students, who did not really understand the meaning of the songs. An attempt was made to replace the festival of the Three Wise Men with Santa Claus and his sled and snow. The practice of law was also affected by the new order of things, for the penal and political codes of the states of Nevada and California were adopted in place of the respective Spanish codes.

As is natural, a policy of this nature would not be complete without an attempt to rewrite the history of Puerto Rico in light of the criteria of the occupiers. The result was Miller's *History of Puerto Rico,* used for a long time as a text in our schools. Its interpretation of the history of our people was in perfect accord with the assimilationist designs of the North American empire. As was to be expected, the book magnified everything North American and minimized everything Hispanic and Puerto Rican. Against the black legend of despotic, authoritarian Spain, the new democratic liberal regime bequeathed to us by the Anglo-Saxon countries rose majestically.

It was the Republicans, led by Dr. Barbosa—the "rock of North Americanization," as he came to be called—who fought with greatest tenacity for assimilation, even when this meant the cultural suicide of the island. Thus arose that type of North American "one hundred percenter" known here as the *pitiyanki*, whom Llorens Torres ridiculed in his famous poem:

A *jíbaro* came to San Juan
and a few *pitiyankis*
stopped him in the park
wishing to conquer him.
They spoke to him of Uncle Sam,
of Wilson, of Mr. Root,
of New York, of Sandy Hook,
of liberty, of the vote,
of the dollar, of habeas corpus,
and the *jíbaro* said: "Uh-huh."

Barbosa and his followers knew as well as anyone else that federated statehood would inevitably bring the destruction of Puerto Rican national identity. The distinguished Puerto Rican jurist, Luis Muñoz Morales, could not have been more explicit on the matter when in 1921 he wrote that North American history showed

. . . that the admission or incorporation of territories and states has invariably been carried out by request of the North American element, when it has predominated in a country or when it has taken over all the resources of its government, annulling the native element (example: Texas, Louisiana, New Mexico, Hawaii); and likewise we must note the circumstance that, on being admitted to the Union, as a constitutional precept the English language has been imposed on them as the official language and as the basis for the school system (New Mexico, Arizona).[5]

[5] Luis Muñoz Morales, *El status político de Puerto Rico* (San Juan: Imprenta El Compás, 1921), p. 62.

Nevertheless, Barbosa's admiration of North American institutions was so great that until his death in 1921 he upheld the annexationist doctrine with all its cultural consequences. His successors at the helm of annexationism have not really departed from this line.

Albizu Campos said once that annexation by way of statehood would mean the "final triumph of colonialism." He thus put his finger on a matter deserving of commentary. What he meant to say was that if the total cultural assimilation of Puerto Rico to the colonial power was perpetrated—that is, if the mother country managed by her annexationist designs to overcome all attempts to resist the destruction of our national identity—statehood would merely be the culmination of that process. Or, to put it in another way, annexation through statehood would follow cultural assimilation, would be its effect rather than its cause, its conclusion instead of its beginning. Furthermore, seen from the perspective of colonization, federated statehood would not be an anticolonialist solution to the problem of Puerto Rico's status, but the most colonialist of all solutions, since in the face of the assimilationist offensive of the colonial power it would mean the total demise of Puerto Rican national identity.

Perhaps the best parallel to this situation is that presently provided by the struggle of North American blacks, for they are fighting to preserve their identity and dignity through the affirmation of their own values in the face of a racist society attempting to negate these values. The Black Power movement is only the attempt to establish a front of militant resistance to the repeated efforts of white North American society to assimilate the black—that is, to make him more docile, more malleable, more in conformity with the image they have of him. In the idiom of the North American blacks, Uncle Tom is what *pitiyanki* is in the Puerto Rican idiom. Both, in their willingness to submit to and in their feelings of inferiority, are representatives of a personality type which always bows before the dominator. Indeed, North American blacks are the victims of an "internal colonialism" imposed by a North American power elite. In this sense, the Black Power movement and the Puerto Rican struggle for independence have an indisputable connection.[6]

But the colonial mentality is not the exclusive patrimony of the annexationists. We also find it in many autonomists who, although they defend Puerto Rican culture, accept the basic premise on which the power of the colonial power rests. One of the stereotypes we find frequently depicted in the writings of men like Mariano Abril and Muñoz Rivera is that of the enterprising, bold Anglo-Saxon as opposed to the more indolent, quixotic Latin. Accepting the validity of some racial interpretations of history in vogue during that period, many autonomist intellectuals witnessing the arrival of the new order frequently took for granted the entire picture the colonial power sought to present to the world—stability, democracy, liberty, etc.—while they received just the opposite impression from the Latin American republics. The logical conclusion was that Puerto Rico should choose to continue to be tied to a civilization that in its most fundamental aspects was superior to ours. This vision—it should be pointed out—continues to be accepted as accurate by many liberal intellectuals of the present day.

Another fundamental premise of imperialist ideology is that of geopolitics. Perhaps no other concept has been so widely accepted—even by some *independentistas*—as this

---

[6] See Stokely Carmichael and Charles V. Hamilton, *Black Power* (New York: Random House, 1968). On blacks as a group subjected to internal colonialism, see Tom Hayden, "Colonialism and Liberation in America," *Viet-Report* (Summer, 1968).

one. This concept, when applied to Puerto Rico, implies that Puerto Rico will never be able to be independent due to the scarcity of her resources, to her inability to govern herself, to the presence of her powerful neighbor, and to the geographic realities that will always make her a strategic bastion of the United States. This geopolitical approach—now discredited in the world generally—was nevertheless very much in vogue at the turn of the century. The geopolitics of Hitler's *Lebensraum* is nothing new. The ideologists of U.S. expansionism had already verbalized it during the nineteenth century. With the exception of Betances, the Puerto Rican leaders of that period accepted the validity of the theory. Consequently, independence had to be—as it was for Muñoz Rivera and even for Barceló—"the last recourse of our dignity and our honor," but always that: an unreal and unrealizable last recourse because it was so utopian.

Inherent in the geopolitical vision of international reality is the ingenuous acceptance of the United States as the champion of democracy in the Western Hemisphere. This vision of the United States—from which not even De Diego was free—is the product of an almost abysmal ignorance of contemporary North American society. Liberal autonomists and even the most extreme pro-North American unconditionalists suffer from this delusion. To justify this statement, it should be sufficient to point out that in the United States racial relations are scarcely given the attention due them in a country with such a large number of blacks and racially mixed people. North American imperialism—as it was begun by McKinley and continued by Roosevelt, Taft, and Wilson—was called by this name by Matienzo Cintrón and De Diego only in the last years of their lives. They all—including the great leader from

Aguadilla—lacked a theory that would permit them to explain the imperialist phenomenon as something intimately bound to monopolistic capitalism. But he and the others were men of their time and of their society. Puerto Rico has always suffered from an ideological lag in her contact with the ideological currents being debated in the world. This ideological lag causes new philosophical, literary, and scientific currents to reach our country several years after they are conceived. This is another fatal consequence of colonialism: an area culturally blindfolded and earmuffed by the colonizer is isolated from all but that which the colonizer allows it to see and hear.

During the first two decades of this century the most "advanced" social thought was represented by Santiago Iglesias' Socialist party. Fatally located within the North American orbit, our labor movement thus remained out of contact with the radical intellectual currents in the international labor movement. After all, if the colonial power was behind the times in the question of social demands, what could be expected of the colony? Iglesias was a faithful spokesman for North American trade unionism—as represented by Samuel Gompers—and its powerful imprint was indelibly stamped on the Puerto Rican labor movement. Linked with annexationism, Iglesias headed a movement which made social demands at the same time as it supported North American imperialism. The profound contradiction that this entailed spelled the end of the Socialist party itself.

De Diego, Matienzo Cintrón, Manuel Zeno Gandía and Luis Llorens Torres[7] on the one hand were representative

[7] In 1967, on the occasion of the centennial of José de Diego's birth, the Institute of Puerto Rican Culture edited a two-volume set of the

figures of the pro-independence thinking of that period. All of them supported nationalism; reminded us of our Hispanic ties, and warned us of the economic absorption of our country and of the destruction of our culture through North Americanization. The militant poetry of De Diego and Llorens Torres, the prose and speeches of Matienzo Cintrón, the novels of Zeno Gandía—were all spiritual expressions of the realities of our colonial problem. For them the material and spiritual salvation of our country was to be found in independence. In these men, desperation alternated with fatalism, and impotence with the cry of rebellion, as they hopelessly watched extremely powerful forces make the attainment of their ideal impossible.

The next two decades under North American colonialism did not alter the scope of its fundamental aspects. In some allusive lines, our greatest poet, Luis Palés Matos, expressed his alienation from the degrading spectacle he witnessed:

> cage of tropical parrots
> politicking among the trees

---

complete works of the Aguadillean leader: one volume of his prose, the other of poetry. In addition, two of our finest literary figures, Drs. Margot Arce de Vázquez and Concha Meléndez, published books on De Diego. That of Dr. Arce, entitled *La obra literaria de José de Diego,* is the definitive work of literary interpretation of De Diego. *José de Diego en mi memoria* is the tribute Dr. Meléndez makes to her former teacher.

As for Matienzo Cintrón, we have the study by Dr. Luis M. Díaz Soler, *Rosendo Matienzo Cintrón, orientador y guardián de una cultura,* to which we have referred in previous chapters. The work of Zeno Gandía, especially *La Charca* and *Redentores,* has been edited by the Institute of Puerto Rican Culture and the Book Club of Puerto Rico, respectively. And the Institute of Puerto Rican Culture has just published the first volume of the poetic work of Llorens Torres, with an extensive prologue by Dr. Carmen Marrero.

This was so true of our politics at the time. We also find Palés desperate and pessimistic at the fate of his people:

> Pity, Lord, pity on my poor nation
> where my poor people will die of nothing.

A man of poetic sensitivity, Palés Matos also expresses in his verses the anguish of one who witnesses a spectacle without being able to do anything about it. To him, Puerto Rico seems at times to be a worthless thing, a mixture of elements without any clear definition. As our greatest poetic figure, Palés offers us another picture of Puerto Rican life during the crucial decade of the thirties. His interest in "blackness," however, sometimes took him far from reality. In *his* black man—because it cannot be said that Palés accurately describes the Antillean black—the poet found the figure to represent the vital, fiery, musical element whose irrepressible virility made Uncle Sam rage. But unlike Nicholás Guillén, Palés Matos lacked a radical social concept. As a result he gets lost in the evocation of a black who only dances and fornicates and who ends up by grotesquely imitating the white dominators. As for the destiny of Puerto Rico, his "Canción festiva para ser llorada" ("Festive Song To Be Wept") offers a hopeful note in Don Quijote Antillano, who out of his folly constructs an ideal. But the colonial world—as an hermetic and constrictive world—eventually led Palés to take refuge in the erotic poetry with which he concluded his poetic works.[8]

Of all the writers of the period which concerns us, perhaps there has been none more influential than Antonio S. Pedreira. A highly gifted essayist, his work *Insularismo*

[8] See the poetic works of Palés Matos, as edited by Federico de Onís in *Luis Palés Matos: Poesía 1915–1956* (San Juan: Universidad de Puerto Rico, 1957).

(1934) constitutes—along with the *Prontuario histórico de Puerto Rico* (1935) of Tomás Blanco—one of the books indispensable to a better understanding of Puerto Rican history. All the despair and desperation which Puerto Rico lived through during that crucial decade can be observed in Pedreira's book. In the beginning of the book he asks "What are we?" and "Where are we going?"—the questions that had to be asked of the period that began with the North American occupation, a period Pedreira called one of "indecision and transition." The answers are in his statement that "in our day, we cannot do without the Anglo-Saxon gesture, which through the United States is slowly filtering into our Hispanic presence." Pedreira also attacks the "rhetoricism" of our politicians, telling us that "it is time to live with a closed fist threatening the prostituted word. A good collective slap on the mouth will take our fatherland off our lips, and then we may be able to find asylum for it within our hearts."

Nevertheless, Pedreira's analysis of Puerto Rican realities succumbs to the fatalism of one who does not see a way out of a situation of timidity and servility except through the coming of a messiah, a charismatic leader capable of shaking Puerto Rico out of her apathy. "The men of my generation," he wrote, "have looked in vain for a man superior to our internal fights, in whose protective and pure shadow we might hear with clarity the voice of our myth." Pedreira—whose aristocratic vision, in the style of Ortega y Gasset, categorizes him as a spectator who is "above the conflict"—lacked the necessary vision to see in Albizu Campos that very "man superior to our internal fights." Given the political vision presented in his work, it is understandable. The greatest weaknesses of his book are his almost playful vision of Puerto Rican reality, his anthropological conception of the "fusion" of our races as the source of our prevailing "confusion," and his inability to become indignant at the double spectacle of our extreme poverty and the colonialism which produced it. In attempting to place himself on the margin of politics in that crucial decade, Pedreira ends his book with his hands empty of solutions. Consequently he too cannot answer his own question: "Where are we going?" In fact, nothing illustrates better than *Insularismo* the vicious circle of colonialism from the mouth of one of the most influential writers of the period. For precisely because of his refusal to "call things by their name"—as he proposed to do in his book—the ideological limitations of a conception of our reality which offers merely the raising of the issues, not the perspective for their solutions, become evident.[9]

Influenced by the work of Pedreira, in his *Prontuario histórico de Puerto Rico* Tomás Blanco gives an analysis that is better than Pedriera's to the extent that it speaks more unequivocally of our crucial problems: economic and political dependence and the utilization of our nation as a "bridge between the two cultures of the hemisphere." Tomás Blanco describes our dilemma in this way: "We must either accept our destiny calmly and firmly, or submit ourselves, like the mentally retarded, to a slow death agony, prolonged by palliatives and orthopedic apparatus, till we reach the limit of physical misery and moral prostration, till the total, complete transformation of the islanders into a

[9] Edil Publishing Company has just published the *Obras completas* of Antonio S. Pedreira in seven volumes. The edition of *Insularismo* appears with a prologue by Professor María Angélica Barceló de Barasorda, who knows Pedreira's work very well. As for Pedreira's sociological notions, I refer the reader to my article, "Visión y revisión de *Insularismo*," *Asomante*, Vol. XXX, no. 1 (January–March, 1963).

work gang of pariahs, a band of coolies. Then only the dead would be saved." In this clear enunciation of an anticolonialist program, he proposes an "appropriate program of national reconstruction," for we have to begin "to liberate ourselves from domination, foreign interference and compromise." Furthermore, the author rejects the so-called thesis of the "bridge"—just as Pedreira had done when he denounced this attempt of "everyone to pass right over us"—a favorite theory of the ideologists of colonialism who saw in that ideological mixture an intermediate solution between nationalism and assimilation. "Behind that phrase —a bridge between two cultures—and some well-intentioned persons who coined it, there lies in wait for us the danger of eternalizing ourselves in a cocktail of mediocrities, in a mosaic of chipped fossils and ultramodern, dazzling trinkets, in a loud, useless thing."[10]

As can be seen, both Pedreira and Blanco diagnose a reality. Going farther than Pedreira, Blanco proposes a solution to the problem. But both attempt to view the politics of their time as impartial spectators. Neither of them sees around him an efficacious instrument of struggle capable of transforming Puerto Rican society and of bringing it out of its state of material and spiritual prostration. As a consequence, their works did not contain an enunciation of a plan for the future, the creation of an alternative to the existing order of things. What is unquestionable is the extremely important gesture of Puerto Rican affirmation

---

[10] Dr. Tomás Blanco is a singular figure in Puerto Rican letters, whose works reveal not only the eager researcher but also the master stylist. Unfortunately, his complete works have not been collected as they should have been. My references to his *Prontuario histórico de Puerto Rico* are to the second annotated edition of the Biblioteca de Autores Puertorriqueños.

which these two works represent—not only for that historical moment, but for the generations to come. Faced with
the dissolving tendencies of assimilationism, Pedreira and
Blanco call attention, through their brilliant essays, to the
authentic ethos of Puerto Rican culture. Men of a generation which reached its political maturity under the North
American empire, they represent the anguished clamor of
those who do not find in the future a vision of Puerto Rico
free from the colonialist yoke.

Therefore, the true creator of the Puerto Rican national
consciousness—after De Diego was dead—was not a
writer, but an exceptional orator whose passion in speaking
before the public will leave written in indelible words the
demand of Puerto Rico for the salvation of its culture and
of its personality as a nation. That man was Pedro Albizu
Campos. From a radical perspective, his militant nationalism raised the idea that the survival of our national identity
was not a negotiable matter, nor was it subject to the
fluctuations of the vote. The goal of Albizu Campos—
achieved in part only because of the limited time he was
allowed in Puerto Rico during the thirties—was to create in
fellow Puerto Ricans a sense of belonging and a pride in
being Puerto Rican. Deeply aware of the prevailing attempts to juggle our true history, the great man from Ponce
revived the celebration of our great holidays—deliberately
ignored by the defenders of colonialism—and the preservation of our traditions and values in the face of those of the
colonial power. If on occasion this action seemed impru-
dent, if at times his criticism of foreign things threatened to
become an obsession, it is no less certain that a country
whose culture was under the most brutal attack had to seek
at home, in its own roots, the path of its regeneration. As a
defender of the Puerto Rican culture against assimilation,

Albizu Campos was one of those who is able to grasp the fact that the denaturalized character of the colonized country is in the true spirit of colonialism. With singular clarity he also grasped the fact that the problem of Puerto Rican culture is political, not merely "cultural." Therefore he could not conceive of a solution to the Puerto Rican problem other than independence, for only through independence could national identity be preserved.

With his imprisonment and the repression unleashed by the North American government against the nationalists, the instrument of struggle for the firm building of a national consciousness suffered a rude blow. With the dissolution of the Liberal party and the creation of the Popular party by Muñoz Marín in 1938, the defenders of Puerto Rican national identity thought they saw in this new grouping the effective instrument for the defense of our culture. At this historical juncture men like Vicente Géigel Polanco and Ernesto Ramos Antonini—to give only two examples—followed Muñoz Marín. On doing so, they consented to putting independence "between parentheses" until a future date would make their final success more viable. The words of the manifesto which Muñoz Marín had presented to the Puerto Rican people only two years before still resounded in the ears of the *independentistas* who formed the PPD along with him:

Since statehood is impossible, the only alternative to colonialism is independence, no matter how much it is doubted, no matter how much it is feared, no matter how much it is misunderstood. There is, then, not even an effective alternative. Independence is the only solution—with dangers or without them—for those who believe in it as much as for those who doubt it. The most serious problem before the Puerto Rican people is not to form factions in their struggles for or against independence, but instead to attach to their patriotic feeling an equal measure of responsibility as citizens; to work for independence with that spirit and purity necessary for the Republic of Puerto Rico to be a republic of economic stability, of social justice, of deep and lasting civilization, of civic order, and of the fullest and most sacred individual liberty. Before the destiny of my country, before the mysterious force of forgiveness and peace which we men call God, I today declare solemnly to my people: that if there is only one Puerto Rican who annuls in his soul and in his spirit the hatred and petty ambitions created by the colony, and who dedicates himself with his whole body and soul to peace, to individual liberty, to the democratic civilization of Puerto Ricans freed in their own country . . . I shall be that man. I appeal to my people that that man shall not be I alone but that it be all of Puerto Rico.[11]

In 1938 Muñoz Marín proposed that his people immediately forget the colonialism he had denounced so vehemently before, and as time passed all that generation which followed him found that independence, far from being "just around the corner," was gradually put further off by their leader once he was in power. Thus the most effective instrument against cultural assimilation and its highest leader— so anticolonialist in the nineteen-thirties—during his almost thirty years of governing unleashed as never before the annexationist forces that before he came to public power he had promised to restrain. But this is already a subject for another chapter.

[11] *El Mundo,* June 25, 1936.

Part III | *From 1940 to the Present*

7 | Economy and Society: New Forms of Economic Dependence

Our painful situation under the empire of the United States is the situation which North America is trying to impose on all our sister nations on the continent. Our cause is the continental cause.

ALBIZU CAMPOS (1926)

It suits no empire to exercise tyranny openly, and it always uses the natives of the occupied nation as a shield for despotism.

ALBIZU CAMPOS (1933)

How are you, Puerto Rico,
you associated associate of society?
Underneath coconut palms and guitars,
under the moon and next to the sea,
what a sweet honor to walk
arm in arm with Uncle Sam!

NICOLÁS GUILLÉN (1958)

The elections of November 1968 have put an end to the practically absolute hegemony of the Popular Democratic party (PPD) in Puerto Rican politics for the last twenty-eight years. Although it is still premature to make predictions, there is no doubt that the overwhelming triumph of annexationism in many districts through the New Progressive party (PNP) (presided over by Luis A. Ferré) is an indication that the process of decay is already well under way in the party whose highest leader—in spite of the formation of a party composed of deserters from the PPD ranks who followed the present governor Sánchez Vilella—unquestionably continues to be Luis Muñoz Marín. The incident is edifying precisely because it raises the question of how a party that monopolized the political life of this country for so long could fall victim to the very social forces it had helped to form by means of its economic program of "industrialization by invitation." In fact, a process similar to the gradual buildup and subsequent decline of the PPD could already be observed in a study of the PPD's ideological development.

In a brilliant analysis predicting the "ideological future" of the PPD, Dr. Nieves Falcón pointed out: "The leadership of the party that began as a living part of the people's reality lost contact with the very people who gave it life, made it grow, and nourished it with creative capacity. Its leaders shut themselves off in ivory towers and preferred to receive a diluted, statistical vision of the people via bureaucrats and technocrats, who think about perfect, foolproof schemes and forget the human elements. The average, the middle way, became the norm, and fundamental necessities have gone unperceived."[1] In fact, this article shows to what extent the PPD became a party serving North American economic interests—an ideological turnabout which can only be described as circular. The result of this has been the

[1] Luis Nieves Falcón, "El futuro ideológico del Partido Popular Democrático," *Revista de Ciencias Sociales,* Vol. IX, no. 3 (September 1965), p. 261.

accentuation of our economic dependence, the precipitous surrender of our national patrimony, and the galloping rhythm of assimilationism.

How could this *volte-face* happen in scarcely three decades in a party that at its beginning had a progressive ideology and came to count on the unquestioned loyalty of the great masses of Puerto Ricans? In what he calls the "conservative tendencies of every organization," Roberto Michels has outlined the process by which the process of bureaucratization of a political party ends by rigidifying it: in its movement toward becoming the political organization in power, the party gradually modifies itself and slowly loses its original "radicalism." The PPD was undoubtedly a victim of this process; its hardening and incapacity to rise above the old clichés has recently become apparent.

Another possible explanation for the decadence of the PPD is the cult of personality prevailing in the party, illustrated until very recently by the iron control of Luis Muñoz Marín over its destiny. The consequence of this policy was the institutionalization of bossism: the establishment of a hierarchy of great and small bosses, little czars who had their own dominions. Not having been able to or wanting to institutionalize power, Muñoz Marín gave in when faced with the problem of a successor, for it was clear that for him anyone who was going to govern Puerto Rico had to be his alter ego. When Governor Sánchez Vilella resisted that idea, the party had its greatest crisis and divided.

But there is a matter which the author considers of greater significance than those mentioned above. I refer to Muñoz Marín's original decision to put the issue of Puerto Rico's independence in abeyance while he resolved the more urgent economic problems of the island. With this policy Muñoz attracted to his party the *independentistas* as well as others. But it was understood that as soon as Puerto Rico's basic problems were solved, the moment of independence would come. Convinced of this, thousands of *independentistas* followed Muñoz and helped make him the victor in the 1940 elections. Once in power, the ideological shift began. And with the PPD triumph of 1944, Muñoz felt sufficiently strong to expel or bring about the exodus of the most militant *independentistas* in the PPD. From that point on his policy of maintenance of colonial status went on uninterrupted, even when, thanks to his efforts, it was disguised with the name of Commonwealth of Puerto Rico.

In the attempt to carry out certain reforms within the colonial framework, Muñoz Marín and those who followed him along this path believed they had found the solution to the economic and social problems of Puerto Rico. When he spoke against "rampant absenteeism" and the "greed of the North American sugar corporations," the leader of the PPD used a political rhetoric which was very popular with the Puerto Rican people. But in place of our extrication from the colonial condition through independence, the *independentista* and socialist of other times tried to substitute a reformist program that in the long run was unable to bring about any structural changes tending to reduce or eliminate the economic dependence from which we had suffered during the first four decades of U.S. domination. Even further, with the program called Operation Bootstrap—initially directed by Teodoro Moscoso from the Administration for Economic Development—the result was a definitive accentuation of that dependence and, as a corollary of what was said before, of Puerto Rico's being less Puerto Rican every day.

When we speak of this, we must be conscious of a very significant fact. On coming to power in 1940, Muñoz

Marín and the PPD counted on the effective support of Roosevelt's administration in the United States. In spite of the precarious nature of its majority in the legislative chambers, the PPD nevertheless won its objective of governing the island freely, thanks to the appointment as colonial governor of Rexford Guy Tugwell, the last of the North American colonial governors of Puerto Rico. In fact, Tugwell—who figured prominently in Roosevelt's Brain Trust—was without a doubt the most intelligent and well-prepared governor we had had up until that point (1941). In his collaboration with Tugwell, Muñoz Marín had in the occupant of the Fortress* a man with whom he could communicate and through whom he was able to cultivate his relationship with Roosevelt. Tugwell's influence during the years 1940–1944 should not be viewed lightly by students of the period. On the contrary, Tugwell was the mentor and adviser of men such as Moscoso, Picó, Descartes, Benítez—those men whose vision of economic development is that which prevails today in the PPD.

In his autobiographical work, *The Stricken Land,* the colonial governor of that period wrote of not being able to understand why there were those who desired independence for Puerto Rico—except for sentimental reasons, a motivation which he attributed inclusively to all *independentistas*—but he did praise all those realistic, unsentimental men, "mostly those who had been educated or who had worked in the States, who to a degree, at least, recognized the difficulties and dangers involved in the situation. It was they who possessed the power to transform. They recognized that the balance of power in the Puerto Rican community

---

* La Fortaleza, the name of the governor's official residence. (Translator's note)

must pass from the politician and the landed and moneyed dons to the technically trained and realistic younger group whose ambition was not to exploit the *jíbaro* and the *obrero* for the benefit of himself and his connections but to develop as a people in one co-operative effort, with leadership but not with dictatorship. This was the American idea."[2] Tugwell thought the salvation of the country was in those men capable of putting the "American idea" into practice: the technocrats and "realistic" men who did not see the Puerto Rican problem "romantically." He meant, in short, those who were willing to serve the colonial regime in power disinterestedly and efficiently.

It was also Tugwell's idea to encourage industrialization in Puerto Rico. Consequently, he must be considered one of the intellectual fathers of the Administration for Economic Development and Operation Bootstrap. As a matter of fact, his book is an extremely interesting chronicle of how the United States saw the role of Puerto Rico within the broader framework of the Caribbean. His language unimpeded by the rhetoric of the cold war, the author can speak of "our colonial policy" toward Puerto Rico without causing a commotion in Washington. He has also documented our character as a "strategic pontoon" during World War II; one can also observe Tugwell's extremely important role in the fortunate conclusion of the most important aspects of the PPD's legislative program. Naturally, on establishing this fertile collaboration both the PPD and the colonial governor were merely offering evidence of a change of tone in the prevailing regime. No longer was a Winship or a Gore in charge of supervising colonial affairs, but an educated

---

[2] Rexford Guy Tugwell, *The Stricken Land,* (New York: Doubleday, 1947), p. 489.

man, an ex-professor. With Tugwell, North American colonialism entered the stage of dissimulation, of the velvet glove—as long as all behave well and no one tries to change the system . . . And as a party dedicated to the preservation of the system, the PPD—during its twenty-eight years of being in power—played the role of effective ally of the colonial power. After their original determination to serve as a force of resistance to the colonial regime faded away, the PPD and its highest leader halted their liberation activities to preside over the surrender of the Puerto Rican national patrimony to the North American capitalists and bankers.

Given the direction that they decided to follow, it could not be otherwise. The colony was utterly defenseless in its economic relations with the colonial power; it was impossible to carry out an authentic program of social reforms— not to mention revolutionary changes—when the basic powers to legislate and implement such reforms did not exist. Up until the program of economic development and Operation Bootstrap were established (1948), there were two fundamental reforms planned by the PPD: agrarian reform and the island government's operation of some public services—the telegraph and some telephone services, water, lights, mass transportation, etc. (as well as a brief experiment to establish a cement and bottle factory under governmental auspices).

The question of agrarian reform in Puerto Rico had already come up in the thirties, above all in the famous Chardón plan, but it could not be implemented at that time. When the PPD came to power in 1940, this was one of its first concerns. The result was the Land Law (1944), among the goals of which were those of breaking up the great estates and redistributing the land to the peasants. With such a goal in mind, eighty-three profit-sharing farms were created; a program making it possible for farm hands to become owners of their own farms was carried out; and another program was begun to create small, family-sized plots of land—between five and twenty-five *cuerdas**—that could be bought by the farmer over a period of forty years. Among the provisions of the land law was a prohibition against monopolizing land. This provision set the size limit for landholding by corporations at five hundred acres. Today this program of agrarian reform is in its death agony; with its last gasp it has dragged down all of Puerto Rican agriculture, especially the cultivation of sugar cane. In his excellent study on agrarian reform in Cuba and Puerto Rico, Dr. Thomas Mathews says that the salvation of the sugar industry requires that "serious consideration be given . . . to the possible nationalization of the industry"—without taking into consideration, perhaps inadvertently, that for its fulfillment any proposal of this nature would require not only legal but political powers which our people lack. The failure of agrarian reform in Puerto Rico and her inability to deal with the problem of the great estates can be seen in the statistics offered by Dr. Mathews: when the Land Authority—an offshoot of the Land Law of 1941—was established, it was calculated that in Puerto Rico there were 194,500 acres of land the owners of which were violating the maximum legal limit of five hundred acres. Today there are about 100,000 acres in great estates, which gives an idea of the effectiveness of the law.[3] An illustration was offered by the now-deceased leader of the PPD, Ernesto Ramos Antonini, when in 1962 he claimed

* A West Indian land measure (3.93 centiares). (Translator's note)
[3] Thomas G. Mathews, "The agrarian reform in Cuba and Puerto Rico," *Revista de Ciencias Sociales,* Vol. IV, no. 1 (March, 1960), pp. 118, 121.

that the Central Aguirre Sugar Company owned 17,976 *cuerdas*, had taken 8,817 *cuerdas* in rent from farmers, and by an administrative contract was utilizing 7,150 *cuerdas*, for a total of 33,943 *cuerdas*. He concluded that the town of Santa Isabel, where the corporation was located, was "an estate of the Central Aguirre Sugar Company,"[4] but the matter didn't go beyond that, his protest remaining a mere verbal outburst.

Nevertheless, the true reason for the decline of our agriculture goes beyond the great sugar plantations. The reason must be sought in the very nature of our relation to the United States—as one of her captive markets. An official group, the Planning Board, touched the heart of the matter when, on discussing the possibility that the replacement of imports might be the answer to the Puerto Rican agricultural crisis, it said candidly, "The goal of obtaining a source of jobs and income in the agricultural sector through the replacement of imports becomes rather difficult due to the fact that the free market [sic] between the United States and Puerto Rico provides that agricultural goods produced by a high technology in the United States compete with local products. And due, furthermore, to that fact that in Puerto Rico the limitation of lands available and adequate for the mechanization of production makes impossible— even with public economic assistance—the adoption of an agricultural technology similar to that of the United States."[5] Or the same idea in simpler terms: Puerto Rican agricultural products cannot compete with North American products, and (although the report doesn't say so) we do not have the means to protect our agriculture from the ruinous

[4] *El Mundo,* May 28, 1962.
[5] Junta de Planificación, *Informe económico al Gobernador, 1967* (San Juan: Junta de Planificación, 1968), p. 111.

competition that has placed it on the verge of bankruptcy. All the superficial answers proposed by the present government are incapable of truly solving the problem, because they always remain on its surface. But that is what power is in a colony—superficial, ephemeral, ineffectual most of the time.

The social result of this process of progressive deterioration of Puerto Rican agriculture has been the mass exodus of the peasant population to the cities and to North American ghettos. Puerto Rican emigration—which a prominent demographer has called "one of the greatest exoduses of population recorded by history"—has brought as a consequence the fact that "if we add to the total number of emigrants the number of children they would have had, had they stayed on the island, we come to the conclusion that as a result of this mass emigration between 1940 and 1960 the island failed to gain around one million persons." We should add that the same source indicates that during the decade from 1950 to 1960 70 per cent of the emigrants were persons from fifteen to thirty-nine years old.[6] This migratory process can also be observed in the growth of the slums in the metropolitan zone of San Juan, for the disruption of their milieus forces great groups of peasants into the cities and into the resultant unemployment, extreme poverty, and marginality—as dramatically illustrated by Oscar Lewis in his recent book, *La Vida*. In this way an urban lumpen

---

[6] José Luis Vázquez Calzada, "La emigración puertorriqueña: ¿solución o problema?" *Revista de Ciencias Sociales,* Vol. VII, no. 4 (December, 1963). On the problem of Puerto Rican emigration to the United States, see also the study of José Hernández Álvarez, *Return Migration to Puerto Rico* (Berkeley: University of California, 1967), as well as the special number of *The International Migration Review* dedicated to the Puerto Rican experience in the United States: Vol. II, no. 2 (1968).

proletariat is created, a group supportive of—as demonstrated in the recently held elections—the political reaction which annexationism represents in Puerto Rican life. On breaking the communicative ties which served him as a means of orientation in the country, the migrant dwelling in the slums of San Juan or the ghettos of New York finds himself without points of reference for the orientation of his behavior. The result is the phenomenon of alienation: a feeling of impotence and fatalism in the face of the surrounding world.

This mass emigration is a forced emigration in the greatest number of cases. Due both to the high degree of unemployment and to the colonial government's encouragement of emigration, the country's poorest inhabitants are forced by circumstance to submit to an even worse ordeal in a society which scorns them.

As I pointed out above, the government's administration of public services, such as light, water, transportation, etc., was carried out under the administration of the Popular Democratic party. But the case of the cement and bottle factories was different. As soon as the program for Operation Bootstrap was authorized, these enterprises were sold into private hands, and a new chapter opened in the economic history of the island: that of "industrialization by invitation" of the Administration for Economic Development. As we shall soon see, Operation Bootstrap marked the crucial point in the turning of the PPD to the right; 1968 shows the results perfectly: the accentuation of our economic dependence and the creation of an economic absenteeism making the absenteeism of the first decades of this century look small and meager.

Basically, Operation Bootstrap is the result of a conjunction of two factors. On the one hand is the provision of the organic law in force (Section 9 of the Law on Federal Relations, the old Jones Act), which allows for the application to Puerto Rico of all laws approved by the United States Congress "which are not locally inapplicable," exclusive of internal revenue laws of the U.S. Federal Government. This means that a North American resident of Puerto Rico—unless he works in a branch of the Federal Government here—does not have to pay taxes to the U.S. Treasury Department. On the other hand is the local legislation that exempts from payment of income taxes, excise taxes, and patent payments corporations established under the Administration for Economic Development in Puerto Rico. The period of industrial tax exemption is seventeen years. This is the greatest incentive for the establishment in Puerto Rico of industrial and commercial firms from the United States. Not obligated to pay taxes to the Puerto Rican treasury, almost completely exempt from the payment of taxes to the North American government, these firms find in Puerto Rico the "adequate industrial climate" for their investments: political stability guaranteed by a submissive and obsequious colonial government and the presence—as if it were necessary—of a very powerful military contingent, lodged in ten military bases, and of the political police, who maintain a close vigilance against any "subversive" outbreak.

That the manner in which Puerto Rico is viewed is as an extremely lucrative business can be seen with perfect clarity from the pamphlet published in 1967 by the Administration for Economic Development entitled *Advantages of Plant Location in Puerto Rico*. In this pamphlet the administrator of the AED, Rafael Durand, announced to investors that profit on investment in Puerto Rico is 24 per cent. The organization he directs offers personnel training, rents the industrial locales which serve as factory sites, and also provides the infrastructure necessary for the good operation of the factories—such as highways, hydroelectric energy, facilities for the transportation of merchandise, etc. In addition, investors are informed that "the richest manufacturing resources of Puerto Rico are her 807,000 workers able and willing to work"; the diagram next to this information places the number of unemployed at 90,600—although in reality it is even greater than that. The Puerto Rican labor market is, of course, cheaper than the colonial power's, this difference in salary scale being indispensable, because in this way "the opportunities for the higher profit margin which the Associated Free State needs for its continued growth" are not destroyed. In short, the report of the AED concludes its call to investors with the following words: "The availability of labor, the lower production costs, the tremendous savings in an atmosphere of excellent conditions and services—all within the control of the Federal Government of the United States—make of Puerto Rico a unique opportunity for industrial investment."

In fact, in its report entitled *Industry in Puerto Rico* (July, 1967), the Chase Manhattan Bank, after pointing out the rosy perspective for investment in Puerto Rico, indicates that "those industries under the economic program of the AED have become increasingly tied to the continental United States. They import raw materials and semi-manufactured products from the United States, generally from their affiliates, they turn these items into manufactured products on the island, and they ship back to the continent almost all the finished products." That it is propitious for North American investors to see in the island a means of multiplying their wealth—"Accumulate, accumulate, that is Moses and the prophets," said Marx of the capitalist creed—nothing less than *The Wall Street Journal* indicates when it says, "The alarming rate of unemployment, which is estimated at between 12 and 30 per cent, is helping to attract industries from the United States to Puerto Rico at what can be considered a record rate, given the labor shortage which affects our country. On the one hand, personal and property taxes, not to mention excise taxes and license payments, are suspended often for a period of up to seventeen years, depending on the company's product and on how much it helps the industrialization of the area. In addition, the Puerto Rican government grants generous subsidies for everything, from transportation to training."[7]

This process of industrialization—which the ideologists of the regime consider their most sacred cow—has very important limitations. Its precarious balance has to be maintained by one concession after another in terms of incentives and tax exemptions and by continuous lobbying in Washington to keep the U.S. Congress from knocking over in one fell swoop the whole castle of cards dreamed up by Muñoz Marín and Moscoso. And it is no longer just the U.S. Congress in Washington, but, for example, a treaty of commercial reciprocity between the United States and the Common Market—I give as an example a not-hypothetical case—that can cause permanent damage to the Puerto Rican economy. But we Puerto Ricans have no part whatsoever in these decisions. Should the United States enforce strictly the minimum wage law in Puerto Rico, or should she choose to amend some section of her internal revenue laws to make them apply to Puerto Rico, or should the Kennedy Round in Geneva take measures on the present

[7] *The Wall Street Journal*, December 27, 1966.

tariffs without taking into consideration the industrial development of Puerto Rico—any one of these would be enough to bring the whole building tumbling down. And it could not be otherwise. For by means of a kind of hothouse capitalism the United States has attempted to erect here a gigantic economic structure operating directly and indirectly for the benefit of North American monopolistic capitalism. To the degree that Puerto Rico is an appendage of that system it can be said that she receives some benefits from it; these, however, do not filter down to the base of the social pyramid, but are in reality trapped by a minority of intermediaries and bureaucrats who are really those profiting from the prolonged dependence of the island on the colonial power.

I am assuming, naturally, a premise that almost all nations in the world accept: that the national wealth of a country should remain basically in the hands of its inhabitants. Put another way, a country like ours should control the resources necessary to permit her to make the basic economic decisions that will determine the life chances of the population groups most vulnerable from an economic standpoint. It is calculated that in the AED industrial development program 78 per cent of all the firms established in Puerto Rico belong to foreign stockholders—in the great majority of cases, North Americans. Now that great petrochemical complexes have begun to be established on the island and consequently we are witnessing the establishment here of North American heavy industry, the process of economic penetration is in its most imposing stage. For that shows that multi-billion-dollar corporations such as Sun Oil Company, Shell, Texaco, CORCO,* and others,

---

* Commonwealth Oil Refining Company. (Translator's note)

find here a place where they can invest millions and millions of dollars without being subject to U.S. revenue laws. So Puerto Rico—as can be observed—is North American for some things but not for others. The important thing is the service she provides to the U.S. military-industrial complex. As a "factory and a strategic pontoon."

And that's what we are.

For the continuation of this situation, the continuation of Puerto Rico's status as a Commonwealth is absolutely necessary, for only this political formula guarantees the enormous profit from investments as well as the atmosphere propitious for the establishment here of branches of the great North American manufacturing consortiums. Another aspect of this problem is one which we can no longer observe in industrial capital but can see in business, retail as well as wholesale. Due to the establishment in Puerto Rico of branches of the great supermarket and department store chains, the small businessman has been ruined, since he cannot compete with these very powerful consortiums. The number of cases before the bankruptcy courts has increased alarmingly during recent years. The displacement of the small and average businessman contrasts markedly with the rosy reports of Grand Union, Pueblo Supermarkets, Sears, J. C. Penny, etc., The fertile ground of the Puerto Rican market has become the favorite field of the most important U.S. business firms. In spite of the fact that while president of the House of Representatives, the lawyer, Ernesto Ramos Antonini, warned of the danger and even spoke of a thirty-eighth parallel beyond which supermarkets could not pass, the truth is that the prophecy made in 1962 to a journalist by Dr. Carlos J. Lastra—then Secretary of Commerce—has come true. Dr. Lastra predicted that "the establishment of so many retail stores, as well as their gigantic size, constitutes a serious danger to the country, because profits and retail sales will be greatly reduced; and probably there will be an increase in failures and bankruptcies."[8] More than fulfilled, the prophecy has become reality and the future of the Puerto Rican businessman is today even more uncertain than when Dr. Lastra commented on the matter.

In his excellent book, *Puerto Rico: Freedom and Power in the Caribbean,* Dr. Gordon K. Lewis has written: "Puerto Rico produces what she does not consume, and consumes what she does not produce." In fact, the Puerto Rican economy is increasingly an economy of consumers, with a minimum capacity for saving and a maximum capacity for going to the sources of credit facilitated by the capitalist system itself. Nevertheless, the Puerto Rican consumer finds himself in the position of only being able to buy in the North American market, while our people—lacking the necessary power to make commercial treaties with other countries—have to buy in the most expensive market in the world. Referring again to the *Economic Report to the Governor, 1967* we find that "the United States continues to be our principal source of supplies. In 1966–67, of a total of $1,798,900 in imports, 80.6 per cent was imported from the United States, 18.1 per cent from foreign countries, and 1.3 per cent from the Virgin Islands . . . during the past year almost 88 per cent of the total value of taxes on durable goods was attributed to imported articles."[9] To illustrate what has been said, all one needs to do is add that we are the fifth-ranked market of the United States in the entire world, and that in U.S. commerce with Latin America, we even surpass Brazil in volume of purchases. That is to say, the Puerto

[8] *El Mundo,* May 28, 1962. The article quoted appears signed by Pedro Hernández, Jr.

[9] *Op. cit.,* pp. 62, 181–82.

Rican market is one of the largest available to the United States as an outlet for its excess products, and in that sense it is one of the richest commercial veins for United States entrepreneurs.

Things being like this, it is not surprising that for those involved the maintenance of our present political status is in perfect accord with their best interests.

Generally, defenders of the system argue that through the establishment of North American industries and business in Puerto Rico massive unemployment is avoided and the country's wealth is increased through the payment of salaries, dividends and interest, etc. In the *Report* we have already cited, it is pointed out that for each dollar of withheld earnings, the equivalent of thirty-two cents was invested in Puerto Rico, and—what is still more significant— 49 per cent of the withheld earnings was spent on savings certificates and other forms of financial investment, *not* on direct industrial expansion.[10] That is to say, the volume of reinvestment is near a third, while half of the withheld earnings is not distributed in dividends, etc., but is withheld in the form of liquid assets through mortgages, savings certificates, etc. In the *Economic Report to the Governor, 1966* the same source offers us the following statistical information: "In the functional distribution of income, salaries and unilateral transferences basically predominate (for example, Social Security or unemployment insurance payments), in contrast to the payment of dividends and interest and other capital retributions. There is one main reason for these statistics: *the majority of industrial earnings, although they originate in Puerto Rico, leave the country and do not, as in other countries, flow to family units in the form of dividends* [Emphasis is the author's]"

10 *Ibid.,* pp. 86–87.

Given this fact, it is not surprising that we suffer a chronic deficit in our balance of payments, to the point that Secretary of Commerce Jenaro Baquero—in his days as a university professor—sounded the voice of alarm at the threatening phenomenon which the accentuation of this process represented. This is illustrated in the following information from the Planning Board (*Report* of 1966): in 1965 the income on Puerto Rican capital abroad was $26,900,000 while the income on foreign capital in Puerto Rico was $238,900,000. Therefore, the net outlay in terms of capital income for the year mentioned was $212,000,-000. This precipitous flight of our wealth abroad can also be seen in the operation of North American financial capital and how this works in Puerto Rico. Because our government cannot negotiate loans with other countries nor with international organizations, her public debt grows each year through loans floated on Wall Street. Once more let us quote official sources. In 1960, the net external (financial) debt of Puerto Rico—that is, after having deducted the capital in Puerto Rican hands but invested abroad in securities—was $573,000,000, but in 1965 it had already gone up to $1,280,000,000. The total amount paid in interest to foreign banks in 1965 was $44,900,000 and it is expected that by 1975 this will have gone up to $241,000,000. As the *Report* of 1966 says, "Only as interest the Puerto Rican economy will pay a net quantity equivalent to 3.3 per cent of the gross national product." But the process is so accelerated that the *Report* of 1967 shows that these payments increased in 1966–1967 to $105,700,000, or 25.5 per cent more than in the previous year. And what is more alarming is the following information from the Planning Board: "In Puerto Rico, of each $100,000,000 of public debt, $95,000,000 are owed abroad and only $5,000,000 are in the hands of local creditors (*Report to the Governor*,

1966)." Faced with this reality, an organization without real powers, such as the above-mentioned Board, can only offer timid suggestions for the use of small palliatives. Within the strait jacket of colonialism, what else can be done?

From what has been said it can be clearly observed that not only does our wealth continually and persistently emigrate to the colonial power, but also U.S. capital extracts from our country enormous quantities of money in the form of interest that never returns to the island. Needless to say, this pronounced dependency of necessity places the bankers, investors, and business proprietors of the island in a situation in which they attempt to maintain the status quo at all costs.

The propitious "industrial climate" of course cannot exist to the degree that there is a strong and vigorous organized labor movement, which demands for itself those economic and social rights which are the patrimony gained from centuries of bloody struggle. As a way of achieving "industrial peace," the Administration for Economic Development discourages the formation of workers' syndicates in factories belonging to its industrial program. Consequently, the following statistic offered by the island's Department of Labor should not be surprising: Of the 575,200 salaried workers in Puerto Rico only 108,500, or 18.9 per cent of the total, are unionized.[11] Today the workers' unions—as César Andreu Iglesias has pointed out in a zealous analysis of the subject—are mere appendages of the North American unions and the workers' Internationals (called this because they recruit workers in Canada), because of which the interests of the Puerto Rican worker are passed over in

11 *San Juan Star,* November, 1968.

the interests of a gigantic organization over which neither he nor his companions have any control.[12] The PPD has emasculated the Puerto Rican labor movement and has encouraged a form of union colonialism, setting back the struggle for workers' demands by several years. This is understandable if we take into consideration that this party is basically interested in benefiting the North American capitalists and not the great worker and peasant masses. Furthermore, the emigrant peasant and industrial worker share only marginally in the goods of that "showcase of democracy" so proudly presented to the world by the ideologists of North American imperialism. And if there is any doubt about this, let us take into consideration the following information.

Let us accept the fact that the per capita income of the island is already more than $1,000 a year. That should not surprise us if we take into account the point to which the Puerto Rican economy is integrated into the North American economy. There were many in the decade of the fifties —perhaps reflecting the prevailing ideology in the colonial power—who proclaimed the "miracle" of the "peaceful revolution" which had been carried out in Puerto Rico. In the euphoria of the moment, poverty seemed to have disappeared, as if by magic—or by Muñoz Marín . . . But the sixties were another case, and suddenly, with the coming into the limelight of the Black Power movement, the Vietnam war, and the problems of the ghettos, the ideologists of "the end of ideologies" in the United States were shown up. And one fine day they discovered poverty. Like a delayed echo, the same thing has happened in Puerto

[12] See César Andreu Iglesias, "El movimiento obrero y la independencia de Puerto Rico," *La Escalera,* Vol. II, nos. 8–9 (January–February, 1968).

Rico. The supposed "miracle" of the "peaceful revolution," which was meant to serve as a source of wonder and as an example to other underdeveloped countries, suddenly broke down, showing the face of misery and—what a problem!—revealing that the much-touted progress stopped at the porches of the brand-new urban developments for the middle class. In 1960 the U.S. Federal Government census gave the following statistic: 47.9 per cent of Puerto Rican families had an income of less than $1,000 per year, while 31 per cent had incomes of less than $500 a year. In what way that income is distributed per capita can be gathered from the study made by Dr. José Luis Vázquez Calzada, in which he shows that in 1963 20 per cent of the richest families in Puerto Rico received 51 per cent of the total personal income, while at the opposite extreme, 20 per cent of the poorest families received only 5 per cent of the total personal income.[13] Cases of extreme poverty are already so obvious that the ex-Sub-Secretary of Labor, Silva Recio, found it necessary to admit that a fourth of the population "suffers from extreme poverty."[14] The truth is that the situation is much worse. A good proof of what has been said is the distribution of surplus foods by the United States Department of Agriculture, which Puerto Ricans call *mantengo*.* According to an article signed by Stewart Kellerman, the number of people who received allotments of food during 1966 was 910,502; thus approximately one out of every

[13] José Luis Vázquez Calzada, "El desbalance entre recursos y población en Puerto Rico" (mimeographed). Centro de Estudios Demográficos, Universidad de Puerto Rico (November, 1966).

[14] Quoted in *El Mundo*, August 23, 24, 29, and 30, 1967.

* *Mantengo:* an untranslatable term referring to the "maintenance" given the poor through the distribution of surplus food by the U.S. Department of Agriculture. (Author's note to the English edition)

three persons on the island received surplus food on
mantengo.[15] The humiliation inherent in the receiving of
these allotments undermines every attempt to present
Puerto Rico as the paradise of the Caribbean. In his book
on the "culture of poverty" in San Juan, Oscar Lewis finally
gave the *coup de grâce* to all official complacency about
poverty and its consequences on the island. The reaction
which his book created in official government circles is a
good measure of how deeply he had probed a sensitive spot
in the system.

None of this should obstruct the understanding of the
fact that under the protection of the present government
there has arisen a workers' aristocracy, a privileged elite
within the Puerto Rican labor movement. Nor does it mean
that the generation growing up within the protective
warmth of the PPD and experiencing a real improvement in
their living conditions should not consider that there has
been progress since the times of the Coalition. If Sidney
Mintz's book on the sugar cane worker shows anything, it is
that for this worker the PPD triumph served as a kind of
liberation from the yoke which weighed him down under
the old regime, and that the perception of change toward
something better left its imprint on him in terms of his
political orientation.[16] This attitude contrasts markedly
with that held by the inhabitants of the slum Oscar Lewis
described in *La Vida.* It is a question of two worlds, of
two different and even antagonistic world views. The
process of industrialization has altered the balance between
country and city to the point that in 1960, of a population
of 2,349,357, 1,039,301 people lived in urban areas (ac-

[15] *El Mundo,* January 6, 1967.
[16] See Sidney Mintz, *Worker in the Cane: A Puerto Rican Life History*
(New Haven: Yale University Press, 1960).

cording to U.S. census figures). In the 1966 *Report to the Governor,* the Planning Committee noted that in 1965 the number of white-collar workers had increased from 141,200 to 226,100 employees, at that point making up 33 per cent of the components of the occupational structure of the country. This process parallels the increase in the urban population, which is expected to increase until by 1970 it reaches 1,569,000, equivalent to 53.2 per cent of the total population of the island.

A study of the growth of the middle class is essential for an understanding of the period we are analyzing. As sociologist and linguist Germán de Granda Gutiérrez tells us in his brilliant book, the middle class is composed of "employees of the innumerable federal and state bureaucracies—which grew up in great numbers right after the establishment of the Commonwealth—of the technicians and functionaries of the state and para-state agencies, and of the employees in the service of private firms—increasingly more numerous and important, more specialized and at the same time more ubiquitous in present-day Puerto Rico."[17] This middle class has a life style oriented around "the quality and quantity of their . . . belongings, the cult of happiness, the ideology of adjustment, and the image of the well-rounded individual."[18] Twenty-five centuries ago, in his *Politics* Aristotle discussed the stabilizing, essentially conservative character of the middle class. During this century we have witnessed how in moments of crisis for capitalism

[17] Germán de Granda Gutiérrez, *Transculturación e interferencia lingüística en Puerto Rico contemporáneo* (Bogotá: Instituto Caro y Cuervo, 1968), p. 45.

[18] Melvin Tumin and Arnold Feldman, *Social Class and Social Change in Puerto Rico* (Princeton, N.J.: Princeton University Press, 1961), p. 463.

there have been countries like Germany and Italy in which this class has turned reactionary, becoming the spearhead of the fascist movement. Phenomena like the careers of Joseph McCarthy, Barry Goldwater, and George Wallace —all men of a proto-fascist character—have been nourished precisely by that element of the population.

Puerto Rico is no exception to this rule. In fostering the rise and development of the small bourgeoisie, the PPD created the class that presided over its most crushing defeat. A class fundamentally oriented toward the life style of its counterpart in the colonial power, a fierce consumer of the mass media, a tenacious defender of law and order and fearful of popular elements, an anticommunist and *anti-independentista* group, the Puerto Rican middle class is in general as pharisaical and anti-intellectual as we could expect of a class which grotesquely imitates the most vulgar aspects of North American mass culture. The children of this small bourgeoisie are as a general rule educated in private schools in which the teaching is done in English and in the cloistered halls of which are cultivated attitudes of scorn and belittlement of Puerto Rican culture and history. For the generation born around 1945, the experience of pre-1940 agrarian Puerto Rico is something remote and insignificant. Television, movies, radio, and the mass media are the soporifics that keep them in the sealed, hermetic world of the "satisfied young gentlemen." The greatest danger that exists in terms of the assimilation of the Puerto Rican and the push for the final annexation of Puerto Rico to the United States lies precisely in this social class, whose qualitative—and even quantitative—importance in Puerto Rican politics has just been shown in the recently held elections.

In Puerto Rico a vigorous national bourgeoisie with class

interests antagonistic to the interests of the colonial power has never been able to develop. Rather it can be said that the PPD laid the groundwork for the rise of the "new rich," who have taken advantage of the process of industrialization to make a profit in the construction industry, in real estate speculation, in mortgage and loan businesses, and as intermediaries and agents for the great North American companies. (I mention only these few examples because I consider them the most important. But a more exhaustive list could be compiled.) This group of *nouveaux riches* has a life style which contrasts markedly with the aristocratic life style of the "best families" of Puerto Rico, those who in the beginning of the forties accumulated their fortunes from the traditional sources of wealth in the island: sugar cane, coffee, real estate, etc.[19] There have been many bureaucrats in the PPD who—following the example of the North American power elite so ably described by C. Wright Mills —on giving up their positions enter private enterprise to enjoy in it the profitable sinecures which the leaders of industry offer to their faithful friends and servants. The "new rich," the traditional "best families," and the managers and administrators of AED factories constitute a sector also oriented toward the colonial power and North American know-how; with some notable exceptions their political attitudes are in favor of annexation. In fact, with evident pleasure, this sector sees the United States as the most zealous guardian of international capitalism and therefore as a supporter of their own class interests.

Needless to say, in comparison to their counterparts in the colonial power, this group of the Puerto Rican bour-

[19] See in this regard the interesting article by Raymond Scheele, "The prominent families of Puerto Rico," in *The People of Puerto Rico,* Julian Steward, ed. (Urbana: University of Illinois Press, 1956), pp. 418–62.

geoisie plays a subordinate role. The basic decisions affecting the life chances of even this minority group, which is indisputably powerful on the local scene, are made on the committees of stockholders of the great United States monopolies—if we speak from the strictly economic point of view—or in the halls of Congress in Washington—if we speak of political decisions having an effect on the Puerto Rican economy. Thus, for example, the earnings of a construction company, such as Rexach Construction, could be affected by an extension of the Federal Wage Law to Puerto Rico, or by a measure—like that taken several years ago by the Federal Reserve Commission—imposing credit restrictions and increasing interest rates. Of course these measures affect not only the North American economy but also the international economy, given the role of the United States as the most powerful of the capitalist countries. But in Puerto Rico there is no other way—except lobbying and the inevitable trip to Washington—by which the Puerto Rican bourgeoisie can safeguard its interests in case of conflict with the interests of the colonial power. If the Puerto Rican bourgeoisie—dependent as it is—continues to look to the United States, it is because the latter guarantees security in Puerto Rico—and throughout the world. Security, of course, means an indisputable guarantee that the bourgeoisie will be permitted to continue their profitable activities without any more interference than is necessary for the maintenance of the capitalist system of production. Therefore it was not accidental that the theme of security should figure prominently in the ideological arsenal of the annexationist party of Mr. Ferré, and that the large and small bourgeoisie have closed ranks around its flag—and that of the stars and stripes.

Another unit in the Puerto Rican social structure is the

intellectuals, a group which in the main comes from the middle class and which historically has been the vanguard of the pro-independence movement as well as the essential standard-bearer of Puerto Rican culture as opposed to cultural assimilation. As a group, Puerto Rican intellectuals—above all the writers and artists—have also been one of the most effective voices of protest against colonialism in Puerto Rican society. From the University of Puerto Rico, the Puerto Rican Atheneum, the Institute of Puerto Rican Culture, and the Department of Public Instruction, they, along with the university students, have marched in the ideological vanguard of the struggle for our independence. Spurred on by annexationism therefore, the most conservative groups in our society consider control of the university and the purging of *independentistas* from state organizations of vital importance to the achievement of their ends. McCarthyism—with its concomitant anti-intellectualism—thus makes its appearance in the demand for persecution of "subversives." Totally dominated by these same interests, the press echoes the demand along with the other mass media (which are in the same condition).

Although the Puerto Rican peasantry is a group whose political importance is decreasing due to the aforementioned changes in the rural-urban ratio, it continues to be a very large part of our population. As such, it continues to be one of the mainstays of the Popular Democratic party. Without any peasant organizations to represent him collectively, without any pressure to apply other than that sporadically applied in the elections every four years, the Puerto Rican peasant is presently the element of our society which has most suffered from the PPD's program of industrialization. Although it may seem paradoxical, the peasants—who were and to a great extent still are the backbone of Muñoz Marín's party—are those who have felt most strongly the impact of the debacle of agriculture and those who have been forced to emigrate en masse to the cities or to the United States. Fundamentally a conservative party, the PPD still keeps the figure of the *jíbaro* on its flag, but the *jíbaro* is increasingly the victim of a process which he barely manages to understand and which deprives him of his means of subsistence. In this way, a party that began with the goal of agrarian reform has ended up changing those most heartily in favor of its goal into a rapidly disappearing class.

The urban phenomenon, on the other hand, has brought in its wake the formation of a lumpen proletariat, within the framework of a "culture of poverty," whose special condition is alienation from the society in which it lives. For the inhabitant of the slums of San Juan—equivalent to the ghettos of other latitudes—the vicious circle of poverty, unemployment, a low level of education, drugs, delinquency, etc., has been the daily reality for a long time. All the politicians of the colonial parties—from the PPD to the New Progressive party—have made political capital out of this wretchedness. The interesting thing is the fact that in the elections of November, 1968, these sectors voted heavily against the PPD and greatly in favor of the PNP. The conservative, even reactionary character of the lumpen is a commonplace in Marxist theory. Therefore it ought not to surprise us that political opinions in the slums lean more toward annexationism than toward radical solutions. As a matter of fact, the PNP triumphed in San Juan and Ponce —the two cities of greatest importance on the island—by gaining the votes of the middle class, the upper bourgeoisie, and the inhabitants of the slums. (Naturally this phenomenon has deeper roots than those shown here. The pro-independence movement has not really been able to establish a firm base in these popular sectors. This has been traditionally one of its most serious failings. The very vulnerability of the urban proletariat when faced with repression by political police is an indisputable factor in the formation of this group's attitudes. Whatever the reason may be, the fact is that the independence movement has not taken root in the worker and peasant sector of Puerto Rican society. As we will see later on, this is one of the most important reasons for its present state of political vulnerability.)

Another factor in the Puerto Rican economy deserves a separate paragraph because of its indisputable influence on Puerto Rican society and politics; it also reflects the state of colonial defenselessness in which we are placed. The *Report to the Governor, 1967,* by the Planning Board, says the following:

The composition of Puerto Rico's population is in its turn influenced by the flux of immigrants to the island. In April 1967, there resided in Puerto Rico some 78,200 persons born in the United States, about 24,600 Cubans, 9,800 Dominicans, and 19,200 from other countries like Argentina, Spain, etc. . . . On classifying immigrants according to the industry in which they were working, it is striking that more than a third—both of the North Americans who come to live in Puerto Rico and of the other foreigners—are businessmen. The majority of the foreigners dedicated to business activities are Cubans.

By December of that same year the number of Cuban exiles residing here had increased to 30,000, according to a column signed by Harry Turner in the *San Juan Star.*[20]

[20] *San Juan Star,* December 25, 1967.

These two groups—the North American residents and the Cuban exiles—carry much weight in our present economy. Because the colonial government lacks the power to regulate immigration to Puerto Rico, the number of Cubans entering Puerto Rico each year depends on a decision made by the U.S. government through its Bureau of Naturalization and Immigration. This policy has created a serious problem of competition for Puerto Ricans, who with an already high percentage of unemployment, are often displaced from their jobs by Cuban exiles. In a "Study on the Impact of Immigration in Puerto Rico," made public in July 1967 by the Bar Association of Puerto Rico, it is noted that "should the present rate of foreign immigration be maintained, concentrated as it is precisely in the occupational areas in which there are already too few jobs in Puerto Rico, the Puerto Rican workers in these job categories will receive strong competition from the foreigners and in these job areas the danger exists of a displacement of Puerto Rican workers by foreigners." The problem is rooted in the local government's absolute dearth of power in the determination of who enters and who leaves Puerto Rican territory; according to the quoted report, "the Commonwealth lacks the power to establish an immigration policy of its own, duly established by laws which a) assure adequate protection against social undesirables; b) assure the economic stability of the working and professional classes; and c) keep the population growth of the country in equilibrium with long- and short-range plans of economic development." As a consequence of this, Cuban exiles have taken over many businesses and jobs, in this way displacing many Puerto Ricans from their jobs.

In addition to his indisputable impact on the country's economy, the Cuban exile has helped to further accentuate the prevailing conservative and reactionary attitudes, particularly among the middle and upper classes. Coming preponderantly from these classes in Cuba, his basic orientation coincides roughly with that of the forces supporting colonialism in Puerto Rico. Entrenched in the press, radio, television, and public relations agencies, Cuban exiles have contributed not only to the progressive vulgarization of commercial television, but also to the promotion of the blindest, most obscurantist anticommunism and anti-independence sentiment that the island has seen in a long time, thus fanning the irrationalism so insidiously cultivated by the mass media at the service of the empire. The majority of them look back with nostalgia to the situation of prerevolutionary Cuba; they have had relative success in following the current so that this recently found "paradise" resembles as much as possible the Cuba of the good old days. The century-old struggle of our people for independence does not mean anything to them, and they don't hesitate to praise and build up everything that is contrary to our desires for liberty. At the University of Puerto Rico, the majority of the Cuban exile professors voted against university reform and resolutely supported the authoritarian regime of Chancellor Jaime Benítez. So this exile could be compared with that other counter-revolutionary exile that hardened conservative attitudes in Puerto Rico during the nineteenth century: the exile of those who fled from Bolívar's liberating actions. The Puerto Rican experience has been really sad in this sense, for today we find ourselves in a similar situation without being able to do anything about it. The political consequences of this process are already being felt here through the strengthening of the cause of annexationism in our land.

The reader should recognize that a system like the one

described above could not be maintained if it could not count on a coercive apparatus capable of preventing any change in the status quo. The system itself sets the rules of the game, which contenders for political power must follow. Within this framework, political action can be carried out, with the condition that the contenders respect the rules as well as the final results of the game. He who is not prepared to respect the rules or who refuses to play will be effectively penalized for his failure. In a colonial regime, those who are fighting against the eradication of the system are thus confronted with a problem: if they decide to respect the results of the game, they must be governed by its rules. But if they are not prepared to do so, they must face the consequences.

To guarantee that the system can only be changed within the framework provided by the system itself is why we have on the island a repressive apparatus which goes from the local political police (CIC) to the Federal Bureau of Investigation (FBI), from a local military force (the National Guard) to the presence on our territory of military, naval, and air bases of all kinds—including those which have thermonuclear weapons. There are also courts of federal jurisdiction that can try and convict Puerto Ricans for the violation of laws of the United States Congress, which are applicable to Puerto Rico.

Because the colonial regime is not seriously threatened at the moment, repression of the *independentistas* is being carried out primarily against their more radical organizations, such as the Pro-Independence Movement (MPI), the Nationalist party, and the Puerto Rican Socialist League.*

* This is no longer true. The Puerto Rican Independence party has encountered severe repressive tactics during the last two years. (Author's note to the English edition)

The process of intimidation is particularly acute in the case of university and pre-university youth. At this time there are countless Puerto Rican youths facing the possibility of five years in a U.S. prison for having flatly refused to serve in the U.S. armed forces. One of the most common ways the political police proceed is by visiting the bosses, neighbors, and parents of these young people, on occasion preventing them from earning a living through their work. *Independentistas* have denounced these practices time and time again before national and international public opinion.

In Puerto Rico they practice what Marcuse has called "repressive tolerance"—that is, the tendency to tolerate the presence of some elements critical of the system to serve as examples of its liberalism and generosity. Other comrades of mine in the struggle within the university can attest to this form of tokenism—so perfectly illustrated by the example of the author of this book.

The best way to find out how far this tolerance goes is through a study of the occasions on which the regime has been threatened or perturbed. We saw earlier what happened in the thirties to Albizu Campos and the nationalists. When the nationalists made an attempt at insurrection on October 30, 1950, the entire repressive apparatus went into action, and Puerto Rico witnessed one of the most extraordinary and fierce displays of force in her history. Years later, the Commission on Civil Rights—created by the same person who had trampled on these civil rights in 1950, Luis Muñoz Marín, who at that time was governor of Puerto Rico—gave eloquent testimony of the indiscriminate violation of the supposed civil rights of the participants and those suspected of being sympathizers of the October 30 attempt at revolution. This repressive action was followed by the application of the infamous Law of the Muzzle, by which nationalist and communist leaders were imprisoned. Once the nationalists were condemned—three of them are still serving time, in some cases amounting to as much as four hundred and sixty years in prison—Muñoz Marín and his party could return to normality, and in 1957 the Law of the Muzzle was abolished.

But that did not end the process of repression. It has merely made it less obvious, less visible. When on October 28, 1964, the university students carried out a protest in support of university reform, the police raided the campus and clubbed them just as they had done during the university strike in 1948. On September 27, 1967, the Federation of University Students for Independence (FUPI) demonstrated in front of the local office of the Association of University Students for Statehood (AUPE) to protest the insulting declarations of the annexationist group when it accused the FUPI of engaging in the narcotics traffic. The police entered the campus and intervened, making use of their firearms and billy clubs. During the night, two volleys of fire were opened up against the students, and during the last volley a taxidriver, Adrián Rodríguez, was killed.

The repressive nature of the colonial regime can be seen with greater clarity in the militarization of Puerto Rican territory through the compulsory recruitment of its youth into the U.S. armed forces, as well as the construction of some twelve military and naval bases which cover some one hundred thousand acres of Puerto Rican national territory.

The process of military recruitment is one which does violence to our people by obliging the young men, once they are eighteen years old, either to register with the armed forces of the United States or to face a five-year federal prison sentence. Note that it is compulsory military service. Many were the young nationalists who served such sentences, refusing to serve in the army of a country which kept Puerto Rico in the most abject colonial state.

The building of military bases—for which the government of the United States did not pay a single cent to the Puerto Rican people—is another form of doing violence to our people. A naval base of vital importance—that of Roosevelt Roads—has replaced Guantánamo as the most important of all the U.S. naval bases on these shores. The other bases serve as training areas for naval and aerial maneuvers, training of recruits, etc. The government of the Commonwealth can do nothing about this fact, for the Pentagon doesn't consult its functionaries when it is a matter of disposing of *its* territories.

Before closing this chapter, I would like to refer to a matter which cannot be overlooked in any discussion of Puerto Rico's economy. It has to do with the existence of mineral deposits rich in copper, nickel, zinc, and cobalt recently discovered in Puerto Rico. According to the economics which I learned in my university days, Puerto Rico had only water, air, and its population as its natural resources. That is, it was a poor, small country that had only its beauty to offer. Today, the discovery of these rich mineral deposits, the value of which in the case of copper is calculated at three billion dollars and at an equal amount for nickel, zinc, and cobalt, has provoked the inevitable scramble for their exploitation. The local government has already entered into negotiations with a subsidiary of the powerful U.S. consortium, the Bear Creek Mining Company. What was about to be one of the most scandalous turnovers of the national patrimony has become—thanks to popular pressure—such a bone of contention that the government still has not signed the contracts. According to what we have been able to find out, this copper—which will be exhausted in thirty years—would be ceded to these companies, with a tax exemption, in a transaction which after three decades will leave us with our hands practically empty and with a big scar in the very center of our land. Far from demanding—like Chile, for example—government control of 51 per cent of the stocks of the exploiting corporation, the colonial government has decided to adopt a timid and submissive attitude toward North American investors. As the contract has not been signed, the new governor-elect will bear the responsibility for it. Given his orientation, we do not believe the prevailing situation will be altered fundamentally—perhaps the contrary. But that is beyond the scope of this book.

This fact, together with the establishment in Puerto Rico of the petrochemical complexes, is of profound significance for the economic and social future of Puerto Rico. Also exempt from the payment of taxes, the already established petrochemical companies, such as Commonwealth Oil Refining Company and Phillips Petroleum—plus those yet to be established, such as Sunoco, Texaco, etc.—mark a new phase in the program of industrialization: the establishment of heavy industry in Puerto Rico and the already definitive entrance into our country's political milieu of the great United States oil companies. As the reader must have noticed, during the next few years copper and the petrochemicals will be the axis around which the Puerto Rican economy will revolve.

On the basis of what has been said here, the reader may judge whether Puerto Rico is or is not a colony in the classical sense of the term. Furthermore, Puerto Rico is an example of what the application of the term imperialism means in its classical sense. In the first place, we find the military occupation of our country. In the second, we have a supply of cheap and abundant labor. In the third, we are a principal market for the colonial power's surplus products. Fourth is the direct exercise of the colonial power's political power through its legislative, executive, and judicial bodies. Lastly, we have the exploitation, due to the colonial power's economic interests, of the colony's raw materials. It is not a matter, then, of an insulting epithet, but of an economic and social reality. Puerto Rico is a colony of the United States and the United States practices an imperialist policy with reference to our island. It can be called something else if that is so desired, but the reality remains the same. The problem is not, as some would have us believe, a problem of semantics. The important thing is the radical, undeniable reality that slaps us in the face. To those who continue in their solipsistic determination to deny the radical fact of our existence as a nation, we can only offer the famous test of the philosopher, whose kick at a stone explained more with regard to the existence of the external world than all possible high-flown rationalizations.

8 | The "Commonwealth of Puerto Rico": A Fiction

Oh, I know your enemy well,
he's the same one we have here,
partner in blood and sugar,
partner associated in society.

NICOLÁS GUILLÉN

Oh, poor Puerto Rico, Puerto Pobre,
nailed with the nails of torment
by your traitorous sons who hammer
your bones on a cross of dollars.

PABLO NERUDA

In 1947, the last of the North American colonial governors of Puerto Rico, Rexford Guy Tugwell, published a book about his experiences on our island. In it, he plainly refers to "our colonial policy" in regard to Puerto Rico. Today the rhetoric of colonial administrators and their Puerto Rican allies must contend with new anticolonialist currents across the international scene. It would be inconceivable today for Henry Kissinger to speak of "our colonial policy" (not, to be sure, because the United States does not have one, since it does) because this rhetoric would offend the countries who have become recently liberated from their former imperial masters. The rhetoric has changed, but the reality is still the same. Today when the proconsuls of the North American empire speak of self-determination for nations, what they mean is the right of every nation to give itself the form of government the United States thinks it should have.

This rhetorical change must clearly be seen as a consequence of the political changes that have occurred since World War II. Throughout the world the former "wretched of the earth" have been liberated. As a result, the colonial problem of Puerto Rico has become more sharply defined and the United States must face once more the question of our independence.

The colonial policy of the United States after World War II reflected the beginning of the so-called cold war. A general rule is that to the degree the military and economic hegemony of the United States in the world is threatened, she will attempt to prevent the loss of another bastion of the "free world." The Truman Doctrine clearly enunciated this goal—as old as U.S. foreign policy itself—to prevent the establishment through force of regimes that threaten North America's position as the guardian of and principal stockholder in international capitalism. The creation of the United Nations, however, raised additional problems for the North American empire, for as a signatory of the Charter of San Francisco, the United States was obliged to make account of its territories or colonies. This accounting, of course, included Puerto Rico.

In December 1947, Albizu Campos returned to Puerto Rico and was received by an enormous crowd. Addressing an audience at the Sixto Escobar Park, the great leader from Ponce reaffirmed his belief in revolution as the only means of liquidating colonialism in Puerto Rico. A year earlier, Muñoz Marín had stated that it was incompatible to believe in independence and also belong to the government party. As a consequence, Albizu Campos also stressed the need to fight against the PPD. For those PPD members who still believed in the ideology of the *independentistas* had left the Popular Democratic party that year and helped to found the Puerto Rican Independence party (PIP). On July 25, 1948, this new party gathered in the Sixto Escobar Park. It proclaimed its goal of working "peacefully for the constitution of the nation of Puerto Rico as an independent, sovereign and democratic republic," and also stated that "once this party obtains the majority in both Houses of the Legislative Assembly, its first official act will be to pass a resolution demanding that the government of the United States immediately recognize the independence of Puerto Rico." In addition, it vowed to name a commission to work toward the fulfillment of this resolution and to arrange a basis for a new relationship between both nations.

No negotiation shall have as its base the loss of integrity of our territory, nor any limitations to the sovereignty of Puerto Rico. To be efficacious, every negotiation should be finally approved by the people of Puerto Rico.[1]

Thus divided between the revolutionary tendency of the Nationalist party and the reformist tendency of the Independence party, the Puerto Rican independence movement remained fragmented.

On October 16, 1945, President Truman addressed a message to the Congress of the United States in which he said that "the present form of government on the island

---

[1] Bolívar Pagán, *Historia de los partidos políticos puertorriqueños* (San Juan: Librería Campos, 1959), Vol. 2, p. 270. Robert W. Anderson, *Party Politics in Puerto Rico* (Stanford: Stanford University Press, 1965).

seems unsatisfactory to a great number of its inhabitants."
He proposed to set up a referendum of the Puerto Rican
people, offering them the choice of statehood, independence, dominion, or greater local self-government, including "the right of Puerto Ricans to elect their own governor." In his message, Truman asked Congress to be
prepared "to carry out any options submitted to the Puerto
Rican people, once they have manifested their preference."
A second plan for granting independence to Puerto Rico
was also presented to the U.S. Congress by Senator Joseph
Tydings. In both of these measures, however, we can observe how the colonial power—pressured internationally
and in Puerto Rico to liquidate our colonial condition—
still attempted to silence the voices of protest rising na-
tionally and internationally in favor of Puerto Rico's independence by making long-overdue reforms. The colonial
power counted on the cooperation of Luis Muñoz Marín
for success. Muñoz Marín had been able to silence the
independentistas in his party, expelling those who refused to
be quiet. He was in a good position to request of the colonial power a form of government which without fundamentally altering the latter's control over the colony would
nevertheless eliminate the most flagrant signs of that control. In other words, he was able to bring about a change in
form without altering the substance of the colonial power's
control over the colony. This colonialist hodge-podge—
wrapped in reformist rhetoric—made Muñoz Marín the
first Puerto Rican colonial governor in 1948. Late in
1952, he became the first head of the so-called Commonwealth of Puerto Rico. It was the supreme creation in the
art of political mythology.

What the Commonwealth of Puerto Rico was to be like
was foreshadowed by Muñoz in several articles published in

El Mundo during June of 1946 under the general title, "New Roads Toward Old Objectives." He first declared that "independence, without special economic conditions, is impossible." He then warned that "we must be very careful not to get involved in the futility of getting our people out of foolish [sic] political imperialism merely to subject them, in their present political development, to economic, financial, diplomatic, aggressive, intelligent, controlling, and overwhelming imperialism." Given this "foolish imperialism," Muñoz had no difficulty suggesting that "the Congress of the United States, without changing—or amplifying—the present desirable economic relations, pass a law establishing complete local government, which we have named the *Associated People of Puerto Rico*. This government will be democratic and will have complete internal authority, which will be irrevocable until said economic indexes set by the law have been reached. When these economic indexes have been reached—such as, for example, per capita income, volume of industrialization, minimum family incomes—the people of Puerto Rico will vote—and their decision will be respected—on whether they want statehood without special conditions or independence without special conditions."[2] In this proposal, the highest leader of the PPD suggested certain reforms of the Jones Act and proposed to indefinitely postpone a permanent decision on our political status. But soon after the Commonwealth was established, Muñoz Marín argued that the decision had already been made. Independence was categorically impossible for Puerto Rico. The ideal that he had defended before coming to power he now renounced.

In 1948, with Muñoz Marín in the government, the stage

[2] Quoted in Pagán, *op. cit.*, pp. 255–56.

was set for the creation of "The Commonwealth of Puerto Rico." The first act was the prerogative, naturally, of the U.S. Congress, who on July 3, 1950, passed the law known as Public Law 600. This law provided "for the organization of a constitutional government by the people of Puerto Rico." Preparations were made for a referendum in which the people were to decide whether or not "to organize a government in accordance with the Constitution which they themselves adopt." If the people vote yes, then "the legislature of Puerto Rico will be authorized to convoke a Constituent Convention that will work out a Constitution for the island of Puerto Rico. The said Constitution will provide for a republican form of government and should include a declaration of rights." This law, however, provided that "once the Constitution has been adopted by the people of Puerto Rico, the President of the United States is authorized to transmit that Constitution to the Congress of the United States. On being approved by Congress, the Constitution will go into effect in accordance with its own provisions."[3] This "constitution," then, was by virtue of a law passed by the governing body of another country, the very body dominating the people who are going to give themselves the said "constitution." In addition, the constitution is subject to approval by the body which authorized it in the first place. It is not only absurd to talk of a country without sovereignty giving itself a constitution—if the term is taken in its generally accepted sense —but in this case, it is a lie. The U.S. Congress guaranteed its plenary powers over the island in Law 600, by providing that what one might call the "Law of Federal Relations"

[3] The complete text of Law 600 translated into Spanish appears in the book by M. Fraga Iribarne, *Las Constituciones de Puerto Rico* (Madrid: Edición Cultura Hispánica, 1953), pp. 482–85.

would be in force in Puerto Rico. This law was a summary of the provisions of the old Jones Act, which granted plenary powers to the legislative body of the colonial power. Section 9 of the new (but really old) law provided—as did the Foraker and Jones Acts, to which we have referred before—"that the statutory laws of the United States which are not locally inapplicable, excepting what has already been provided in this respect and what in the future may be provided, will have the same force and effect in Puerto Rico as in the United States, except for the internal revenue laws."

In other words, what was really the very essence of Puerto Rican colonialism was not altered: the power of the Congress of the United States to legislate for the Puerto Rican people without their consent. After half a century of domination, the powers of the colonial power continued unchanged. The supposedly autonomous measures of the new "constitution" paled because of their ridiculous insignificance in the face of the might of the colonial power. Once more history would repeat itself. The exalted reforms granted by the imperial power amounted to no more than a hill of beans. Nevertheless, all the gigantic Madison Avenue style publicity apparatus and all the party machinery of the PPD was wound up. An all-out effort was made to demonstrate that this arrangement would do away with the colonial character of Puerto Rico. What was really being attempted by this ruse was a means by which the United States could present to the United Nations authentic proof that the Puerto Rican people had exercised their right of self-determination.

As a means of dramatizing to Puerto Rico and the rest of the world the colonial character of the new "constitution," as well as in defense of independence as an inalienable right of the Puerto Rican people, on October 30, 1950, a group of Puerto Rican nationalists attacked the residence of Governor Muñoz Marín, and later brought about several outbursts of violence in Arecibo, Jayuya, Utuado and Adjuntas, Ponce, Naranjito and Mayaguez. On November 1, 1950, the nationalists Óscar Collazo and Griselio Torresola attacked Blair House and made an attempt on the life of President Truman. Muñoz Marín mobilized the National Guard and the state police to put the insurrection down. He also ordered the mass arrest of all nationalists and communists, and even of those suspected of being nationalist sympathizers. With that decision made without having suspended constitutional guarantees, Muñoz Marín made a mockery of all the "rights" consecrated in the organic law in force. Years later, a Commission on Civil Rights created by Muñoz himself came to the same conclusion.

The true history of the nationalist insurrection of October 30, 1950, is yet to be written. Poorly armed, watched closely by the police, few in number, the nationalists—emulating the revolt of Lares in 1868—did not have a chance of successfully launching a revolution at that time—and they knew it. Men and women of matchless courage and admirable patriotism lived the words of Albizu Campos: "The fatherland is courage and sacrifice." Those who did not lose their lives were imprisoned for many years, receiving sentences that many are serving even today. The police fired at and inundated with tear gas Albizu Campos' residence in San Juan. He had to be taken out almost unconscious—after being disarmed by the police who entered his house—but not without first saying to the press: "Our country is passing through a glorious transfiguration." On succumbing to numerical superiority and an extraordinary show of force (it is calculated that a total of three hundred nationalists participated on October 30; with the mobilization of the National Guard, Muñoz Marín put into service two hundred and seventy-two officers and four thousand and seventeen soldiers, and assigned four pursuit planes to help the infantry troops),[4] the Puerto Rican patriots left no doubt that the revolutionary tradition started by Betances was kept alive in the figure of Pedro Albizu Campos.

The colonial regime gladly took over the job that the North Americans themselves had to carry out in 1936—the trial of the surviving insurrectionists. Included among these survivors was Albizu Campos. As a consequence of the university strike of 1948, the Legislative Assembly of Puerto Rico had met in special session and approved the infamous Law 53, known as the Law of the Muzzle. Since this was, as representative Benjamín Ortiz admitted at the time, "merely a translation of the text of Section 2" of the Smith Act of the United States, it was clear that its only purpose was to persecute the most radical sectors within the independence movement. This law made it a serious crime (drawing up to ten years in prison) to "promote, advocate, advise, or preach voluntarily and knowingly the necessity, desirability or suitability of overthrowing, paralyzing, or subverting the insular government or any of its political divisions, by means of force and violence." Furthermore, the law in question made it a crime to print, publish, edit, circulate, sell, distribute or exhibit publicly any writing or publication where the above-mentioned acts were advocated, as well as any attempt to organize an association, group, or assembly of persons to carry out these acts.

Under the Law of the Muzzle, there began a period of

---

[4] All this information is from the article by Dr. David M. Helfeld, "Discrimination for political beliefs and associations," in *Revista del Colegio de Abogados,* Vol. XXV, no. 1 (November 1964), p. 36. See also in this regard Ramón Medina Ramírez, *El movimiento libertador en la historia de Puerto Rico* (Santurce: Imprenta Borinquén, 1954), Vol. 2.

persecution against militants of the Nationalist party and the Communist party. Many of them were sentenced to prison on the strength of the fact that there were recordings of their speeches in the police archives. Albizu Campos was sentenced to fifty-six years in prison. The ferocity of the prosecuting attorneys at these trials, their total disdain for the law so conveniently invoked on other occasions, and the severity of the sentences—all indicated how far the Puerto Rican custodians of North American colonialism were prepared to go.

As a consequence of his solitary confinement for about a year in San Juan, Albizu Campos became seriously ill. Because of this he was pardoned by Muñoz Marín in September, 1953. His pardon was revoked by Muñoz Marín a year later after four nationalists, Lolita Lebrón, Rafael Cancel Miranda, Andrés Figueroa Cordero and Irving Flores Rodríguez shot their way onto the floor of Congress, shouting "Long live free Puerto Rico!" Albizu Campos was not let out of prison a second time. The hospital in which he spent the last years of his life served as a prison until a little before his death on April 21, 1965. At the time of his death he had been imprisoned for various acts for about twenty-two years. But the persecution of his person and his party began long before he was jailed. It was Muñoz Marín's dubious privilege to be the hangman and jailer of Albizu Campos during the greater part of his term as governor of Puerto Rico.

But to return to the "constitution" of the Commonwealth of Puerto Rico. Once the nationalists had been imprisoned for the events of October 30, 1950, a "Constituent Convention" was called to give legitimacy to the new "constitution." In addition, a large number of "experts" in constitutional and international law were contracted—and stupendously well paid; they did not take long to discover the essentially "creative" character of the new political formula, not without first congratulating our country for its good fortune in having a leader of the stature of Muñoz Marín. Among the many experts who visited us on such a great occasion was Dr. Carl J. Friedrich of Harvard University who, like a modern Plato coming to his Syracuse, pontificated to us about that new invention that had revolutionized the traditional concepts of federalism. After many discussions, the "founding fathers" of the new constitution edited and submitted this constitution to a referendum. It was approved by a majority of votes. The Puerto Rican Independence party refused to participate in the Constituent Convention and denounced it for what it was: another inconsequential reform which left our colonial situation unchanged.

The Constitution of the Commonwealth of Puerto Rico became our new law. In reference to the term "compact" appearing in Law 600, Muñoz Marín compared it to the cosmetic compact of a woman. By doing so, he unwittingly hit the nail on the head. For the Constitution of 1952 is nothing but an attempt to hide the most obvious wrinkles of colonialism through the use of cosmetics, which cover reality with a smooth mask. Dr. David Helfeld, Dean of the Law School of the University of Puerto Rico, came to the same conclusion from his examination of the intentions of the U.S. Congress in approving Law 600.[5] As long as the U.S. Congress retains the power to legislate for Puerto Rico without the consent of the Puerto Ricans there is no real

[5] See David M. Helfeld, "Congressional intent and attitude toward Public Law 600 and the Constitution of the Commonwealth of Puerto Rico," *Revista Jurídica de la Universidad de Puerto Rico* (May–June, 1952).

change in the relationship between the island and the colonial power. Everything else—including the question of whether or not there is or is not a "pact" between Puerto Rico and the United States, or whether or not this "pact" cannot be altered unilaterally—is pure legal sophistry. And those who practice it end up looking ridiculous. Many are the talents that have been wasted in the dishonest labor of this legal juggling. For this reason, and to illustrate the extent of the powers which the mother country has at her disposal over Puerto Rico, I direct the reader to the following enumeration of powers made by Yamil Galib in his testimony before the Status Commission (1965):

By virtue of that unlimited power the Congress [of the United States] recruits our young men and sends them off to war; it determines who can enter and leave our country through the laws of immigration and emigration; it maintains here a Federal Court which tries and judges Puerto Ricans under federal laws; it controls radio and television, and without its consent a broadcasting tower cannot be erected in our country nor can any message be sent or received through these means of communication. It censors books and works of art through its agents in the federal customs; it controls our commerce and our economy through monopoly, as far as is possible, as a consumer's market. It maintains an absolute and incredible control over maritime and air fleets between the United States and Puerto Rico, which imposes on our country an extra charge calculated at between forty and fifty million dollars annually.

It intervenes with exclusive rights in the laws respecting bankruptcy, naturalization and citizenship. It maintains an unlimited power of expropriation of our lands and property, and although it could be alleged that it has not always exercised that power in an abusive way, the fact that there exists no limitation in this respect is an unequivocal sign that our territory and our wealth are at the mercy of and continue to be the possession and belonging of the United States.

It controls the delegation of power in air and maritime matters. It directs foreign relations with exclusive rights. It forbids us to set our own tariffs by Article 3 of the Federal Relations Act, reserving for itself the only weapon we could brandish to protect our production enterprises against ruinous competition from the very powerful producers in the United States, leading us to the paradoxical situation that a poor country buys at the prices of the richest country in the world; in the interchange of merchandise we have annually an unfavorable balance in a sum that fluctuates between 250 and 300 million dollars, and our balance of payments has been, systematically and endemically, adverse to Puerto Rico ever since the North Americans set foot on our land.

Congress maintains control over the sugar industry. It does not permit us to take a part in commercial treaties which the United States negotiates with other countries, not even in those aspects which affect us adversely; it controls the mails and currency and establishes the fundamental decisions on the norms which prevail in the banking business. It covers Puerto Rican land, sea, and air with its army, navy and air force, without even asking for our opinion or our consent to cover up the appearance of a system which pretends to be democratic.

It can be sustained, in short, that almost everything which directly or indirectly affects the life of Puerto Rico is in the hands of the U.S. Congress.[6]

It is obvious to anyone familiar with such matters that a constitution and a constituent convention which leave untouched the recently enumerated powers cannot be any-

[6] *Hearings before the United States—Puerto Rico Commission on the Status of Puerto Rico.* Vol. 1: Legal-Constitutional factors in relation to the Status of Puerto Rico. San Juan, P.R. (May 14–18, 1965), pp. 215–16.

thing but a gigantic joke. This constitution violates the most elementary principles of a free nation, as consecrated in the Charter of the United Nations: that is, the freedom from non-intervention and the right to self-determination. The Constitution of the Commonwealth of Puerto Rico is just one more attempt to confer legitimacy on a regime predicated on the principles of legal and political inequality. As long as the North American empire has military, political, economic, and cultural power over Puerto Rico, to speak of the self-determination of the Puerto Rican people is more than ridiculous—it is a monstrous fraud.

But notwithstanding the manifestly colonial character of the Commonwealth, the United States appeared before the United Nations in 1953 to ask that Puerto Rico be declared a "territory with self-government." Muñoz Marín and Fernós Isern spoke as part of the North American delegation. Notwithstanding the manifest opposition of the socialist and recently liberated countries—of the Latin American countries, only Mexico, Uruguay and Arbenz' Guatemala voted against the resolution blessing our colonial status—a resolution was passed declaring us to be a territory with "self-government" and exempting the United States from submitting reports on Puerto Rico to the United Nations. On that occasion the colonial legislature committed one of its most shameful acts. President Eisenhower sent a message by way of his delegate to the United Nations also saying that the United States would be willing to give independence to Puerto Rico if the Legislative Assembly of Puerto Rico so requested (knowing beforehand, of course, that the legislature was controlled by the Popular Democratic party). In a unique case in the annals of the history of liberty, the colonial legislature rejected independence. From then on the United States has declared repeatedly that the status of Puerto Rico is an internal affair of the United States over which the United Nations has no jurisdiction at all.

As a consequence of the obvious defects of the Commonwealth, from the very moment of its inception the problem was raised in PPD circles of which way the ELA* was going to "grow"—toward independence or toward statehood. This was a sign that the problem of our political status, far from having been buried by Muñoz Marín in 1952, was still alive and kicking. As a result, in 1959 a bill which has gone down in history as the Fernós-Murray Bill was presented to the U.S. Congress. This was an attempt to liberalize the relations between Puerto Rico and the United States: establishing a greater flexibility in the setting of tariffs by the United States (so, for example, the island could buy salt cod from countries like Nova Scotia), transferring the public debt to Puerto Rico, and allowing direct appeals on legal decisions to go to the Supreme Court of the United States. Muñoz Marín stated in testimony that the modifications proposed by the bill were not very significant. Still, the Fernós-Murray Bill did not manage to overcome the obstacles in Congress and was stillborn. An examination of the testimony given at congressional hearings indicates that the body which held sovereignty over the island was not very inclined to give up one speck of its power.

Nevertheless, dissatisfaction did not die with the Fernós-Murray Bill. On December 3, 1962, the Legislative Assembly of Puerto Rico passed Joint Resolution No. 1, in which it was stated that "the people of Puerto Rico are in favor of resolving the final status of Puerto Rico in a way

---

* ELA: *Estado Libre Asociado* is the Spanish term that we have herein translated as Commonwealth. (Author's note to the English edition)

that leaves no doubts as to the uncolonial nature of said status." This resolution proposed to the Congress of the United States of America a procedure for establishing the final political status of the people of Puerto Rico, and furthermore provided for the "recognition and reaffirmation of the sovereignty of the people of Puerto Rico, so that there will be no doubt at all of her capacity to make agreements in terms of legal equality."

An additional sign of the preoccupation with the colonial character of the ELA manifested itself at the general assembly of the Puerto Rican Bar Association. On February 21, 1963, this assembly affirmed that "the sovereign nation is the one in which resides the ultimate source of power." Clearly, this meant that "the Congress of the United States must renounce all its power over Puerto Rico, transferring it to the Puerto Rican people." About this time there was, moreover, an exchange of letters between President Kennedy and Governor Muñoz Marín in which the need to resolve definitively the problem of the political status of Puerto Rico was discussed. But the only consequence of this exchange of letters and the submission of the previously mentioned resolutions was the creation of another commission designated, for the *n*th time, to study the political status of Puerto Rico.

One such commission created by a law of the U.S. Congress was the Joint Commission of the United States and Puerto Rico for the Study of Status (STACOM). This commission was composed of seven North Americans and six Puerto Ricans. The North American representatives were named by President Johnson. The Puerto Rican members represented the three political formulas: ELA, statehood, and independence. (The *independentista* delegate, Dr. Gilberto Concepción de Gracia, retired in protest before the commission finished its work.) After voluminous studies and extensive public hearings. STACOM concluded its work in a predictable fashion. Its conclusions were weighted in favor of the Commonwealth. But it ended by proposing that a plebiscite be held to determine the preference of the people. This plebiscite was boycotted by the *independentistas* and by a sector of the annexationists. In spite of the fact that its results did not oblige the U.S. Congress to respect in any way the will which would be expressed, the plebiscite was hastily held on July 23, 1967. As was to be expected, the ELA won. Muñoz Marín immediately declared the problem of political status to be resolved and completely closed.

The plebiscite of July 1967, like the plebiscite held to ratify the Constitution of the Commonwealth of Puerto Rico in 1952, attempted to confer legitimacy on the colony. Both, of course, were supported by Muñoz Marín and the Popular Democratic party. But neither complied with even the most elementary requirements imposed by the United Nations. What the North American government should have done and should do is comply with the provisions of Resolution 1514 (XV) passed by the General Assembly of the United Nations on December 14, 1960, which in its most relevant passages reads as follows:

The subjection of peoples to foreign subjugation, domination, and exploitation constitutes a denial of fundamental human rights, is contrary to the Charter of the United Nations, and compromises the cause of peace and world cooperation. So that dependent nations can exercise peacefully and freely their right to complete independence, all armed action and all repressive measures of any kind directed against it should cease, and the integrity of the national territory should be respected.

In all territories in trust and not autonomous, and in all the other territories which have still not achieved their independence, measures should be taken immediately to transfer all power to the people of those territories without conditions or reservations, in conformity with their will and their rights freely expressed, and without distinction of race, creed, or color, to permit them to enjoy absolute freedom and independence.

A plebiscite held with the presence on our soil of North American power is necessarily in conflict with the declaration just quoted. It denies the inalienable right of the Puerto Rican people to their independence and to the exercise of their sovereignty, a right that cannot be juggled away by a spurious plebiscite directed toward perpetuating colonialism in our country.

Muñoz Marín's defense of this inferior status was to talk of it as a reality and to relegate independence to an illusion. He constantly spoke of the "permanent and irrevocable union" with the United States, based on common citizenship, common money, common defense, and a "free market" between Puerto Rico and the United States. He defended his resistance to any attempt to alter this "union" stating that any alteration would seriously harm Puerto Rico by frightening away North American investors. Hemmed in by his own creation—and by history, as César Andreu Iglesias has said—Muñoz Marín found that each day the North American investors demanded more and more unconditionalism or complete loyalty as a precondition for establishing themselves in Puerto Rico. It was not enough to offer them extraordinary earnings without their having to pay a single cent in taxes to the Puerto Rican treasury. It was also necessary to guarantee to them that the flag of the United States would perennially float over Puerto

Rican soil. Pressured by the annexationists who accused him of harboring hidden pro-independence sentiments, Muñoz Marín was forced to sponsor resolutions similar to the following: "to reiterate the expression of unbreakable will of the Puerto Ricans to fulfill their obligations as citizens, civilian as well as military, at all times and places, and to condemn every act which serves as an obstacle to or tends to weaken the armed forces of the United States of America, and [to be willing to serve under] the circumstances which in any time or place would demand, as they do today in Vietnam, the fulfillment of their responsibilities to the world and to history, and to contain communist aggression, or which tends to debilitate the will of the citizens in the fulfillment of the military and civic duties which law and morality impose on them."[7] In this resolution (even the U.S. Congress has not passed one like it) one can observe what is really meant by "common citizenship" and "common defense": the sacrifice of Puerto Rican youth in the wars of the United States. Extracted through laws which are passed without the consent of the Puerto Rican people, this "blood tribute" is the very essence of the Commonwealth. And the conversion of our territory into an atomic powder keg and a training base for imperialist aggression in the rest of the world is another earlier example of the very same thing. Of course, the United States defends this earlier action as necessary for our "common defense," as if the Pentagon had consulted the Puerto Rican people before they made the decision to store atomic bombs in the air base at Aguadilla. But once one has started on this road of concessions, there is no place to stop. The appetite of the

---

[7] This resolution was passed by the Puerto Rican Senate on February 3, 1966 (*El Mundo*, February 5, 1966) with only one vote against it. The House of Representatives passed a similar one unanimously.

investors and of the Pentagon—the military-industrial complex, as even Eisenhower called it—will always be insatiable. And colonial appeasement will only encourage those in power in the United States to take a greater part of our national patrimony and to increase their militarization of our territory.

To the degree to which the Commonwealth is fertile soil for U.S. aggression will its character as a legal and political fiction and its essential moral corruptness be revealed. Nevertheless, everything seems to indicate that this colonialist creation will not live beyond the life of its creator (who is already seventy years old). Therefore, when future generations—once we have won independence—study the history of this period, they will not be able to keep from seeing in Luis Muñoz Marín the pathetic case of a man devoured by his own creation: the annexationist middle class. He will be scorned by those who saw in him a hope for the liberation of Puerto Rico; pointed to as the man who perpetrated the opportunistic and colonialist policies of his father; and relegated—together with the ELA, his creature —to the place which history reserves for those who were not truly great, although they had it in them to be so. In the history of free nations his name will be inscribed with those who turned their backs on a noble, sacred, and morally just cause to serve unconditionally the worst enemy of liberty— not just of his people, but of all the peoples of the world.

Fortunately, for our people, their honor and their dignity have remained untarnished. Throughout our country's history our best sons have carried out a campaign of resistance to colonialism. As Martí said on one occasion: "When there are many men without honor, there are always others who have in them the honor of many men. These are the ones who rebel with terrible force against those who rob the people of their liberty, which is their honor." Visible throughout the dishonorable spectacle carried out by Muñoz Marín and his cohorts for the last four decades has been the brilliant figure of Puerto Rican national consciousness: Pedro Albizu Campos. He and those who suffered death, prison, and persecution with him constituted in their time the essential, strengthening element represented by all those who are the bearers of liberty. Their honorable example lives today in the spirit of our young people who are resisting colonialism, as in all those Puerto Ricans who insist on saying *No* to the repeated attempts to destroy Puerto Rican national identity and to convert us into pariahs in our own land. The struggle against the independence of Puerto Rico is corrupt and sterile. The principles of world-historical validity cannot be annihilated because it reflects the desire of all people to be free. How anti-historical, how retrogressive, to fight against that principle! Our people—like all the other peoples of the world—will prevail as they have prevailed against the antihistorical pull of the colonialists, thanks to the liberating action of all those who will one day be able to understand the profound meaning of Albizu Campos' statement, "The fatherland is courage and sacrifice."

9 | "The Bridge Between Two Cultures," or the Siege of Puerto Rican Culture

Porto Rico is the only country in the world where North American ideals are being put into operation in a Latin American civilization of high type. There is no other region where the two civilizations can touch each other and influence each other so effectively as in Porto Rico.

J. J. OSUNA (1923)

The latest fashion taking advantage of geographic position and the Anglo-Hispanic graft is to preach our mission as interpreters of the two cultures of the New World: a task of intermediaries which places us as diplomatic arbiters—*amicus curiae*—in the acrid intercontinental debate.

ANTONIO S. PEDREIRA (1934)

Behind that phrase [bridge between two cultures], and some well-intentioned souls who must have produced it, lies in wait for us the danger of becoming eternalized in a cocktail of mediocrities, in a mosaic of broken fossils and flashy ultramodern trinkets, in a strident piece of junk.

TOMÁS BLANCO (1935)

I wish to pay tribute to some of the men who have given shape to the extraordinary social and economic revolu-

tion which in twenty-five short years has made of Puerto
Rico an oasis of peace and progress in the troubled
basin of the Caribbean . . . This is the revolution
which is converting the experiment of Puerto Rico into
the pattern of the peaceful and democratic future of the
Hemisphere.

> VICE-PRESIDENT HUMPHREY (*in a speech at the
> $100-a-plate banquet given in his honor by the
> Democratic party of Puerto Rico* [El Imparcial,
> *November 29, 1965*])

In 1940, with the assumption of power by the Popular
Democratic party, a certain change in the setting of the
Puerto Rican cultural problem becomes apparent. Later,
the era of the Commonwealth inaugurated by Muñoz
Marín incorporated the national anthem and the single-
starred flag—up to that time symbols forgotten by all but
the *independentistas*—as part of the new order. Naturally
these symbols were to be accompanied by the anthem and
flag of the United States. Although we were "free" we
remained indissolubly "associated" with the colonial power.

Changes in the attitude of North American officials came
even more slowly. In 1948 President Truman applied his
own veto to a bill that would have made Spanish the official
language in the schools. This bill had been passed over the
colonial governor's veto by a two-thirds vote of the Puerto
Rican legislators. However, the North American government was forced to swallow the substance of the bill.
Through an administrative ruling, the schools were directed
to teach their classes in Spanish, and a new administration
in Washington was finally forced to go along. By 1952,
then, after more than fifty years of struggle, we were allowed our anthem, our flag—*associated,* let it be under-

stood—and our Spanish tongue. Furthermore, in 1955 the government created the Institute of Puerto Rican Culture, to encourage and perpetuate the study of our cultural heritage. The creation of this institute, the recognition of our flag, our anthem, and our native language—all were important concessions made during the assumption of power by the PPD. But we may wonder to what extent these concessions also reveal a guilty conscience among the leaders of the PPD, many of whom were *independentistas* in their youth. These advances all helped to ease the consciences of the members of the PPD administration and enabled them to appear as protectors of "Puerto Ricanism" without compromising their status as loyal North American citizens.

But Puerto Rico is still a colonial possession; despite the adoption of these forms of appeasement, Puerto Rico's cultural problems continued to be as complex as they were before these and other partial, timid measures were taken. For none of these measures directly confronts the real threat to Puerto Rican identity—its total absorption by the colonial power. On the contrary, these measures only served to hide the island's true cultural problems behind a veil of ersatz Puerto Ricanism without authentic roots.

In addition to the internal cultural problems besieging Puerto Rican identity, an additional strain was placed upon us. The North American government began to present Puerto Rico to the world as the "showcase of democracy" in the Caribbean, "the best answer to Castro," and, from the cultural point of view, a bridge between the two great cultures of the hemisphere. A country as small as ours thus gained an unnatural international importance. For we were not only forced to offer the wooded mountains of El Yunque for the anti-guerrilla-warfare training of the Green

Berets, but had to annually provide the site for the world-famous Casals Festival. Although the "bridge" business is not new, the period of the cold war sharply defined the callous and selfish way in which the U.S. continues to use Puerto Rico to promote her own interests.

To implement this new image, programs of cultural interchange sponsored by a spurious "State Department" of the Commonwealth were set up. Every year thousands of visitors were brought to our island under the Point Four Program or under the auspices of AID, ORIT,* and other organizations. These visitors were shown examples of the progress that can be achieved under the protective mantle of the North American flag. But they were led from one site to another by trained guides who shielded them from all that might burst the magic bubble.

The University of Puerto Rico and the Department of Instruction also joined in the promotion of Puerto Rico as the "showcase" of the Caribbean. The Institute of Labor Relations of the University of Puerto Rico held seminars and training programs for labor leaders sponsored by AID, ORIT, etc. The School of Public Administration provided similar training for Latin American students who had been given scholarships by the Organization of American States. Latin-American teachers began to come to the Department of Public Education to receive basic training in "the American way, Puerto Rican style."

This arrangement, since its beginning, has allowed the colonial power to use Puerto Rico to demonstrate the benefits of the "American way." On a small scale Puerto Rico has become what C. Wright Mills once called "The Ameri-

---

* AID: Agency for International Development; ORIT: International Labor Organization. (Translator's note)

can Celebration." Even writers and artists take part in this celebration of the Commonwealth. Thus, for example, Julián Marías, the Spanish philosopher and knight-errant of liberal democracy, sporadically abandons gloomy Madrid to come to our country to tell us that for his Spain he would like an institutional arrangement similar to the one which exists between Borinquén and the United States. The Catalonian cellist, Pablo Casals, has allowed his picture to be used in a full-page advertisement in *The New York Times,* luring North American investors to the propitious "industrial climate" of Puerto Rico, a climate which of course includes the Casals Festival as one of its principal attractions. The political status of Puerto Rico has also been celebrated by the Latin-American democratic left, but particularly by those two great lovers of democracy as it is practiced in the United States: Rómulo Betancourt and José Figueres.

And as is to be expected, the North American liberals—from Hubert Humphrey to John Kenneth Galbraith—have been an integral part of the celebration of the "peaceful revolution" that has taken place in Puerto Rico under the leadership of Muñoz Marín, a revolution which, they note, has ended poverty and colonialism in a single stroke and has bridged two cultures without destroying either.

But if Puerto Rico is a bridge between two cultures it is a bridge with three lanes going in one direction and only one in the other. The culture of Puerto Rico must constantly reconcile itself to the crushing presence of the culture of the colonial power. Even with the creation of the Institute of Puerto Rican Culture or with the Puerto Rican Atheneum we are unable to counteract the accelerating pace of cultural assimilation, with its manifestations on all levels of our collective life. Part of the problem lies in the fact that exposure to the "American way" begins in the public schools. If we examine the orientation of those officials responsible for elementary, secondary, and higher education in Puerto Rico—public as well as private—and if we analyze even in a superficial way the influence of the mass media on Puerto Rican popular opinion, we can see why we have not been more successful in slowing down the rate of assimilation.

Primary and secondary education in Puerto Rico is, as we have said, the responsibility of the Department of Public Education. In its definitions of what is and what is not Puerto Rican, this department has reflected the political vision of the party in power. Consequently, the textbooks, the curriculum, and the presentation in the classroom of Puerto Rican history are slanted toward the views of the colonial regime. Puerto Rican history is seen through the deforming glass of the latter's political inclinations. We cannot stop here for an in-depth study of the problem. It is sufficient to say that the colonialist mentality—the fruit in many instances of the disproportionate influence of the educational and political attitudes at Teachers' College (a branch of Columbia University) in New York City (where many of Puerto Rico's educators received their training)—permeates the whole bureaucratic structure. And in the hands of this bureaucracy lies nothing less than the intellectual and moral formation of the Puerto Rican child. Always afraid of being exposed as nationalists or subversives, the higher functionaries of the Department of Education have moved timidly and with characteristic ambiguity before any attempts to revise the presentation of the subjects of Puerto Rican culture and history in the schools.

In addition, these same functionaries have given accreditation to those private schools using English as a first language because of political pressures brought to bear by those middle-class citizens in favor of the assimilation of Puerto Rico to the colonial power. This antipedagogic and anti-Puerto Rican practice has been one of the major influences contributing to the cultural assimilation of our nation, since it is these schools from which the majority of candidates for a university education comes. (In a study done by Dr. Luis Nieves Falcón, it was found that only 1 per cent of the children of workers and peasants manage to get to the university, even though they represent the largest single group in the population.) Education in these private schools and institutions makes use of North American textbooks, with the consequent belittling of everything Puerto Rican. Yet the Secretary of Public Education has chosen to adopt a hands-off policy and by this decision has in effect helped to lower our culture to a position of secondary importance.

The attitudes of those in charge of higher education in Puerto Rico follow the same pattern. I quote two distinguished Puerto Rican writers discussing higher education at the University of Puerto Rico:

The University of Puerto Rico, in existence since 1903, has tended preferably to copy and reflect the methods and programs of study existing in the universities of the United States, avoiding European and Latin-American models, to the point of stating in an ordinary demogogic way the arbitrary comparison between the concept of the university in Spanish-American countries and the concept of the university in the United States, sifting out the motives of an urgent university reform on the basis of those extremes, side-stepping the responsibility of creating a university which would satisfy the spiritual appetites and legitimate needs of Puerto Rican society. Besides the University of Puerto Rico, located in the towns of Río Piedras and Mayaguez, there exist on the island other prestigious Catholic and Protestant universities in which predominates, as in the University of Puerto Rico, the criterion of turning to account the English language, educational patterns imported from the United States, the system of schools and academic degrees existing in Chicago, California, New York, or any other city of the nation, to the detriment of humanistic studies and the belittling of Puerto Rican culture and the values embodied in the Spanish language and literature.[1]

In the perpetuation of the outdated and authoritarian structures of the University of Puerto Rico, the former chancellor and president, Jaime Benítez, has played a dominant role during the historical period that concerns us. Benítez was appointed in 1942 to the chancellorship. In 1948 Benítez put down a student movement which had begun that year and had turned into a general strike. For the next two decades Benítez imposed an autocratic regime on our highest educational center, depriving professors and students of all influence in the decision-making process. During his regime, which lasted uninterruptedly from 1948 to 1966, the University of Puerto Rico was treated by Benítez and his followers as their exclusive property. University procedures were strictly controlled by Benítez, and the *casa de estudios* ideology,* which he helped to mold, dominated university thinking. Naturally, this ideology received the unconditional support of the press. It can be said, however, that no other ideology has better served the interests of those who wish to perpetuate colonialism on our island than this one has—except perhaps the ideology of the Common-

---

[1] María Teresa Babín and Nilita Vientós Gastón, "La situacion de Puerto Rico," in *Sur* (Buenos Aires) (March–April, 1965), p. 118.

* Literally, house of studies. Figuratively, similar to the expression the intellectual ivory tower.

wealth. Though Benítez is no longer president, his ideas still permeate university thinking. The actual president, named by a political body created by the Legislative Assembly known as the Council on Higher Education, insists that the institution be "depoliticized," that the student body and faculty of the university be "pacified," that the concerns of both be channeled along the "legitimate" paths created by the colonial regime through its recognized bureaus of higher education.

The consequences of this educational policy are many. The ideological and political currents now running through human society come later to our country than to the rest of the world. Because of our political status we are isolated— especially from changes occurring in the countries of Latin America. Yet all the most burning issues which today divide humanity into hostile camps or create new blocks of solidarity do finally reach our country. In Puerto Rico it is most often the college generation which serves as the antenna for those currents and tendencies. No group experiences a more profound and restless concern for the destiny of its country and humanity than do the most alert sectors of Puerto Rican college youth. As a center of higher education, the University of Puerto Rico is particularly vulnerable to those signs of discontent or restlessness originating from causes of dissatisfaction beyond the purely commonplace. As a result, it is most important that at the university freedom be allowed. For only to the degree that the university is a catalyst of the restlessness, the problems, and the desires of the thinking sectors of society does it fulfill its complete function. But this also explains why those who choose to defend the status quo are unwilling to give the university the right to function as it should.

What has been said up until now applies with singular

acuteness to the restrictive framework of present-day Puerto Rican society. We all know that the university is the favorite target of those interests attempting to perpetuate the colonial situation of our country. Yet the University of Puerto Rico is still one of the last strongholds of national resistance and remains so despite repeated attempts to suppress the student movement on the Río Piedras campus. (In fact, the University of Puerto Rico has become a stronghold of resistance to oppression, exploitation, and dehumanization in Latin America and—we gladly point it out—in the United States.) As a social institution, the University of Puerto Rico is a product and reflection of Puerto Rican society. At the university, we can observe on a minor scale the prevailing attitudes and political ideologies in fashion, the structure of classes and of power; in short, we can see the general and basic outlines of the Puerto Rican society at large. But at the same time the university is something more than a miniature copy of society (that's what the defenders of our colonial situation wish it was); it is the place where the dissident groups in Puerto Rican society can present their points of view with greatest liberty. In that sense, we can say that the university, while a product of the establishment, is at the same time its goad.

What seems at first glance to be a contradiction is merely the result of our inability to reason dialectically. Let me explain.

In any society, the dominant ideas and beliefs of the society will be those held by the people with economic and political power. These ideas and beliefs, once given credence, will serve as spiritual support for the economic and political policies promulgated by the powerful classes or groups in the society. This so-called spiritual power then becomes the ideological weapon utilized by the dominant groups to offer a justification, a rationalization for the privileges freedom of action confers on its exercisers. The university, situated in the very center of that political power, nevertheless represents a challenge to its spiritual basis. For the university, if it functions faithfully, criticizes and questions, while others merely accept. Like Faust's Mephistopheles, it is "the spirit that always denies." Critically, it goes to the root of problems, examines them, turns them upside down and—why not—subverts them. Let us say it once and for all. When the university is not merely an academic center—academic in the sense of sterile—when it is not, as some pretend, an innocuous institution in which a moratorium is declared on all authentic student restlessness for four years, then it is, of necessity, a center for subversion of the existing system. Not in vain is the lewd dream of all the oligarchs, military men, policemen, gentlemen of the press, etc.—from the North Pole to the South—that of intervening in the universities with military or police power.

What are the problems of Puerto Rico and who are those who try to mystify them, hide them, or make them disappear? It is easy to answer the last part of the question. They are those in whose interest it is that Puerto Rico continue in her present condition of political inferiority. That is why it is these individuals who do not want to go to the root of all our problems, to the basic problem that weighs like a millstone around our collective neck: the problem of colonialism. Here is the most fundamental question, the most urgent problem we as a group have faced for more than four centuries. It is precisely this problem that most concerns our thinking young people, our college generation. Yet is is this problem that the colonialists wish to tuck away and hide.

Puerto Rico is not immune to the intellectual and political currents that are presently shaking this earthly globe. One of those currents—perhaps the strongest and most vigorous—is the struggle to liquidate colonialism throughout the world. In fact, the world today is the scene of one of the most heroic and glorious struggles recorded in the history of humanity: the struggle of the Vietnamese people for the full exercise of their right to be free and to have the type of government they, as a majority, choose. What is happening in Vietnam cannot be ignored by Puerto Rican youth—not simply because the flower of this youth unwillingly pays tribute with its own blood in a fight against a people with whom we have no cause to fight. But because these youth know that in the swamps and jungles of that small country of Southeast Asia, the destiny of humanity is at stake, the destiny of all countries under colonial or neocolonial domination is at stake, the destiny of Puerto Rico is at stake. The college generation of Puerto Rico— Puerto Rican youth in general—cannot remain indifferent before the magnitude of what is happening there. Despite the entrenched conservatism of the majority of university students the issue of the war in Vietnam has begun to move a growing sector of college students to militant protest. These youth still represent a minority of the student body. But they are an intelligent, brave, alert, and determined minority.

But it is not just the war in Vietnam that arouses their concern. They are also attempting to come to grips with racism, the role of the United States as policeman of the world, the deterioration of our natural resources, the precipitous surrender of our national patrimony, and the dishonesty of the generation of men in whom Puerto Rico put its faith in 1940. The masks are falling, and youth—which has nothing to loose but life—is seeing the hypocrisy and falseness of those who were once its mentors. The crisis which grips our society—a faithful reflection of the crisis which grips the colonial power—stirs youth to dethrone its old idols. Unfortunately, only to find that the surrounding panorama has become more and more gloomy. It is the hour of truth and youth knows it. Because youth and only youth—not the legislators who unconditionally supported a resolution backing the genocidal war the United States is waging against the Vietnamese people—will be the ones called to die or forced to go to jail because of Vietnam.

Strangely enough, the same young people required to go to Vietnam are considered incapable of making intelligent decisions about those university matters which most affect them. By a curious, twisted logic, after the age of eighteen a young man can serve in the armed forces of the North American empire but cannot—because he lacks maturity— have a voice and vote in university matters for a period of at least four years. On entering the University of Puerto Rico, the student—according to Jaime Benítez' *casa de estudios* theory—should declare a moratorium on all "political" activity on the campus. It is obvious that the word "political" is to be defined in line with the interests of the colonialist groups in our society, since Mr. Benítez is one of their spokesmen. Therefore, to keep politics out of the university means to keep those with an ideology other than the ideology of the defenders of colonialism off the campus.

This presumptuous academicism of the *casa de estudios* thesis is not only a farce but is violated daily by its own proponents. No matter how much Mr. Benítez and his allies opt for the contrary, politics cannot be eliminated from the university, either in Puerto Rico or in any other part of the world. All decisions regarding university curriculum—what courses should be taught and what should be the content of each course—are made as a result of political decisions. For example, at the University of Puerto Rico the humanities and the social science courses reflect the ideological bias of those supporting liberal democratic governments. This bias is the cause and product of the development in the West of certain institutions and political ideas. It is the representative ideological expression of a particular economic system: capitalism. Therefore, the education of the professors themselves, the stress placed on certain subjects of study—including what thinkers are and are not to be discussed—is in itself an institutional decision that has a political basis. Not to mention, of course, the fact that the legislature of Puerto Rico and the Council on Higher Education—bodies that exert tremendous influence on the structure of higher education in Puerto Rico—are political bodies in the most exact definition of the term.

Our college students recognize that the doctrine of the *casa de estudios* is unattainable, that it is a doctrine of expedience created only to eliminate all relevant activity on the university campus.

Let us not lose sight of the fact that a university created within a colonial context will to a great extent reflect the ominous influence of colonialism. If the nation is not in control of the ultimate decisions affecting its destiny, the university within this nation will not be able to channel its intelligence toward the solution of the nation's *authentic* problems. In a colonial system the university will be made to serve the twisted interests of the colonial power and her native defenders.

A relevant example is the case of ROTC, a program created by the U.S. Congress under the so-called Land Grant Acts to provide trained officers for the U.S. Army.

Although Puerto Rico had neither voice nor vote in the passage of this bill, in the operation of the armed corps to which these young people will later belong, or even in the subjects which are to be taught to the cadets, an ROTC program was instituted at the University of Puerto Rico and academic credit is now being given for learning to handle a firearm.

Like every colony, our island epitomizes and possibly magnifies the worst evils of the colonial power. The pressures in our environment to conform are greater than those in the United States. The suppression of forces actively opposed to the political powers is also greater—except when those in opposition in the colonial power are North American blacks. We all know that colonialism is not merely a system based on the economic exploitation and political domination of one people by another. It is also— and this is vital to its survival—a system based on the repression of the authentic cultural heritage of its colonies and it is a system that will apply psychologically aggressive methods to achieve its goals. The Puerto Rican university student must therefore fight against a double tyranny: the physical presence and power of the North American government (who could deny the visibility of the North American presence in Puerto Rico?) and its more subtle attempts to indoctrinate Puerto Rican youth with positive attitudes toward the North American presence in Puerto Rico. Now, after more than a hundred years of colonial domination, the students and many Puerto Rican university professors have been exposed to long-term psychological as well as political indoctrination. And with each passing year, the United States begins to appear in a more positive light. (Perhaps those who resemble the Puerto Ricans most in this sense are the North American blacks, whose identity problems in a society oppressing them are very similar to the identity problems of Puerto Ricans. The struggle that has most helped to liberate North American blacks from their colonialist mentality—that is, from their feelings of inferiority —has been the Black Power movement. This movement has had an undeniable impact on the struggle of blacks for liberation.) The authentic liberation of the Puerto Rican university student—that is, the overcoming of his alienation from an educational system unresponsive to his needs—can only be achieved when Puerto Rico has attained her final liberation. Only then will we be able to have an authentically Puerto Rican university at the service of Puerto Ricans.

Therefore, the Puerto Rican student cannot remain passive or indifferent to the destiny of his own nationality. He also cannot remain on the edge of the struggle of the Vietnamese people and the black people of the United States. Whether those in power like it or not, each and every one of the youth born in the forties has his life at stake in the struggle for freedom. And, even more important, Puerto Rico's life is also at stake.

The problems of Puerto Rican society are urgent and serious. They are not the problems of who will be governor in the next election or whether or not legislators' salaries should be raised. They are the authentic problems of a nation whose decision-making power is not in the hands of its people.

But these problems are not the object of debate in the mass media. By a curious and grotesque distortion of priorities, the media will discuss whether or not there should be pickets at the University of Puerto Rico, but will not even talk about whether or not there should be hydrogen bombs at Ramey Base in Aquadilla. In addition, several words have been eliminated from the common vocabulary of respectable society—fatherland, revolution, nation, nationalism, sovereignty, independence, imperialism, colonialism, etc.—with the result that the political struggle in Puerto Rico has been reduced to a contest in which there appear to be no burning issues. There is a conscious attempt to "depoliticize" our society, to have it reflect the North American dream of a utopia. But university students resist this attempt and that is why the immemorial cry is raised: "We must intervene in the University."

In addition, the mass media—press, radio, and television —functions as another arm of the colonial rulers. Puerto Rican radio and television are regulated by the Federal Communications Commission and operate within the rules set up for radio and television in the United States. The cultural level of Puerto Rican stations—if we exclude WIPR, which is a body of the Department of Education—is really depressing. Most of the films and programs are in English or are translations of programs originating in the United States. The Cuban exiles, who are particularly involved in our entertainment media, have brought here and placed on our television screens all the bad taste and vulgarity of prerevolutionary Cuba. They promote and encourage the values of North American society and the political illiteracy of the snobbish middle class.

The Puerto Rican press, on the other hand, is basically dominated by North American capital. Of the four existing newspapers, the one put out in English, the *San Juan Star,* belongs to the newspaper chain of Scripps-Howard. The arch-reactionary paper *El Mundo*—our equivalent to the *Diario de la Marina* of prerevolutionary Cuba—is tied to the Knight newspaper chain. *El Imparcial*—which began as an independent newspaper and remained so during the lifetime of Antonio Ayuso Valdivieso, its founder—has been sold to North American interests. The first act of its new publisher, Clem Littauer, has been to fire the notable journalist and independent fighter, César Andreu Iglesias. Lastly is *El Día,* belonging to Luis A. Ferré, the governor of Puerto Rico for the New Progressive party and leading spokesman for the Puerto Rican annexationists.

In no other country is "freedom of the press," as defined by the SIP*, so unfree as it is in Puerto Rico. Here the press can lie, conceal, vilify, vituperate, and destroy reputations, without the groups or persons mentioned—usually the *independentistas*—being able to do anything to prevent these actions. Our press is so one-sided in its coverage that if you have read one paper you have read them all. Most story coverage is based on UPI and AP reports, so the only variations from paper to paper are the result of mistranslations of the news releases. These same criticisms can be applied to the magazine *Bohemia Puertorriqueña* and to others of a similar type and orientation.

It should now be apparent to the reader why I have entitled this chapter "The Siege of Puerto Rican Culture." In Puerto Rico, the press, radio, and television are at the service of the colonial regime. The public educational system serves the United States' goal of spiritual domination. The University of Puerto Rico has been subjected at all levels to colonialist intervention.

Anthropologists and sociologists—such as Eduardo Seda Bonilla, Eugenio Fernández Méndez and Luis Nieves Falcón—who have dedicated their sharp intellects to this task, have come to the same conclusions I have. Even more recently, a keen student of the problem, Dr. Germán de

---

* Inter-American Press Society. (Translator's note)

Granda Gutiérrez—a linguist who approaches the subject from a sociological perspective—made an observation which other Puerto Rican scholars, such as Nilita Vientós Gastón, María Teresa Babín and Margot Arce de Vázquez, have already demonstrated from other perspectives: that the thesis of Puerto Rican bilingualism is totally false, that on our island the language has been so corrupted that we are in danger of becoming a nation of stammerers.[2]

Puerto Rican writers and artists concerned with this problem have testified to its seriousness. René Marqués, Pedro Juan Soto, Emilo Díaz Valcárcel, José Luis González, Enrique A. Laguerre, José Emilio González—to mention only a few—have dealt with this subject in plays, essays, novels, fiction, and poetry. The deep concern with the spectacle they are witnessing is evident.[3] The same deep concern is depicted in the artistic works of Lorenzo Homar, Carlos Raquel Rivera, Rafael Tufiño, Augusto Marín, José R. Alicea, and others. Each of their works expresses the intellectual who sees a gloomy scene but can do nothing to change it.

With the recent electoral triumph of the annexationists, survival of Puerto Rico's cultural identity is in even greater danger. Octavio Paz has described the social phenomenon of Mexican *pachuquism** in his brilliant essay, *The Labyrinth of Solitude*. There is the danger, in my opinion, that as time passes we will have in our country a situation analo-

---

[2] Germán de Granda Gutiérrez, *Transculturación e interferencia lingüística en el Puerto Rico contemporáneo* (Bogatá: Instituto Caro y Cuervo, 1968).

[3] I refer the interested reader to my article, "La temática social en la literatura puertorriqueña," *La Torre* (San Juan, P.R.) Vol. XXI, no. 2 (April–June, 1963).

* *Pachuco* is one word used to describe the half-assimilated, Americanized Mexicans of the Southwest. (Translator's note)

gous to that of New Mexico, that the Puerto Rican *pachuco* will be born. It is enough to speak with Puerto Ricans born in New York to observe how deep is this identity split when cultural and political ambiguity reigns over the spirit of a whole generation. Governor Ferré speaks of *"jíbaro* statehood" for us, believing that we could perpetuate our culture even when part of the United States as a state of the Union. But this is an act of wishful thinking on his part. It is unfortunately in conflict with our historical experience of almost two centuries of North American imperialism. At any rate—as I have said before—annexation to the colonial power will not be the cause of Puerto Rican cultural assimilation but one of its effects—that is, the total intellectual and spiritual colonization of our people is the result of a much deeper political phenomenon.

It is still too early to predict all the consequences of the educational and cultural policies of the PNP, which now holds executive power. It is clear, of course, that the ascendancy of the PNP to power will open our country even further to cultural penetration by the United States. But our condition will not be *essentially* altered. During the thirty years of government under the PPD, annexationist and assimilationist forces were given strength by the ambiguous and equivocal educational policy of the PPD, the inevitable result of those who thought they could have their cake and eat it too.

The resistance of Puerto Ricans to their cultural assimilation has been truly admirable. Spanish is still spoken on this island despite seventy years of concerted effort to undermine the very foundations of our national identity. This is proof of how solid was the base of our culture at the time of the North American invasion. Even in our abject colonial defenselessness we continue to be a nation. Today, the danger of our loss of heritage comes from those in our elephantine middle class who tend to imitate blindly the cultural patterns of their counterparts in the colonial power. Even though the attitudes of this middle class do not really affect the masses, their influence is still much more marked and consequently more inclusive than the influence of the intellectual groups who have attempted to stop cultural assimilation. It is truly a sad comment on Puerto Rican reality that the question asked by Pedreira in 1934— "What are we?"—must still be asked by present and future Puerto Rican generations. To the degree that our people have been victims of intellectual colonialization, they have lost contact with their cultural and historical roots. Regarding their past they suffer amnesia. A people who do not know from whence they have come or how they have come to be cannot know where they are going or what they are going to be. Here is the most ominous consequence of colonialism in its Puerto Rican version: the cultural and historical vacuum that threatens to leave us the mere shell of our culture, the mere form empty of substance.

Only a people who can make themselves masters of their destiny can confer on present and future generations the roots necessary for a common national identity. The cultural problem we have described is, consequently, essentially political in its origins and solution. It has to do with the problem of power. Colonialism is, by definition, the lack of power, collective impotence. Puerto Rican national identity will only be able to flourish fully when our people are powerful enough to make the basic decisions which affect their existence as a people. As long as that day—the day of our independence—does not come, the threat of our cultural extinction must weigh upon our national identity. Our culture will remain what it has become and still is: a culture under siege.

Part IV | *Approaching a Conclusion*

10 | "The Unfinished Poem of Bolívar": Puerto Rico's Struggle for Independence in Historical Perspective

The great are only great because we are on our knees.
Let us arise.
BETANCES

Puerto Rico is extended into the heavens by this Yunque*
And there is no hammer in the world which can sink this
anvil.
DE DIEGO

To take away our fatherland they will first have to take
away our lives.
ALBIZU CAMPOS

In spite of the fact that the last vestiges of colonialism of the classical type are being liquidated throughout the rest of the world, Puerto Rico is still as we have tried to show—a

* *Yunque* literally means "anvil," but it is also the name of a great rain forest on the northwestern end of the island of Puerto Rico. (Translator's note)

colony. After five centuries of colonial domination—first under Spain and then under the United States—a national liberation movement capable of ending our situation has not managed to crystallize. To what can we attribute this failure, which marks Puerto Rico with an indelible sign among the nations of the world? Why is this century-old struggle not now able to take advantage of the present favorable historical juncture to break the vicious circle of colonialism, joining Puerto Rico to the international community of free and sovereign nations of the world?

In the development of this essay we have seen that our past liberation movements have moved by two distinct methods: through armed insurrection and militant resistance to the established system; and through the electoral process—working within the legitimate channels for the liberation of our nation. Betances and Albizu Campos were the main standard-bearers of the insurrectional theory. The theory of struggle "against the regime within the regime" was a contribution to the independence movement of José De Diego. These two methods were indicative of the two different tendencies of those within the Puerto Rican independence movement—or, in current language, those with revolutionary and those with reformist tendencies.

During the nineteenth century, there is now no doubt that the only way we could have attained independence was through armed revolutionary struggle. Betances and Martí, the two great leaders of that historical period, were revolutionaries. Two elements were of vital importance to the success of their actions: the continued disintegration of the Spanish Empire as a consequence of Spain's internal and external weaknesses; and the development of an indigenous insurrectional struggle capable of working *from within* to undermine the rotting colonial structure ruling Puerto

Rico. To achieve those ends, Betances and Martí worked on both fronts: with the émigrés outside the country working for Puerto Rican liberation, waiting for the propitious moment to join forces with those inside the country; and with those progressive forces in the Caribbean prepared to offer support and solidarity to a revolutionary movement. The Spanish Empire was not prepared to easily relinquish her hegemony over our islands. The long and bloody war waged in Cuba gives us an idea of how far Spain went to prevent the loss of even one of her colonies.

But Puerto Rico's revolutionary struggle was different from Cuba's for a number of reasons, some of which we have already discussed in Chapter Two. The insurrectionary movement in Borinquén scarcely managed to get off the ground. Attempts by outsiders to liberate Puerto Rico— first by Simon Bolívar and later by Rius Rivera—either met tenacious opposition in U.S. governing circles, or failed to build the revolutionary unrest among the masses indispensable for a successful revolution.

That's where the trouble lay: in the lack of popular support within Puerto Rico for a liberation movement. Despite the countless abuses of authority committed on countless occasions by the Spanish authorities—even against those Puerto Ricans who, like the autonomists, did not really endanger Spanish hegemony on the island—this support could not be mustered. The liberal reformists of the time held out to the people the possibility of obtaining gradual concessions. These concessions did not, of course, challenge the substance of the colonial power's hegemony. And at the same time, the Spanish Empire took advantage of the struggle going on between the autonomists and the unconditionalists to fortify her control of the colony. Later, when at the end of the nineteenth century the very moment of her downfall was imminent, she agreed to recognize the political reality existing in the Caribbean only because her choice was to grant either autonomy or independence to Puerto Rico. The autonomists took advantage of the occasion to reach for power, and Puerto Rico had to settle for autonomy. But the autonomists' power was ephemeral.

With the Spanish-American War the pro-independence movement fostered by Betances and Martí suffered a cruel blow. Along with Cuba, Puerto Rico was annexed to the United States. A neocolonial regime was established on the Cuban island, and a new chapter in our struggle began. What had previously been a confrontation with an empire on the decline now became a struggle with an empire on the rise. In addition, this empire spoke the rhetoric of democracy and freedom.

Under North American domination the pro-independence struggle received its first ideological expression in 1904. As the fifth point in its party's program the Union party of Puerto Rico adopted support of pro-independence movements. Matienzo Cintrón created the first independence party, whose platform supported a movement for independence only, offering no alternatives. When this party disappeared in the elections of 1912, the Union party—the majority party at that time—thanks to the move of José de Diego, discarded the issue of statehood from its platform and leaned decidedly toward independence for Puerto Rico. So strong was this pro-independence sentiment in the Union party that even Muñoz Rivera—who always walked the tightrope on matters of political status—had to inform the U.S. Congress that the party he represented in Washington supported independence for Puerto Rico.

During the first twenty years of North American domination, De Diego carried the ideology of the independence movement to its zenith. The Union party, which served as a

base of support for De Diego, had one defect which se-
verely weakened this movement. I refer to the separation it
made between the struggle of the oppressed classes for
social justice and the struggle of the party for independence. As we have seen, the task of organizing the labor
movement in Puerto Rico was begun under the sign of
annexation. This is a matter of vital importance, for the
Union party, which to a great extent was a spokesman for
the most progressive and nationalist sector in the Puerto
Rican colonial elite, did not really respond to the interests
of the working class. The consequences of this separation of
class and ideology were not remedied until the nineteen-
thirties—and then only temporarily—when a considerable
sector of the Puerto Rican labor movement became independent of the annexationist movement. But this separation
has continued to be one of the most proverbial weaknesses
of the liberation movement of Puerto Rico.

On the other hand, at the crucial moment—when the law
imposing North American citizenship on us by congressional fiat was passed—De Diego decided to respect the
decision. He did not organize a resistance movement, despite the fact that he himself foresaw that this decision
would have extremely serious consequences for our
struggle. On pronouncing his famous dictum, "against the
regime from within the regime," he chose to respect the
discipline of the Union party and to continue the struggle
against colonialism within the legal channels provided by
the system itself. This must have been a very difficult decision for the leader from Aguadilla to make. But to reject
North American citizenship and speak out for its repudia-
tion by the Puerto Rican people would have compelled him
to stir up the people for a rebellion he was not prepared to
carry out.

Although in the beginning of his political career De

Diego leaned toward reformist sentiment, with the passing of time and the unfolding of events, he gradually became more radical in his speeches. His bitter criticism of the Jones Act is an example of his later political philosophy. But the act that would have given meaning to his true "song of rebellion" did not crystallize, and with his death in 1918 independence was orphaned by her most brilliant champion.

In 1922, the Union party abandoned its pro-independence platform in favor of the "commonwealth," and we confronted a historical moment similar to the one we face today. The Nationalist party came into being to fill the void, and in time came to be the political movement which managed to lift the independence movement from its low point in 1922 to the very center of our people's concerns.

Once De Diego was dead, Barceló took over at the helm of the Union party. As a consequence of his equivocal policies, the independence movement suffered a historical retrogression. This historical retrogression was, however, limited in duration. The crucial decade of the thirties—the decade in which world capitalism, led by United States capitalism, nearly fell apart—was to give the cause of independence an unusual push. If we were ever close to obtaining independence in this century, it was during that decade. Breaking with the Alliance in 1932, the Liberal party agreed to support a movement for "unconditional independence." And if we analyze the results of the elections of 1932 and 1936 we will observe that the liberals won more votes than did any one of the other parties that formed the triumphant Coalition. (The Liberal party got 170,168 votes in 1932 and 252,647 votes in 1936.) This was an indication of the degree to which there existed in Puerto Rico a strong feeling for independence—prepared, of course, to follow the reformist path, but nonetheless clearly committed to the fight for the liberation of Puerto Rico.

The Nationalist party, on the other hand, constituted the revolutionary vanguard of the liberation movement of Puerto Rico. And at this juncture the colonial power demonstrated the repressive character of the regime which she had imposed on the island. In the violent suppression of the Nationalist party during the thirties and later on, we can really observe how far the colonial regime was prepared to go to preserve the status quo. At that moment, North American colonialists showed two faces: one with a wink to the reformist *independentistas* and one with a frown for those who did not obey "the rules of the game" laid down by the colonial power.

The policy of Albizu Campos was radical because it did not allow for compromise: independence was an inalienable right of the Puerto Rican people. Since this was a country under military, political, and cultural intervention, it would be foolish to participate in elections in which the colonial power and her creole allies had the monopoly of political power. No solution other than the return to the Puerto Rican people of all the powers of their sovereignty would be acceptable, independent of the fact that colonial elections would show more or less votes in favor of certain parties. Having broken the established rules of the game, the nationalist leader knew that his die was cast. The response of those in power would not be long coming.

The fierce suppression of the nationalists by the North American colonialists marked the beginning of a hard-line policy against dissent which has not ceased until now. As long as independence was a political movement which did not endanger imperial hegemony—that is, as long as it was only the manifestation of a desire for liberty and was expressed most of the time verbally—the repression against the *independentistas* did not show itself for what it was: the last recourse of an empire unwilling to grant power voluntarily to the inhabitants of its colony. But when a group of Puerto Ricans organized behind a charismatic leader determined to put an end to the interminable chain of abuses fostered by every colonial regime, contemplation ended and persecution began.

(On this particular issue no one should be deceived. A contemporary author has written: "Historical experience shows that when the existence of the dominant class is in danger, it does not hesitate to resort to the most extreme violent forms, including mass terror, for no social class is willing to abandon the stage of history voluntarily."[1] It would be most dangerous for us to let ourselves believe that the colonial elite and the power elite of the colonial power are "voluntarily going to abandon the stage of history," yielding up the power which they enjoy over our country. For this would lead us to act as if the colonial system— which is predicated on the principle of violence—will one day be willing to grant us liberty without first trying out all the means at its disposal to preserve the status quo, including the *"ultima ratio"* of political power: violence.)

The Nationalist party led by Albizu Campos was doubtless the most heroic and courageous of all the twentieth-century pro-independence movements in our political history. This party created the Puerto Rican nationalist and anti-imperialist consciousness. The fury with which these patriots were pursued contrasts with the generous treatment received by Muñoz Marín once he bowed to the will of the

[1] Adolfo Sánchez Vázquez, *Filosofía de la praxis* (México: Editorial Grijalbo, 1967), p. 305.

colonial power and put the word independence "between parentheses" in the recently created Popular Democratic party (1938). There is no contradiction between the two policies. Rather, we ought to see them as two sides of the same coin. The hand that closes to some will open to show the expeditious way to others.

Once in power—as we have seen—Muñoz Marín deserted the *independentistas'* camp forever. With Albizu Campos imprisoned the road was clear. Muñoz Marín and those with whom he shared colonial power were the principal agents responsible for the historical retrocession from which the independence movement suffered and from which it still has not totally recovered at the moment these lines are being written. That is, the cause of liberation as manifested in the decade from 1930 to 1940 came to a stop and then went backward for several decades—three, I dare to say—as a consequence of the anti-independence work of the Popular Democratic party, on the one hand, and the virtual destruction of the Nationalist party and its leader on the other. This is a task over which the colonial power originally presided, but which was apparently carried on by the man and the party who most jealously defended North American interests in the colony.

If we examine the basis on which the PPD was created we will observe that its great original stroke of genius was to include in its platform both the causes of the independence movement and the social and economic improvement of the Puerto Rican people. Muñoz Marín successfully created a genuinely popular political movement. But the party which began under the umbrella of independence and social justice gradually divested itself of first one and then the other, until it revealed itself to be just one more annexationist party.

One of the most serious limitations of the Nationalist

party was precisely its failure to associate itself with the problems of the masses—a limitation endemic to all of the independence movements of this century. For example, the sugar-cane workers came to Albizu Campos and asked for his support of a strike they had just called. One of the men closest to the nationalist leader at that time evaluates the reaction of Albizu Campos:

"The Nationalist party did not have leaders—not even one single leader—skilled in labor-union organization. At that decisive moment, the social composition of the leadership of the Nationalist party threatened both the eventual success of the party and the destiny of the country. Noble, disinterested, heroic, the nationalist leadership guaranteed its economic support of the strike to the working class. But it was unable to take the immediate step necessary to consolidate the alliance: to turn over the leadership of the working class to the Free Federation* organizing a new labor union with patriotic spirit. Instead, the Nationalist party, themselves all too aware of the fact that independence was a necessary prerequisite to social justice, told the people the truth about the struggle for independence. Preparing the people seriously for the struggle to win independence, they could not be deceived as to the nature of their own fight—a hand-to-hand fight to the death with the conceited Yankee imperialist. In the heat of the fight, the nationalists, deeply involved in the struggle for independence, progressively diminished the aspect of social justice in their propaganda. It was a lapse, but an unfortunate one."[2]

Muñoz Marín took advantage of this lapse to stress the precedence of economic stability over independence. Fur-

* The Free Federation of Workers. (Translator's note)
[2] Juan Antonio Corretjer, *La lucha por la independencia de Puerto Rico* (San Juan, P.R.: Publicaciones de Unión del Pueblo Pro Constituyente, 1950), pp. 64, 70.

thermore, we can say that to a great degree his economic program could already be found in its germinal form in the 1930 program of the Nationalist party, and that he knew how to incorporate skillfully those aspects which suited him, but in the process leaving independence to one side.

The Puerto Rican Liberal party, successor to the Union party and predecessor of the PPD, originally defined the goal of reconciling the struggle for freedom with the immediate pressing social demands. I do not believe there can be any doubt that Antonio R. Barceló—despite his often equivocal positions regarding independence—was really a man who bore the liberation of Puerto Rico more deeply in his heart than Muñoz Marín. In destroying the Liberal party and Barceló as a political leader, Muñoz Marín struck another blow at those in the reformist wing of the independence movement. Forming his new party with the masses from the Liberal party, he deprived the country of a political party which, as we have seen, counted on a solid electoral backing, while it rested on an unequivocally pro-independence platform. From any perspective, whether it be from the fierce repression of the nationalists or from the destruction of the Liberal party, we can only conclude that the most tenacious enemy of Puerto Rican independence within Puerto Rico has been Luis Muñoz Marín.

I believe that the reader will now be able to understand better what I mean when I say that with the coming to power of the PPD in 1940, the struggle for independence suffered an historical retrocession whose consequences are being felt even today. In facilitating our cultural assimilation, which is now in a rather advanced phase, the PPD has undermined as has no other party in our history *not openly advocating annexation to the United States* the foundations of Puerto Rican national identity.

But despite the historical retrogression of the liberation movement, three decades of government under the Popular Democratic party have not been enough to thwart the struggle for liberation. On the contrary. Everything seems to indicate that with the recent triumph of annexationism Puerto Rican society will be polarized into annexationists and *independentistas*.

By its very nature annexationism tends to place face to face those forces which defend that which is Puerto Rican with those which attempt to deny what is Puerto Rican. Statehood necessarily brings with it the cultural assimilation of Puerto Rico to the colonial power as well as the virtual disappearance of all organized resistance to the annexationist process itself. As long as there exists in Puerto Rico a feeling, however much in the minority, that is clearly opposed to any annexationist solution, the Congress of the United States will think twice before making Puerto Rico one more state of the North American Union. The only thing which prevents a direct confrontation between the annexationists and Puerto Rican forces is the mediating condition of the Commonwealth. Once this disappears or shows its most flagrant defects to the Puerto Rican people, the issue will be clearly between the two basic solutions: independence or federated statehood. Although it seems paradoxical, statehood is even more remote than independence—among other reasons, because statehood depends, not on a decision of the Puerto Rican people as such, but on them and the U.S. Congress. And that, despite the annexationist triumph in November 1968.[3]

[3] In a really extraordinary article, Kal Waggenheim has hit the nail on the head in indicating that the only real alternative for Puerto Rico is independence. See his article "An Absurd Prediction," *Sunday San Juan Star Magazine,* December 8, 1968.

Independence as a future for the people of Puerto Rico depends essentially on the successful outcome of the tenacious fight to conserve the Puerto Rican national identity. That is, the present situation raises the question of the very survival of Puerto Rico as a society with a national culture. If the process of cultural assimilation is not arrested in time, if colonialization continues to procreate the colonialist mentality—a product of seven decades of North American domination—the day may come when only the hollow shell of the Puerto Rico that knew De Diego and Albizu Campos remains. Hence the urgency of the patriotic *independentistas'* actions. For only independence—and not the mediating formula with autonomist aspects—can put an end to the total intellectual and moral colonialization of our people.

In my opinion, the cause of independence is today—with the essential historical exceptions—at the same juncture that it was in 1922 when Albizu Campos took the flag of De Diego and kept the cause of independence alive. The present independence movement must again raise this cause to a prominent place in the consciousness of our people. But without forgetting for a single instant what it personally cost the leader from Ponce and the patriots who followed him.

In 1968, the independence movement is still between the reformists and the radicals. It is the old controversy between those who want to fight "against the regime but within the regime" (De Diego, Concepción de Gracia) and those who seek to carry the struggle against the colonial system along routes not provided for by the system itself (Betances, Albizu Campos).

This fragmentation of the Puerto Rican liberation movement has made unified action by all patriotic forces practically impossible except on very rare occasions. The problem has deep historical roots. And it is aggravated by the fact that neither group appears to have found an effective solution: the electoral process does not seem to offer the most effective way to achieve independence, but neither can it be said that armed struggle will be any more successful, especially today when the independence movement is relatively weak.

Faced with such a difficult and long-term situation, many have shown their desperation and withdrawn momentarily from the struggle. Impatience—the inability to see that the history of a nation is not decided in the period of a generation—often causes internal struggles and conflicts between personalities that weaken the total effectiveness of the struggle and allow the oppressors to "divide and conquer."

There is no reason to doubt that if the present regime should feel threatened, it would resort to the same violent tactics it used against the nationalists in the thirties and fifties. As historical experience shows us, this repression against pro-independence groups is selective. It is used primarily against those who refuse to obey the rules of the game as they are laid down by the regime.

The use of force and violence is the very essence of the present colonial regime. Its police watch and pursue those who defend the cause of independence in a defiant way, not those who defend independence through recognized legitimate channels.

After seven decades of North American domination, it is truly difficult to conceive of an electoral triumph of a pro-independence party in a general election. For all the material and spiritual means for the perpetuation of colonial control still reside in the very empire which rules us. The electoral process itself is in the hands of this regime—including the very machinery by which the results to the elections are supervised and verified. Despite these great obstacles, those in the independence movement are not exempt from responsibility for their failures. Their proselytizing work has not been as efficacious as it could be. Their lack of organization and discipline, their cult of personality, and their internal struggles definitely have weakened this movement. Nonetheless, an essential question remains: given the circumstances within which this patriotic struggle has had to develop in Puerto Rico, would it be possible for independence to come through electoral means? I consider it to be improbable, although certainly not impossible. The decline of the PPD and the polarization which will follow the annexationist triumph will surely strengthen the PIP in the 1972 elections.

At present the Puerto Rican Independence party is under the direction of a young and capable leadership. It has a great attraction for Puerto Rican youth, and it has adopted a socialist platform in order to place itself in a more advanced ideological position than it had before. Perhaps all these factors will contribute to its strengthening as a political party during the next four years.

From my point of view the most crucial problem confronting the liberation movement of Puerto Rico is the vicious circle of colonialism. The colonized man does not have a clear national consciousness because he lacks independence. In turn, he lacks independence because he does not have a clear national consciousness.

The most dangerous illusion, therefore, and the one most contrary to historical experience, is to believe that an empire will voluntarily abandon one of its most valued colonies. The process of taking a conscientious stand against colonialism is not just an intellectual process of the struggle itself against the colonial regime. The colonized person becomes "uncolonized"—Fanon points this out well—when he stops seeing in the colonialist the archetype of human perfection. A long time ago Hostos expressed this in his book, *La peregrinación de Bayoán,** "You shall kill the god of fear and only then shall you be free."

To achieve freedom one must confront colonialism through direct resistance. This confrontation will be as peaceful or as violent as the regime allows it to be. But direct confrontation is the only way to force the regime out of hiding, to bare it of all its "liberal" pretensions. As long as no crisis is created, the colonial regime will be able to maintain its apparent attitude of tolerance toward pro-independence groups. Only if it is confronted with a sweeping crisis that endangers its own hegemony will it put into operation all the repressive apparatus at its disposal, ready for the occasion when its presence is called for.

Since its founding in 1959 the Pro-Independence Movement (MPI) has consistently called for the electoral strike, rejecting resistance through the electoral process as spurious and counter-productive. In its activities against compulsory military service for Puerto Rican youth, in its campaign against the surrender of our mineral wealth to North American consortiums, in the development of a program incorporating the most advanced thinking in social and economic matters into the struggle for independence, the MPI—despite its limitations in numerical terms—has succeeded in creating an anti-imperialist, anticolonialist consciousness and has helped to make known a radical perspective on the problems of the island. This has, of course, driven away those whom the regime considers "respectable" defenders of the cause of independence. And it has brought out the enmity of the reactionary press in this country.

* See footnote, p. 117.

Except for the fact that the MPI has still not resorted to armed struggle as a means of liberating Puerto Rico, the organization has a place in the radical trajectory of frontal resistance to colonialism established by Albizu Campos. Its essential problem is that of incorporating the masses into the anticolonial struggle to precipitate the crisis that will eventuate in the liquidation of the colonial regime. Because as long as the pro-independence movement does not achieve this goal it will continue its marginal life within Puerto Rican society. As a movement of national resistance and as a vanguard in the struggle for independence, the MPI today plays the part that the Nationalist party played in its day—although with the exception that the magnitude of the nationalist effort does not allow comparison with any other pro-independence movement of this century. And I say this because when everything looked gloomy for the cause a decade ago, the MPI kept it alive before the eyes of Puerto Ricans and the international community.

The question of the most effective way to fight for the independence of Puerto Rico is debatable. The answer does not lie in conceiving the question dogmatically.

In my opinion, independence is an inalienable right of the Puerto Rican people. It is not a negotiable matter to be debated in an election or a plebiscite.

The life of a nation cannot be determined in one, two, or many generations. The struggle for the independence of Puerto Rico—a century-old struggle—has in the course of these hundred years enjoyed advances and suffered setbacks; it has had its triumphs and its defeats. But it has been an irresistible struggle, as permanent as the principle which serves it as a guide—the principle that liberty is an inherent right of all nations.

As long as there is in Puerto Rico a large group of people

believing in independence, the annexation of our country cannot be perpetrated. The present colonial regime is as weak as the party which fostered it. Sooner or later the confrontation between the extreme defenders of North Americanization and the genuine Puerto Ricans will crystallize, and in that moment, the Puerto Rican people will respond to independence in a much more favorable way than they have thus far. This reaction would automatically prevent statehood for the island. At that historic juncture, independence would become the only solution to the colonial problem of Puerto Rico.

But liberation will not come like manna from heaven, nor will it come by way of some international organization. It must be the product of the historical resolution of the struggle begun by Betances in 1868 in words whose echo we still hear today: "The great are only great because we are on our knees. Let us arise."

11 | Puerto Rico and the International Community

> The subjection of people to foreign subjugation, domination and exploitation constitutes a denial of fundamental human rights, is contrary to the Charter of the United Nations, and compromises the cause of peace and world cooperation.
>
> In those territories which are in trust and not autonomous, and in all the other territories which have still not won their independence, immediate measures should be taken to transfer all power to the people of those territories, without conditions or reservations, in conformity with their freely expressed will and rights, and without distinction of race, creed, or color, to permit them to enjoy absolute independence.
>
> *Resolution 1514* (xv) *passed by the General Assembly of the United Nations on December 14, 1960.*

As a consequence of her colonial situation Puerto Rico is a country artificially isolated from the rest of the world. Not having been incorporated into the community of sovereign nations of the globe, Puerto Rico must always, of necessity, have her international relations sifted through the U.S. State Department. Our relations—especially with those countries which Martí designated as members of "Our America"—cannot take place directly between one country and another, but in the final analysis are the product of what suits the power which rules us imperially. Not a single citizen of another country may enter Puerto Rico if the Immigration Service of the United States objects. And for Puerto Ricans to travel to other countries they must have a North American passport. This contributes to the "insularism" and hermeticism from which we suffer, as well as to the false notions many of our people hold about other Latin American countries. The stereotypes disseminated by the U.S. news agencies, by the mass media, and even by educational means create for the average Puerto Rican an impression of Latin America that is a tangle of confusions, half-truths, and even the most absurd conceptions. It cannot be otherwise while his impression is kept the same as that of the average North American.

Similar inaccuracies are transmitted in reverse. In the Latin American world two antagonistic notions prevail: that of an abject and servile country which does not dare to fight against imperialism, and that of a prosperous and democratic country in which everyone bathes in the rose water provided by the North Americans. To the degree that this book is addressed to a Latin American public, it is my hope that our brothers understand that we are neither the one nor the other, but a country whose peculiar circumstances put her at a certain historical moment under the direct dominion of an empire at the height of its powers, one that in time has come to be the most powerful empire in the world.

This separation of Puerto Rico from other countries with which she is related by a common culture and language has contributed to our cultural stagnation and spiritual poverty in a world to which we should belong. As a consequence of our political situation Latin America has been made a remote and unknown universe where there is no democracy or freedom.

For the United States, the relations of Puerto Rico with Latin America are conceived of—we have already seen this—as a "bridge" or "showcase" in the cold war. The Muñoz Maríns, the Moscosos, Benítezes, and Morales Carrións are the emissaries of the United States to the Spanish-American nations, bringing word of the virtues of the Commonwealth. It is not surprising, then, that when Latin Americans speak of "Puertoricanizing" Latin America they are not praising us.

That our role as an intermediary suits the North American empire is demonstrated by its determined refusal to permit the Committee on Decolonization of the United Nations to include Puerto Rico on the list of territories which "have still not obtained their independence" under the provisions of Resolution 1514 (XV), passed by the General Assembly of the United Nations in December 1960. Using to good advantage the control which she has over this international body, the United States has maintained—like Portugal in the case of Angola—that the matter of Puerto Rico is an "internal affair" which only concerns her and not the United Nations. Her delegate even threatened in the Committee on Decolonization to abandon the session if the case of Puerto Rico was brought up. That by so doing the North Americans are violating the provisions of the Charter of the United Nations, to which they are signatories, does not seem to bother them.

The same thing is happening in the case of the treaty for denuclearization of Latin America, known as the Treaty of Tlatelolco. In the discussions for the approval of this treaty, the United States refused to include Puerto Rico within the scope of its provisions, thus implicitly admitting the existence of thermonuclear bases on the island. So that Borin-quén—a Latin American country when it suits the empire —is not one when it comes to guaranteeing its security before the prospect of a thermonuclear attack.

But the Latin American governments know all this and do not dare to denounce the situation through which our island is passing. Only the revolutionary government of Cuba,* faithful to the ideals of Martí, resolutely backs our right to independence in the international forum and our struggle against colonialism. The same can be said—if we extend our scope outside the Americas—of the socialist countries and of some countries recently liberated from the colonial yoke.

If Puerto Rico is to become incorporated into the international community it cannot continue in its present dubious role as an instrument of North American foreign policy. Only after the achievement of full sovereignty will we have true bridges everywhere and not be restricted to one bridge which always takes us in the same direction.

The United States has the legal and moral obligation to place in the hands of the Puerto Rican people all those powers that are concomitant with the existence of a sovereign nation. Until that happens, every plebiscite, every election held in our country will have the effect of giving legitimacy or the appearance of legitimacy to the existing order, further postponing the final resolution of our colonial status.

We must remind ourselves, nevertheless, that neither international legality nor morality influence the North American empire when its economic and military interests

---

* We must now add the people and government of Chile to this list. (Author's note to the English edition)

are in danger. Cuba, Santo Domingo, and Vietnam illustrate this elementary lesson. It will not be the United Nations nor any other international body which will undo the injustice, but the Puerto Rican people themselves, although with the committed solidarity of all the countries in the world who are fighting against imperialism.

It will be the Puerto Rican people themselves who will break this tyranny of classical colonialism that strangles us, and who will take the first steps toward the recovery of our national patrimony. Let it be clear that formal independence will be only the first step in the bold struggle against neocolonialism, and thereafter, in the struggle to win finally our national liberation. None of this will take place as if by magic or through the "power of positive thinking," but because the historical development of all nations points toward the final eradication of colonialism and the retaking of the powers and prerogatives which now belong to the imperial masters. Although she may have arrived late, Borinquén will not remain on the margin of the historical development of humanity. The North American empire has been weakened by the internal and external struggles which have shaken its very foundations, and this will advance our struggle for liberation.

On the day when Puerto Rico, the most solid bastion of the North American empire in the Caribbean, is finally liberated, we will be in the twilight of an economic-military structure that has wielded a power besides which that of the earth's ancient empire pales.

One hundred years from the glorious Cry of Lares the future of the fatherland begins to take shape in a definitive form.

In this context, the task of the writer is to create a consciousness of the imminent, to lay open before present and future generations the alternatives of the future. It implies dedication of body and soul to the liquidation of an iniquitous and unjust system at its very source. Consequently, it cannot allow a posture of neutrality before the phenomenon being witnessed. As Frantz Fanon has written: "The colonized man who writes for his people; when he utilizes the past should do so with the intention of opening up the future, of inviting actions, of building hope. But to assure hope, to give it density, it is necessary to participate in action, to commit oneself body and soul to the national struggle."

As long as colonialism exists in Puerto Rico, every attitude of presumed "objectivity" is a way of evading the real situation we are confronting. Where the colony is concerned, "objectivity" is not appropriate, if by it we understand that the writer looks at things from a convenient distance "above the fray." The author of this book does not believe in those postures of Olympian separation from human reality.

Therefore, if this book is addressed to anyone, it is to the youth of Puerto Rico, who are resisting colonialism and who illustrate through their brave actions that the spirit of the revolutionaries of Lares, of Betances, and of Albizu Campos, is always alive. This interpretation of our history is, then, my humble tribute and my salute to the pro-independence youth of Puerto Rico.

HATO REY, *Puerto Rico, December 1968*
YEAR OF THE CENTENARY OF THE PROCLAMATION OF THE
REPUBLIC OF PUERTO RICO IN LARES

Epilogue to the Fourth
Edition of *Puerto Rico:*
A Socio-Historic Interpretation

Two years have elapsed since the conclusion of this manuscript. During this time political events in Puerto Rico have occurred with extraordinary rapidity. The polarization foreseen in my essay, as well as the inevitable period of repression following it, has occurred, causing us to believe we are faced with another "crucial decade" in Puerto Rican history—a decade that could possibly turn out to be even more crucial to the struggle for independence of Puerto Rico than the decade of the thirties.

In the period of time from the appearance of my essay (November, 1969) to the present I have had the opportunity to confront the criticisms made of this book from diverse ideological perspectives. Without a doubt confrontation has contributed to the revision of some approaches possibly excessively schematic and to a serious examination of the limitations of a book attempting to cover so much in so few pages.

Last year, round-table discussions on the book were held at the University of Puerto Rico and the Puerto Rican Atheneum.* The content of the work was discussed, its

* The following professors participated in the round-table discussion at the University of Puerto Rico: Dr. Isabel Gutiérrez del Arroyo, Dr.

methodology examined, and its conclusions, as well as its ideological premises, criticized. It can be said that in general the criticism was favorable, although it should be pointed out that almost all those present had a common ideological basis with the author. One of the main criticisms was directed against the excessively schematic nature of the discussion of the period of Spanish domination, a criticism with which I currently agree. It was praised, however, for its panoramic vision and for the relative success with which it synthesized four centuries of our history. Of course, the most fundamental criticisms at this symposium were those which revealed opposing ideological tendencies and consequently presented contradictory interpretations of the history of Puerto Rico—for example, those of Díaz Soler and García Passalacqua.

In Puerto Rico, where hypersensitivity to criticism results in the virtual absence of what could be considered criticism, it is extremely important for an author to receive the stimulating breeze of a critical analysis which—while being fraternal—helps the author reflect on the imperfections and lacunae in his work. Recently a critical essay on my book appeared in the university magazine *La Escalera* (Vol. IV, no. 1, June 1970), in which many objections to the work were made specific. With the publication of this review, written by my comrade in arms, Gervasio García, debate of the issues was stimulated at a level of intellectual rigor which—it must be said—was absent from some of the discussions on the subject held at the Atheneum and the university.

José Emilio González, Professor Pedro Juan Rúa, Professor Juan Rodríguez Cruz, and lawyer Juan Manuel García Passalacqua. At the Puerto Rican Atheneum the participants were Dr. Louis Manuel Díaz Soler, Dr. Aida Negrón do Montilla, Dr. Luis Nieves Falcón, and Professor Angel Ruiz.

The notes which I have made on the following pages are directed, therefore, towards clearing up some points that I feel were not adequately understood by Professor Gervasio García.

In the first place, I believe that Gervasio García has correctly designated my book an "historical handbook." Many of the book's imperfections are a consequence of this fact. García himself recognizes this when he indicates that "in view of the precarious state of our historiography, the author's ambitious attempt at reinterpreting four centuries of history had to cope with gaps and reflect certain inaccuracies." The truth is that every author has a particular audience in mind when he writes. This book was conceived primarily for the Latin-American public—whose image of Puerto Rico is, in the great majority of cases, distorted—and in particular for the young Puerto Ricans who are eager to find a source of information that demystifies our historical process under colonialism while providing a theoretical combat weapon. Thus the panoramic character of the work, excessively inclusive if you wish, about our historical development. The erudite work which Professor García might prefer surely remains to be written. I did not intend the book to serve as a final reference work on its subject.

Secondly, the "precarious state of our historiography" greatly contributed to my inability to treat certain subjects (such as the labor movement) more extensively. If I had gone to consult the original source material in all areas touched on I would not have finished writing the book in the time the editors and I agreed upon. But I can still affirm that many primary sources *were* consulted, particularly those pertinent to the study of relations between Puerto Rico and the United States of America during the first thirty years of North American domination. This investigation took me to source materials in the Library of Congress in Washington, D.C., dealing with the historical-social circumstances surrounding the first two organic laws approved by the U.S. Congress. However, the very nature of the book precluded concentrated analysis of those historical realities, which might have shed light on particular events at the expense of the general thesis being developed. The controversy about the definition of the individual's role in history and the importance of history as a tribunal is a problem of emphasis rather than ideology, although I am aware of its having an ideological basis. From a strictly Marxist viewpoint like that of Gervasio García, the role of the individual pales in the face of historical-social realities. On the other hand, García clearly approaches the concept of the "tribunal of history" literally rather than metaphorically. When I speak of "determining the pertinent historical responsibilities," I do not attempt to hypostatize nor deify history. I speak of something Fidel Castro spoke of when he said: "History will absolve me." I am simply saying that there are certain forces which retard historic change and others which accelerate it. This attitude conforms with Marx's as related in *The Eighteenth of Brumaire*. In the case of individuals who attain historic significance, their responsibility to future generations derives only from their limited role as representatives of the above-mentioned social forces. But I am in agreement with Professor García when he comments that on occasion my analysis leads me to see the development of Puerto Rican history in terms of its personalities. Most likely, this is the result—probably unconscious—of my concern with the fact that our youth scarcely know anything about those men who have symbolized our struggle for national liberation and of my desire to rescue these men from the oblivion into which they have been sunk by the colonialists. At any rate, García's comments on the problem

of annexation at the end of the past century and the economic factors causing this phenomenon are very illumi-
nating.

The same can be said with reference to his observations
about colonialism. I do not object to a definition of colonialism as an essentially economic phenomenon. But García works with a single aspect of the phenomenon and uses
it as the total basis for his criticism. He loses sight of those
chapters in which I maintain that Lenin's thesis on imperialism could also be applied perfectly to Puerto Rico. Furthermore, I think that on occasion he confuses colonialism with
neocolonialism. At no point do I defend the proposition
that colonialism is primarily a cultural phenomenon. My
feeling is that in Puerto Rico one of colonialism's most
important effects has been to besiege the Puerto Rican
national consciousness with the aim of destroying Puerto
Rico's national identity.

I am completely in agreement with Professor García on
the necessity of writing the history of those "without a
history." We are all awaiting the results of his historical
research into the Puerto Rican labor movement, hoping
that it will fill the gap he points out. The same hope can be
expressed of other aspects of our collective life still secret
and unstudied.

I repeat that the review of my book by Gervasio García
is one of the best I have read. It is a good criticism from a
member of the left of a book with leftist leanings. Comrade
García's analysis should serve as a stimulus for more much-
needed radical criticism in Puerto Rico.

As I said previously, my book begins with the "recent
triumph of the cause of annexation" in the elections of
November 1968. It closes, consequently, before Governor
Luis A. Ferré, who was elected on the ticket of the New
Progressive party (PNP), took office and before the party

that kept colonial power on the island for almost three decades, the Popular Democratic party (PPD), was relegated to a position of secondary political importance. As was to be expected, the triumph of annexationism has brought with it an intensification of the efforts to North Americanize Puerto Rico, even though the declared goal of the government is to preserve our national culture through the introduction and popularization of a concept called "jíbaro statehood." This popularization has taken place primarily through the educational system, as directed by Dr. Ramón Mellado Parsons, who is Secretary of Public Instruction of the PNP government and the ideological chieftain of Puerto Rican annexationism. In reaction against these tendencies leading toward the cultural assimilation of Puerto Rico with the colonial power, a countermovement has been created, one which supports Puerto Rican nationalism and the growth of national resistance to colonialism and imperialism. The polarization Albizu Campos foresaw ("the supreme question: Yankees or Puerto Ricans") daily takes on a more definite character. The bankrupt ideology and practices of the Commonwealth of Puerto Rico have contributed noticeably to this polarization as well as to the disintegration of the PPD since the partisan schism that cost the party its power in 1968.

All that has been said seems to point to a crisis of the colonial system in Puerto Rico, a crisis that appears in a series of "indicators":

I THE ISLAND OF CULEBRA

The small island of Culebra is located seventeen nautical miles east of Puerto Rico. Constituted in 1905 as a municipality of Puerto Rico, Culebra extends some 7,200 acres and has approximately 700 inhabitants.

Originally settled by the Spanish in the 1880's, Culebra was part of the Puerto Rican territory ceded to the United States by virtue of the dispositions of the Treaty of Paris. In 1898, when the North American invaders reached Culebra and proceeded to occupy the island, a town already in existence, San Ildefonso, had a population of around two hundred Puerto Ricans. The U.S. Navy drove the town dwellers from their homes, forcing them to disperse into the rural areas.

Empowered by the Treaty of Paris, the Congress of the United States, after having promulgated the Foraker Act to "provide a civil government for Puerto Rico," passed Law Number 249 (July 1, 1902), which authorized the President of the United States to reserve public lands of the United States for various public—including military and naval—purposes. It was by virtue of this power that the President of the United States, Theodore Roosevelt, issued proclamation Number 4 (June 26, 1903), which made Culebra a zone "reserved for naval purposes." According to the congressional law previously cited, however, *all* public properties and buildings not thus reserved—except for ports, navigable waters, and lands submerged under the latter—were to remain under the direction of the government of Puerto Rico to be administered for the Puerto Rican people's benefit.[1] On February 16, 1903, the colo-

---

[1] I wish to indicate that I am indebted to the Commission on Civil Rights of Puerto Rico for its report on the island of Culebra and its civil rights (1970–CDC-015). A great part of the information here presented comes from this report. I should also mention the legal study of the lawyer, Carmelo Delgado Cintrón, *Las concesiones privadas y las zonas públicas de terrenos en la isla de Culebra: un análisis histórico y jurídico* (San Juan, 1970).

nial legislature approved a law—still in effect—which turned the island of Culebra over to the U.S. Government.

The Governor of Puerto Rico be and is by the present document authorized to transfer to the United States, at their discretion and in the name of the Commonwealth of Puerto Rico, for naval or military purposes and uses all rights, property titles, and interests belonging to the Commonwealth of Puerto Rico, or to any municipality of the same, in and on any or all public lands on the island of Culebra, together with the coasts or boundaries of the same, or any public buildings located on the same, or in and on that part of them which the United States desires for such purposes, and in and on any and all of the roads, streets or highways or other public property of the said island of Culebra, belonging to the Commonwealth of Puerto Rico or to any municipality of the same, together with all the rights, uses, customs, rights of way, benefits and privileges which may belong to them.* (Author's emphasis)

I cite this law to illustrate to what extent the arrogance of power of the U.S. Navy in Culebra was the direct result of pusillanimous and submissive acts by the Puerto Ricans wielding public power in the system under which we live. The U.S. Navy did, of course, claim the prerogatives to which every imperialist country has always considered itself entitled. But acting in collaboration with the North American authorities, Puerto Rican colonialists have aided as well as permitted the development of a situation like that which now threatens Culebra as well as Vieques with virtual dissolution as municipal entities within the Puerto Rican nation. For it was the very Legislative Assembly of Puerto

* Since the law remains in force, the term "Commonwealth" has been inserted by the Legislative Assembly of Puerto Rico in order to put language up to date. (Author's note to the English edition)

Rico that proceeded to expropriate the lands of Puerto Ricans in Culebra and then transferred these lands—by exchange, rental, or sale—to the U.S. Navy for its exclusive use. The result of this disastrous policy has been the slow but sure transferal of control of large areas of Puerto Rican territory to the United States Navy. In this way, the taking of our territory by the imperial power has been made easier and less conspicuous. As an illustration of what has been permitted in the name of Puerto Rico, it is sufficient to cite the resolution of April 22, 1937, made into law on May 6, 1938, which provided for, among other things, "authorizing the Commissioner of the Interior to acquire in the name of the people of Puerto Rico . . . an appropriate surface area of 300 *cuerdas* (in Culebra) by means of purchase, exchange, surrender, or, if necessary, by expropriation, to be transferred to the Government of the United States for federal purposes." (Although it is true that this particular law was approved during the incumbency of the annexationist Coalition, this group was not exclusively responsible for the surrender of Culebra and Vieques. This can be demonstrated by the fact that during the administration of the PPD an endless number of islets or keys, which the U.S. Navy intended to utilize for target practice, were rented for the ridiculous sum of one dollar annually. This is fully documented in the report of the Commission on Civil Rights previously cited.)

As if it were a small thing that the Puerto Rican residents of Culebra have had to continually face the threat of expropriation and eviction for the benefit of the U.S. Navy, on February 14, 1941, President Franklin D. Roosevelt issued Presidential Order Number 8684, designating the island of Culebra as an "Area of Naval Defense." The said Presidential Order—dictated, of course, without consultation with the residents of Culebra, much less with the Puerto Rican authorities—establishes the following restrictions on air and sea transit with Culebra:

At no time may any person . . . not a passenger on United States public vessels enter the Naval Defense Area of the Island of Culebra, nor shall any ship or any type of vessel, other than U.S. public vessels, be navigated toward that area, unless so authorized by the Secretary of the Navy.

At no time may any airship . . . not an airship of the United States be piloted toward the Naval Reservation of the Island of Culebra, unless so authorized by the Secretary of the Navy.

The dispositions of the preceding paragraph will be put into effect by the Secretary of the Navy, with the cooperation of local officials in the public service of the United States and the Government of Puerto Rico, and the Secretary of the Navy is hereby authorized to prescribe those rules which are necessary for carrying out these orders.

Culebra was hereby made virtually incommunicado with the rest of the Puerto Rican community. The Puerto Rican authorities may do nothing to regulate naval or air access to Culebra, since it was made thenceforth the exclusive prerogative of the U.S. Navy.

But the matter did not end there. The Culebrans were not only cut off from communication with the outside world, but the island itself—including its seven hundred inhabitants—was converted into a war maneuver zone and a target range for the United States Navy. Although the slightly incredulous reader may not believe it, this little island has been the object of constant bombardment and target practice with live ammunition, day and night, placing the lives of the inhabitants in constant danger. According to Sub-Secretary of the U.S. Navy Joseph A. Grimes, Jr., "Culebra is an integral part of the field of target practice of the Atlantic Fleet. Culebra cannot be replaced as part of the military complex of Roosevelt Roads not only because its topography and adjacent islets constitute excellent targets but also because it is located near the Control and Command Center and Auxiliary Base of Roosevelt Roads, the Navy training zone in Vieques, and the training zones in the open sea, in which there exists little north and south traffic."[2] Or in other words, Culebra cannot be replaced as a firing range or as a target for U.S. Navy missiles. The Commission on Civil Rights describes the situation facing the Culebrans daily: "These heavy-caliber artillery practices on Culebra or adjacent islets and keys—in particular, those near people and private property on this island—create a situation of constant tension and fear because of the high danger level. Also, the nuisance caused by the deafening noise of firing, of airplanes and helicopters flying at very low altitudes above private property, and of drills until all hours of the night constitutes an onerous condition to the people of Culebra Island."[3] People are killed and wounded by Navy missiles on Culebra; fishermen lose their traps and nets, returning with no catch because frequent bombardments kill the fish; the people cannot use the beaches because of the perennial danger that they may fall victim to a bullet or a missile. Culebra is, then, an island and a people who live under a sign of terror—the threat of their own extinction. In an attempt to fight for their survival as a Puerto Rican community, their Municipal Assembly sent the following ultimatum to the Navy, dated March 12, 1970:

You have mined, bombarded, and torpedoed our fish and fishing grounds. You have dropped fire rockets and napalm

[2] *El Mundo*, July 8, 1970.
[3] *Op. cit.*, p. 32.

bombs on our birds and their nests, even though there exists a prohibition to that effect in the 1909 Presidential Order issued by President Theodore Roosevelt. Human and computer errors have sent your missiles off-course toward our ports and private lands, exposing us to death. Conscious of the presence of our civilian population in the center of the area in which you carry out your maneuvers, you continue and plan to increase and extend those activities in and around Culebra Island.

The intensity, the frequency and type of maneuvers carried out by the Navy of the United States in and around our island in recent years, and especially this year, have created a situation passing the limits of our human tolerance.

We live submerged in an economic crisis and a psychological state of confusion, anxiety, insecurity, and terror, and we are in constant danger of losing our lives.

THEREFORE: We will not tolerate these practices and we will not consent to the situation continuing like this; neither do we nor will we entertain any idea of abandoning our homes, our property, our town, our culture, our island of Culebra.

Noam Chomsky writes that North American imperialism appears to have found a solution for doing away with peoples' wars: doing away with the people. This appears to be the case with regard to Culebra.

The reader should not be deluded into believing that this ultimatum moved the chieftains at the Pentagon. Quite the contrary. Their response has been: we need more land for our activities and if possible we want the Culebrans moved from Culebra to somewhere else in Puerto Rico. As a matter of fact, in accordance with the Navy's plan, the Navy would like to acquire through purchase or expropriation three-fourths of the territory of Culebra. At least this was the action recommended by the Real Estate Sub-Committee of the U.S. House of Representatives after it held public hearings at which most of the Puerto Rican delegates present spoke out against the presence of the Navy in Culebra.[4] And Admiral Norwell G. Ward made clear the Navy's position when he recently affirmed that "the Navy had the power to expropriate all the lands it thought necessary to assure its effectiveness and promptness."[5]

Because the case of Culebra is such a flagrant example of injustice, the colonialist politicians—even those like Muñoz Marín, who at one time contemplated relocating the inhabitants of Culebra and Vieques for the sacred cause of U.S. national defense—have suddenly become openly opposed to the U.S. Navy's continued presence in Culebra. The Pentagon has nevertheless disregarded the pronouncements even of Governor Ferré and is supported in its position by Secretary of Defense Melvin Laird. Muñoz Marín and Ferré are opposed to the Navy's continued use of Culebra as a firing range—that is, as long as it is not indispensable for the "national defense" of the United States, you understand . . . This issue has created a big uproar in Puerto Rico and abroad. Of course, our official politicians are very concerned with how this will affect the "good name" of the United States. In this respect, the views of Muñoz Marín and Ferré coincide, as they always have.

Patriotic organizations have not, however, remained passive. On the contrary, they have carried the campaign against the incredible abuse of Culebra to the very heart of the martyred island. The Puerto Rican Independence party (PIP) has carried out open acts of protest and defiance on

[4] See the complete text of the report in the *San Juan Star,* August 10, 1970.

[5] Cited by the journalist I. Rodríguez Feliciano in *El Mundo,* December 8, 1970.

Culebra—including entering firing zones, swimming at forbidden beaches, holding meetings under the very nose of the Navy—knowing that while they are there, at least, target practice is discontinued. This preaching by direct action has won the PIP and other patriotic organizations the support and admiration of the inhabitants of Culebra.

The Navy will have to leave Culebra. But this will not take place as a result of the entreaties of the politicians who throughout this century have created the conditions that made a Culebra possible. The Navy will leave when the Culebran community itself and the Puerto Rican people demonstrate that they will not back down in the fight for their rights as Puerto Ricans.

There is the possibility that the uproar caused by Culebra may cause President Nixon to take a personal hand in the matter. To judge by the attitude of his Secretary of Defense, the prospects for a favorable solution do not seem very good. But whether or not Culebra can successfully evict the U.S. Navy in the near future, the true nature of the U.S. imperialist regime has been stripped bare in this small community of seven hundred inhabitants. How much the cause of Culebra has contributed to the creation of a patriotic consciousness among Puerto Rican youth is difficult to predict at this time. But what cannot be denied is that Culebra is an issue separating the authentic Puerto Rican patriots from those who still think of the interests of the United States before those of their own country.

Culebra is only the most extreme, the most horribly exaggerated case of the sickness from which Puerto Rico as a whole suffers: the sickness of collective impotence. As an indication of the challenge to colonialism the issue of Culebra presents at this moment, it should be noted that this small island is one of the most fertile grounds for the creation of an anti-imperialist consciousness among our young people. The Culebran community, determined to resist the genocidal designs which hang over it, has warned the Pentagon that if it continues with its plans, it will have to pay a very high price to achieve success. This issue is indicative of the degree to which Puerto Rican patriots will challenge colonialism and at the very least, attempt to strip it of all its aura of supposed benevolence in Puerto Rico. Independent of the outcome of this issue—which will be decided without Puerto Ricans having an effective voice in the final determination—we have certainly demonstrated that the Pentagon can be resisted and that it is not invincible. This is a lesson which the youth of Puerto Rico will not forget.

After I concluded this Prologue, several events occurred with respect to Culebra. On the one hand, Governor Ferré brought in an expert on national defense, Dr. Kilmarx. After a one-week visit to Culebra, Dr. Kilmarx advised that the U.S. Navy be given five years to terminate its target practice. Furthermore, he advocated U.S. Navy acquisition of even more land than it already has on the small island.

Recently an argument has been put forth that the presence of a fleet of Soviet ships in the Caribbean now prevents the departure of the U.S. Navy from Culebra—thus precluding the full vindication of the Culebrans' rights. Both Dr. Kilmarx's argument and the argument based on the presence of the Soviet fleet have called forth the most absurd defenses among the hard-core annexationists. Ostensibly, the whole Western Hemisphere is in danger as a result of Soviet ships navigating in international waters. Worse yet, an annexationist group was set up to request that the U.S. Navy remain in Culebra. Fortunately, the cacophony reached Washington. Several U.S. Senators raised their voices in protest of the real problem in Culebra —the continued military presence of the U.S. Navy in this area. But everything seems to indicate that the issue of using Culebra as a firing range is not to be resolved immediately. Using the excuse of the "Soviet threat," the colonialist politicians are retracting their original demands. As usual, the only ones who today remain friends of the Culebrans—and defenders of Puerto Rico as a nation—are the *independentistas*.

In addition to the problem of Culebra, the issue of ratification by the North American delegation of the Treaty of Tlatelolco for the denuclearization of Latin America has been recently raised. In accord with several press releases issued by the U.S. Government, Charles Van Doren, Director of the Legal Office of the Agency for the Control of Armaments and Disarmament, said before the Committee on Foreign Affairs of the U.S. Senate that the United States "had no intention of signing an amendment to the treaty known as Additional Protocol Number One." This additional protocol amendment would place Puerto Rico and the Virgin Islands within the provisions of the Treaty of Tlatelolco applicable to the denuclearization of all Latin America. During questioning by Senator J. William Fulbright, Van Doren affirmed that Puerto Rico and the Virgin Islands "are much more important to the structure of North American defense than are the territories of the Caribbean to the British" (*San Juan Star,* Sept. 23, 1970). These declarations clearly reveal the intention of the United States to allow Puerto Rico to become a nuclear powder keg and to mock the Treaty of Tlatelolco by means of a clear-cut colonialist subterfuge. From the U.S. position on the above amendment it is apparent that Culebra is only an extreme manifestation of the more general sickness which our country suffers from: North American domination. It can be said without exaggeration that to a great extent all of Puerto Rico is a magnified Culebra.

II STUDENT REBELLION AND THE UNIVERSITY

Many people have commented upon and written about the student rebellion as a social phenomenon of universal scope. In fact, the new college generations are showing signs of growing uneasiness with the world they have inherited. Often taking a violent form, the protest is directed against a system marked by a wide discrepancy between that which it says it believes and that which it really believes. Insofar as the student rebellion aims to threaten the existing order, its power is limited by its very nature as a movement essentially composed of consumers and not producers. (Note that the closest the student revolution had ever come to triumphing in a collective dispute was in the May movement in France—but only thanks to the fact that it was able to incorporate into the protest movement the unionized French workers.) In other words, to the extent that the student protest movement remains circumscribed by a strictly college ambience, it will be effectively isolated and eventually controlled by the system, whether it be through the use of massive force (Mexico) or through the closing of the university and the consequent expulsion of the students (Berkeley). I believe recent experiences demonstrate that the present Latin American governments are not going to fall—if they ever do—through student action. It is therefore important to point out that the university struggle must be seen in a limited context as a social phenomenon, and that every liberation movement that confuses the symptoms of a social revolution with the struggle itself is sadly deceived. The student rebellion, therefore, must be seen as a barometer of social discontent and as a measure of the degree of ferment in the existing social order, the society serving as the framework, but never as the actual cause of that crisis.

With these preliminary warnings in mind, let us analyze the Puerto Rican university situation. It is important to point out that although the Puerto Rican student movement has flourished tremendously in the last five years, it is still based on an experience of its predecessors, the National Federation of Puerto Rican Students (FNEP)—founded in the thirties by the Nationalist party—and the students who led the abortive university strike of 1948. Forged in the midst of the extraordinary rise of the Popular Democratic party and the simultaneous rise of the repressive wave culminating in the McCarthyism of the fifties, this strike left its still visible imprint on Puerto Rican university activities. Police intervention on the campus by the then (and apparently eternal) Chancellor Benítez, as well as the expulsion of student leaders and teachers sympathetic to the strike in the university, laid the groundwork for the autocracy which Benítez would impose on the university until 1966, when he was replaced by Chancellor Abraham Díaz González. To a great extent, the total rise of the subsequent student and faculty movement can be better understood in the context of this one-man regime in which the basic authority of the university flowed from the chancellor, as the unquestionable and unquestioned chief, through the deans and department heads, to the most remote levels of faculty and student life.

The so-called movement of "university reform," which began in the decade of the sixties, is essentially a reaction against that state of affairs. Its very composition reveals its eclectic orientation: personal enemies of Benítez who had fallen out of favor with him (many of them annexationists who earlier had occupied important positions in the administration), some PPD people disenchanted with the university administration because they saw in Benítez a man dedicated to making his political career from the university, and the traditional enemies of Benítez—the *independentistas* or nationalists.

As the decade of the sixties began, these three groups united, constituting an increasingly powerful pressure group in favor of university reform. During the first five years of the sixties, a faculty organization called the Puerto Rican Association of University Professors was founded to direct the struggle. Disorganized and weak, the student body lacked the cohesiveness to enable it to utilize the faculty association in the struggle to recover its rights. During this period, the Federation of University Students for Independence (FUPI), founded in 1956, was the principal catalyst of the reforms desired by the most progressive students in the university—even though in its beginnings it was a small organization anathematized by the administration of Benítez. Throughout the early sixties the student-faculty alliance was very precarious. On the one hand, the student body was disoriented, unaccustomed to struggle after a long period of enforced silence. On the other, the conservative forces within the faculty who advocated university reform viewed with apprehension the potentially radical nature of the student demands.

The University Law of 1966—the result of this agitation for university reform—illustrates the extent to which true university reform was frustrated during this first attempt, and helps to explain the cause of the continued radicalization of the student and faculty struggle which we are witnessing now. Let us examine the matter.

It is essential to point out that contrary to the experience of other Latin American countries, Puerto Rico never had her equivalent to the Reforms of Córdoba. The experiences of a democratically shared university government and of the extraterritoriality of the university campus are completely alien to the history of the University of Puerto Rico. The model of higher education in Puerto Rico has always been the U.S. state university—specifically, one of those belonging to the middle state colleges. A traditional argument against authentic student participation in Puerto Rico has been the supposed anarchic character of the Latin American university.[6] It was precisely this continued insistence on the use of the Latin-American university as model and the consequences this possibility suggested that energized the counter-reform movement and which—it should be said—determined the pusillanimous attitude of certain sectors within the reformist movement when appearing before the public authorities to request a new university law to replace the one in effect since 1942.

The Legislative Assembly of Puerto Rico—dominated by the PPD as a result of the elections of 1964—finally heard the clamor of the proponents of university reform and began the process culminating in the 1966 law. A little before the elections of November 1964—October 28 of that year, to be exact—the reform movement directed by the students had begun seriously.

---

[6] For an excellent analysis of the Latin American university from a comparative perspective, see Darcy Ribeiro—*La universidad latinoamericana* (Montivedeo: Universidad de la República, 1968). The majority of the criticisms of the Latin American university made in Puerto Rico— when they do not have a partisan character—are the products of an absolute ignorance of Latin American reality.

The protest which took place on October 28—together with the success of the FUPI in making ROTC voluntary in the university—is one of the significant events of that first five years of student struggle. Since Benítez had imposed the silent era in the University by breaking the 1948 student strike, all demonstrations, picket lines, meetings, and other activities of a political character had been prohibited on the campus. On October 28, the FUPI decided to demonstrate before the front gates of the university. After a march through the campus, the protest culminated in a demonstration of passive resistance that blocked automobile traffic. The state police entered the campus to force the students out. Several students were clubbed. A police car was set on fire. It was the baptism by fire of the student generation of the sixties. For the first time, they fought the police with whatever was at hand: stones, sticks, fire. But the engagement had a very limited scope. It was only a skirmish. The following day the press thundered against "professional agitators" and warned the public of the dangers inherent in university reform led by this type of student. As was natural, the issue divided the faculty movement along ideological lines. It is difficult to evaluate exactly to what extent and in which direction the events of October 28 influenced the legislators of the PPD; it is clear that from 1964 on, both the reform movement and the backlash it engendered exercised real pressures on public authorities to reform the university law.

In response to these pressures and also as a result of certain internal matters in the heart of the PPD, the new University Law was finally approved in 1966. As was to be expected, this law reflected a series of transactions and compromises in the matter of student-faculty participation. In all essential matters, the structure of university government continued as before: the Council on Higher Education (equivalent to the boards of regents of U.S. state universities) guaranteed the public authorities ultimate control over university affairs. Professors were given a limited participation in the academic senates and in the administration of each campus. These bodies were to be governed by a chancellor named by the Council on Higher Education. The students would have a voice, but no vote, in the decisions and expressions of academic senates and the administration. A president of the university would act as coordinator as well as supervisor of all the campuses that compose the University of Puerto Rico. In addition, there would be a particular procedure established for consultation, for the designation of the chancellor, the deans, and the heads of departments.

As can be seen, the student body was deprived of any effective power. Also provided for was the election of student councils in each school and the election of a general student council, but these councils would have the power only to speak—they would not have the force conferred by the power to vote on vital issues of university life. Consequently, university autonomy turned out to be a limited, diluted autonomy, since the appointments made by the Council on Higher Education define the power to manipulate university life, directly or indirectly.

The University Reform of 1966 was, therefore, only a halfway reform—more likely, an impediment to real reform. As inevitably happens in a colonial society, so many factors extraneous to university life weighed on the minds of the legislators that in the end they created a lame law, again immobilizing the authentic forces for a democratic Puerto Rican university reform. Today we are realizing the effects of this indubitable fact. Because, at the time of the passing of the reform law, the Popular Democratic party believed that it would govern eternally for the colonial power in Puerto Rico, the law was made on liberal suppositions—in the ideological sense of the term—and could function up to a certain point as long as the liberals were disposed to interpret the law in the most generous, broad way possible. But when the power changed hands and the law was interpreted in a restrictive fashion, all its flagrant defects became obvious. And that is the very root of the present crisis through which the University of Puerto Rico is passing. We will return to this subject in a moment.

Once the law of 1966 was passed, we had on the Río Piedras campus of the University of Puerto Rico what I call the brief liberal interlude. This interlude was basically the result of the appointment as chancellor of the campus of an authentic Puerto Rican liberal: Abraham Díaz González. This appointment was due to the fact that at that time the Council on Higher Education was dominated by persons appointed by the government of the PPD. This chancellor, Díaz González, brought to the university the experience of a successful career as a lawyer-businessman, and he immediately surrounded himself with people known for their liberal and progressive positions. During his administration, meetings, picket lines, and demonstrations were held on the university campus, political organizations were officially recognized on the campus, student participation was encouraged at all levels of university life, and the university was given a sense of openness, a broadness of outlook such as it hadn't had for a long time. But in spite of his good intentions Díaz González was limited and his liberalism circumscribed by an antiliberal law. In the end, as a liberal, he found himself caught between the right, which wanted to return to the silent era and the *casa de estudios,* and the left, which demanded a series of radical measures that could not be effected within the legal limitations of the law in force.

Once more the FUPI marched in the vanguard of the student struggle, although now it led not an indifferent student body, but one ready to fight for its rights. In addition, the General Student Council of the campus and the student councils of the respective schools were also ready to fight for authentic student participation and for Puerto Ricanization of the university. One issue arose to polarize student feeling: the existence on campus of a body to train reserve officers of the U.S. Army. The antimilitarist sentiment which was rising in the colonial power (the United States) was also reflected here in Puerto Rico. At the same time, the annexationist right was fighting to revert to the previous authoritarianism and took up the defense of the ROTC program.

In February 1969, a group of ten of us university professors decided to picket the ROTC building in open violation of an existing university regulation. Our purpose in picketing was twofold: to protest the presence of ROTC on campus, and to question the legality of the existing restrictive rule. This demonstration was followed by another in March. On this latter occasion, the Association of University Students for Statehood (AUPE) mobilized in support of ROTC, and a minor confrontation developed between the two groups. In April, the chancellor appeared before the faculty and in his first message set down the position that he would do everything in his power to liberalize the rules preventing marches, meetings, and picket lines on the university campus. But the confrontation was already out in the open. The ROTC announced that there would be an open house at the university for recruitment of future aspirants to a military career. A loudspeaker van from a business firm announced it right in front of the university. Furthermore, ROTC announced a full-dress military parade for May 5, 1967. The FUPI picketed the open house, which was held in the university theater, and there were encounters between the FUPI and the AUPE. Chancellor Díaz González personally intervened to cool tempers already at the boiling point. When the military parade began, the students of the FUPI, the FNEP, and other independence organizations physically obstructed its progress, and the university police reacted by clubbing several students. But the parade was a huge failure and was the last to be held on the Río Piedras campus of the University of Puerto Rico. Chancellor Díaz González took disciplinary action: ten students of the AUPE and fifty of the FUPI were suspended for a period of six months.

May 5 marked a continuation of the actions initiated on October 28, 1964. A greater radicalization of the student body as part of a resurgence of ideological polarization within the university became apparent at this point.

As soon as the 1967–68 academic year began, this phenomenon became even more evident. The right began to ask for Díaz González' dismissal and intervention in the university.

The new confrontation was not long in coming: on September 27, 1967 the FUPI gathered in front of the headquarters of the AUPE to protest statements made by the president of the AUPE alleging that the FUPI was involved in narcotics traffic. Several students were clubbed when the police entered the campus and charged the demonstrators. The FUPI regrouped its forces and went to the Río Piedras police headquarters to protest this unwarranted use of physical force. In answer to them the police again charged.

As the afternoon progressed, the students doubled back toward the university and took it as a sanctuary. From there they fought the police, who had mobilized their riot squad and were threatening to enter the university. Only the stubborn resistance of Chancellor Díaz González—who consistently opposed the expressed wishes of the then Chief of Police Salvador Rodríguez Aponte—succeeded in keeping the police off the campus.

Despite his resistance the police had fired volleys against the university in two separate instances. As a result of the last volley, a taxi driver, Adrián Rodríguez, died of a gunshot wound in the back. After an investigation conducted by one of their own detectives, the police concluded that he had not been killed by a police bullet. But twenty-five students were indicted as a result of the events of the day.*

On Nobember 5, 1968, we Puerto Ricans awoke to a new reality: the era of Muñoz Marín and the Popular Democratic party had come to an end. Annexationism was in power. This historic fact sealed the fate of Abraham Díaz González as chancellor of the Río Piedras campus and gave birth to the period of repression under which we are now living.

(It is necessary to point out that the student movement did not limit itself to fighting the ROTC in the university, but also combated, both on and off campus, compulsory military service in the armed forces of the United States. As the campaign against compulsory military service intensified, a sizable group of Puerto Rican youths were indicted in the U.S. courts for refusing to serve in the U.S. Army. Among these many young men was Edwin Feliciano Grafals, a university student and a militant of the Movement for Independence.)

The academic year 1969–70 was without doubt the most significant in the student struggle since 1948. For it is in that year that the university experienced its worst crisis

* The courts finally decided to impose fines upon the students found guilty. They are all free now after paying the fines. (Author's note to the English edition)

since the strike of 1948. To a great extent, one can say that the university became a microcosm of present-day Puerto Rican society in which the most definitive tensions and tendencies flourished at their extreme.

When classes began in August, 1969, storm winds were already blowing in the university. The FUPI, the University Youth for Independence (JIU), and the General Student Council let it be known in no uncertain terms that ROTC must go from the Río Piedras campus. On September 12— the birthday of Albizu Campos—a meeting and student demonstration were held in front of the ROTC. On September 22—the eve of the anniversary of the Cry of Lares—a larger student demonstration took place against the ROTC. On September 26, 1969, a university student, Edwin Feliciano Grafals, was sentenced to a year in jail by a U.S. court for refusing to serve in the armed forces of the United States. After unfurling the Puerto Rican flag in the middle of the courtroom and singing the national anthem, militants of the FUPI returned to the university, marched across the campus, and ended their march by taking over the ROTC building and burning some of its facilities. At one point there were some three or four thousand students gathered, shouting in unison: "Fire, fire, the Yankees want fire." Students climbed to the top of the building, which architecturally resembles a military fort, lowered the U.S. flag, and flew the Puerto Rican flag alone, while below the multitude sang the national anthem, "La Borinqueña." Once more Chancellor Díaz González refused to call the state police to intervene on the campus. And once more the right and its spokesmen in the press demanded his dismissal.

Chancellor Díaz González urgently convened a faculty meeting to take some definitive action regarding the recent events. On October 2, 1969, the faculty recommended to the Academic Senate of the Río Piedras campus a study to be submitted within thirty days. The study would be directed toward resolving "the status of military instruction (ROTC) on the Río Piedras campus, in light of the university's mission as it is defined in the provisions of the University Law and the goals outlined by its directive bodies." The vote to remit the ROTC study to the Academic Senate was quite close. It showed the deep division existing in the faculty over the issue of ROTC. An additional indication of this split was shown in the general assembly of the Puerto Rican Association of University Professors. When the anti-ROTC faction began to dominate the assembly, the fragile alliance which originally existed between the annexationist "reformists" and the *independentistas* was broken. On the ROTC issue the opposing camps were clearly marked off in the APPU just as they were in the faculty. The old "reformists"—who were only reformists out of antagonism for Benítez—ended up returning to Benítez' fold as soon as he joined the pro-ROTC camp. They finally founded an association of professors opposed to the APPU: The Organization of University Professors (OPU), where all the right-wing factions of the Río Piedras university faculty banded together. One thing remained clear: the University of Puerto Rico was sharply divided not only in regard to ROTC but also regarding the very vision of the university as an institution dedicated to higher learning.

Once the question was referred for study and consideration, the Academic Senate of the Río Piedras campus passed a resolution—after holding public hearings and discussing the question in two successive sessions—on November 5, 1969, in which it recommended to the Council on Higher Education that it "discontinue on the campus the program of the Reserve Officers' Training Corps (ROTC)." The resolution was received with great jubilation by the student body, which was gathered in front of the Academic Senate and which proceeded to march through the campus in celebration of the event.

It is axiomatic that every action produces its reaction and since the September 26 attack on the ROTC the reaction was being put together. An Association of Parents in Favor of ROTC was organized and proceeded to sponsor various activities, all with the dual aims of forcing the dismissal of Díaz González and of achieving permanent status for ROTC on the campus. A senator from the PNP, Juan Antonio Palerm, affirmed publicly at the time that ROTC would remain at the university, "cost what it may." On November 7, 1969, a confrontation took place. A group of parents and ROTC cadets, directed by Senator Palerm, staged a protest march in front of the university. Chancellor Díaz González did not allow all those among the demonstrators who were not students to enter the campus. Hostilities began a little after two in the afternoon. Stone-throwing started between the students who were on the campus and the demonstrators who were outside it. The latter tried on repeated occasions—although unsuccessfully—to take the campus by force. Chancellor Díaz González, fearing for the safety of the students, brought them together in the university theater. On the outskirts of the university and in the town of Río Piedras elements of the lumpen proletariat began to mobilize with Cuban exiles who were leading them. At nightfall, crowds, emotionally worked up and led by rightist elements, tried to take by force the head-quarters of the Pro-Independence Movement (MPI) in Río Piedras. There were some thirty persons on the premises at that time, including the secretary-general of the MPI, the lawyer Juan Mari Bras. The MPI group was completely unarmed. The police surrounded the premises but did not intervene while the crowd threw incendiary bombs, stones, and other objects toward the building. On two different occasions when they tried to take the headquarters by force, the aggression was repelled. Meanwhile the crowds were running unchecked through the city of Río Piedras, accosting all those they suspected of being *independentistas,* destroying automobiles which displayed stickers of the Puerto Rican flag, and indulging themselves in all kinds of abuses in open conspiracy with the state police. This being the state of affairs, a group of students armed themselves with sticks and ran up a side street flanking the besieged building, with the aim of protecting those trapped inside. The police clubbed them. From the rooftop of a nearby building, the police fired toward the headquarters of the movement, wounding with bullets the painter Fran Cervoni and Carlos Padilla Pérez, both militants of the MPI. At that moment the executive secretary of the Commission on Civil Rights, the lawyer José Nilo Dávila Lanausse, intervened. He finally succeeded in prevailing upon the police to let the wounded be attended and to guarantee the departure of the rest of the besieged. The members of the MPI were taken to the offices of the Commission on Civil Rights and were finally freed. That was November 7, 1969. On that occasion, the horrible face of fascism in Puerto Rico was exposed for all to see. The fanaticism, the irrationality, the overwrought crowd, and the complicity of the police authorities during the entire incident leave glaringly clear the length to which the enemies of independence are willing to go in their zeal to stop its momentum.

The decision made by the Academic Senate eradicating ROTC did not prevail. Due to the new composition of the Council on Higher Education (CHE), it was to be expected that it would revoke the decision of the highest representative body of the university community. It did so without giving any explanations, without even bothering to return the report to the Academic Senate with its objections. In an arrogant manner, on November 21, 1969, the CHE approved a resolution in which it said in part: "The ROTC program should continue as an integral part of the university courses offered on a voluntary basis at the Río Piedras campus." But the retaliation was not complete. There was still Díaz González' dismissal. On December 22, 1969, the Council on Higher Education wrathfully dismissed him from his position. As in the case of the restitution of ROTC, the CHE gave no reasons. It went on to name Jaime Benítez as interim chancellor of the university. The brief liberal interlude had ended . . .

The speech of Díaz González before the Academic Senate that same night was the swan song of a chancellor who tried to be liberal when liberalism was in bankruptcy throughout the world. Abraham Díaz González died a quiet death that December 22. His own liberal ideology prevented him from seeing that there was a battle to be fought and that it would have to be fought side by side with students and professors who were fighting for true university autonomy and for the demands of the students. For when the eleventh hour came, he believed that he could be above the battle, and finally lost the support of the only elements who would have backed him if he had decided to face the right firmly. In spite of this, the memory of Abraham Díaz González will endure when the history of true university reform is written.

The dismissal of Díaz González and the restitution of ROTC mark, then, the pendular movement toward the right and toward university counterreform. With the liberal spirit that animated the University Law of 1966 completely gone, one could safely say that this law had fulfilled its historic mission. From then on it would be demonstrated how dead its letter was once its most essential principles had been debunked. From that moment, I repeat, the counterreform began to take over the university, Jaime Benítez presiding once more over the dissolution of university reform. But not without the student movement first showing its new combative spirit and its uncorruptible basis.

The second semester of the academic year 1969–70 began with apparent tranquility. Benítez traveled to Washington; and through conversations with General Evans, he managed to convince the Pentagon that all marches, parades and military exercises on the Río Piedras campus should be suspended. Apart from a brief skirmish in February—brought on by the work of an *agent provocateur*—all seemed to be calm.

This calm was broken on March 7, 1970, when the University Feminine Action Committee held a protest activity against the ROTC. A group of students belonging to the Puerto Rican Socialist League confronted the ROTC cadets who, entrenched in the ROTC building, responded with stones and shotgun fire. A great number of police and military agents were also noted in the university. The university police, armed this time with protective helmets and electrified billy clubs, aligned themselves with the ROTC cadets. The battle was therefore, between *independentista* students on one side and ROTC cadets, the university guard, and undercover agents on the other. At one point the students set fire to a little wooden hut where part of the ROTC equipment was stored; faced with this situation, Interim Chancellor Benítez called on the Riot Squad of the state police. This group quickly began to occupy the university, dislodging the students with their regulation night sticks. Several students were clubbed by the police, who proceeded to dislodge even those who happened to be in the campus libraries. Even after what Chief of Police

Luis Torres Massa called "Operation Cleanup" had been carried out, the student groups continued fighting the police from the streets bordering the university.

At this point, the police fired several times at the students, wounding some of them. When a group of the state police marched along Ponce de León Avenue with the purpose of cleaning the street of students, they were met with shouts of "Assassins!" from the students gathered there. An angry guard responded by firing toward the area from which the insult appeared to come. As a result, fourth-year education student Antonia Martínez Lagares was instantly killed with a bullet in her head. The bullet which killed her also wounded the young student at her side. The balance sheet for the dark, gloomy night: one dead and about ten wounded by bullets. (The police, of course, claimed self-defense, alleging that there were snipers firing at them. The most fanciful even claimed to have heard the sound of bazookas and there was one who swore he had heard the crackling of a Viet Cong machine gun. The investigation into the death of Antonia Martínez Lagares has just been concluded. The result: there is no probable cause against the policeman, although many were able to identify him as the one who fired the murder weapon. Just as in the case of Adrián Rodríguez, it was not the police who fired. A grotesque conclusion worthy of the film *Z*.)

Benítez closed the university for several days. When students returned to classes, the issue was again raised: out with ROTC, out with Benítez. After a tempestuous student assembly it was decided to submit the question to a referendum. The result of the referendum is illustrative of the ideological confusion of the Puerto Rican student body: out with ROTC, let Benítez stay. Moreover, the student body showed itself massively in favor of true university reform. At that point the faculty was also divided along ideological lines: the APPU condemned the intervention of the university, the OPU supported it. In fact, the referendum as well as later events help illustrate how far the University of Puerto Rico was from being a university community. The police occupation of the campus, the continuation of Benítez as chancellor, the presence of the ROTC on campus— all these issues really divided the student body—but above all the faculty—into antagonistic bands.

After the sound and the fury of those fateful moments, the student body decided to wait and see if its wishes, freely expressed in the referendum, would be taken into consideration. A report of the special committee designated by the Council on Higher Education for the study of ROTC, which was finished on March 10, 1970, should have made them think twice before crying victory. This, together with the appointment of Pedro José Rivera as chancellor of the Río Piedras campus, augured very badly for the future of the student-faculty struggle. Faced with student militance, the right began to organize. In May, elections were held for the Academic Senate for the period 1970–72. Solidly entrenched in such schools as Education, Pharmacy, Natural Sciences, and Business Administration, the conservative antireformists succeeded in controlling the Academic Senate in the May elections. With a chancellor who before being appointed had indicated his support for ROTC, and with a Senate controlled fundamentally by the OPU, the time was ripe for the consideration of the special report on the ROTC made at the request of the Council on Higher Education. As soon as the new Academic Senate was constituted, it received the longstanding report for consideration.

Nonetheless, student protests did not cease. On June 14, 1970, graduation exercises were held on the Río Piedras campus. A large section of the student body made its protest evident to the new administration by refusing to receive diplomas from the chancellor—in a few instances tearing them up in front of him. The students dedicated the graduation to the memory of Antonia Martínez Lagares, and unfurled right on the stage a banner which read: "Antonia did not graduate because Benítez killed her." At a certain moment in the graduation ceremony, one student, Carmen Noelia López Avilés, slapped President Benítez across the face. The speech of Chancellor Rivera was interrupted by outcries, whistles, shouts, and other demonstrations of displeasure. The entire university guard was mobilized for the occasion, and the atmosphere prevailing in the university theater was one of extreme tension. When Benítez and Rivera left the theater, they had to be escorted by the university guard.

These events served to dramatize the profound division which split the University of Puerto Rico. It would be deceptive to pass over the demonstration of affection given President Benítez after he was slapped, or the outcries and shouts which interrupted the speech of the Student Council President, Leopoldo Rivera. In fact, it became very evident that there is really a struggle on the Río Piedras campus between two universities, between two totally different concepts of what really constitutes the task of the university. Those who have the power on the campus right now are, of course, those who are fiercely opposed to the democratization of the structures of the university and to its total demilitarization. That is to say, the university is today really in the beginnings of an historic retrogression, a movement back to the stage before university reform.

The present Academic Senate, as was to be expected, subsequently endorsed the report of the special committee on the ROTC, establishing the permanence of said program at the university. Nevertheless, the Senate had to recognize that military drills could not be held on campus—or there would be no classes at the university. This fact is in itself indicative of the extent to which ROTC is hated by the university student body; its mere physical presence constitutes a provocation. Even a counterreformist Academic Senate had to accept this fact, although reluctantly. But no one should be fooled. The Academic Senate is currently controlled by the PNP, and it will continue to respond to the political directives which emanate from the Council on Higher Education through the administration of Chancellor Pedro José Rivera. Once Díaz González was deposed, the alignment of forces in the university inclined in favor of the conservatives, and for most purposes they have already made a comedy out of the provisions of the University Law of 1966. This law—which left much to be desired when it was passed and which was only a kind of mini university reform in its time—is no longer keeping pace at all with the times. Consequently it lacks all force and is no longer able to deal with the situations through which the campus is passing. But because of its very character of watered-down legislation, the 1966 law marvelously allows those who hold power in the university to stifle all authentic student-faculty participation in the processes which determine university life.

At the present, the university crisis is a crisis of authority. The present university administration is one which has been imposed on the university community by the public authorities. For a considerable segment of the faculty and an even greater part of the student body, the problem involves the legitimacy of this administration. The root of the problem resides, of course, in the fact that the student body and the faculty, who are struggling for the democratization and

Puerto Ricanization of the university, are up against a ruling judicial hierarchy that condemns them to humiliating impotence. It is not an exaggeration to say that the only right which can presently be exercised by dissident students and faculty is the right to stamp their feet. Every day the university administration and the Academic Senate close off more channels through which dissident voices can be effectively expressed on the Río Piedras campus. The prevailing attitude in these circles is punitive and repressive. A monolithic structure like that represented by the senate-administration front only understands one language: the one it speaks—the language of power. When the student body spoke that language, it was listened to and respected. In situations of crisis in which communication between struggling factions is broken or hangs by a thin thread, the recourse of the less powerful will be resistance to the powerful, since the latter will otherwise not listen to the former.

In the crisis of authority which is presently afflicting colonialism in Puerto Rico, the university crisis is only the most advanced manifestation of an illness that is beginning to develop and undermine the organism of the system. In the same way that the determination of the Culebrans has put the U.S. Navy in check, the determination and fighting spirit of the *independentista* university student body has forced the elimination of ROTC drills on the Río Piedras campus. Just as in the case of Culebra, the university administration might, like the Navy, disregard the protests and resort simply and openly to the power of physical force. But that would unmask it even more before the student body and the entire university community. When the university student body in its great majority really attains consciousness of the power at its disposal and of the goals which every university reform should strive for, we will be at the dawning of a more authentic university reform. And this can only be fully achieved when Puerto Rico has obtained her total independence.

III THE INTENSIFICATION OF THE UNDERGROUND STRUGGLE AND THE INCREASE IN POLICE REPRESSION

On September 23, 1968, we Puerto Ricans who gathered to celebrate the centennial of the Cry of Lares found a mimeographed sheet signed by a group called the Armed Liberation Commandos (CAL); it announced the beginning of an underground struggle to sabotage North American businesses established in Puerto Rico and to carry out other activities of similar purpose. In this manifesto, the CAL stressed the anti-imperialist nature of its struggle and openly declared itself to be, from that moment on, in a state of war with North American imperialism. Several fires broke out in North American businesses—the losses were calculated in millions of dollars—after that announcement, and the colonial authorities were unable to apprehend those responsible. The CAL has identified itself as the "armed wing of the struggle for Puerto Rican independence." Several explosions that have occurred in the luxury hotels in the tourist zone of El Condado have shown another facet of this clandestine organization's approach. What is more, its leaders announced: "We will not lose sight of the real enemy: the Yankee imperialists. Therefore, we undertake the commitment, which today we renew before the patriotic people of Puerto Rico, that for each young Puerto Rican jailed for refusing to serve in the U.S. armed forces, we will execute one Yankee." As a matter of fact, just after the murder of Antonia Martínez Lagares on March 4, 1970, the CAL claimed credit for the execution of a North

American Marine as reprisal. As is to be expected, this underground struggle provoked the inevitable reaction from the conservative sectors of Puerto Rican society. The press saw CAL as a group whose directions come from Cuba, and loudly demanded repressive measures to apprehend those responsible for these acts.

The existence of the CAL has not gone unnoticed by the insurance firms of these U.S. businesses nor by potential investors interested in establishing themselves in Puerto Rico. In addition to the CAL, another underground group has recently come into being, the Armed Revolutionary Independents' Movement (MIRA), a group which has committed acts of sabotage including that which led to the partial destruction of the U.S. Navy communications system in El Yunque. The authorities have not been able to apprehend those responsible for these acts either.

Until now, the underground movement has been operating in a sporadic, though continuing, manner. On occasion, they have succeeded in coordinating various attempts to destroy North American property. But as of now, the impact of this struggle on those in power continues to be relatively slight, though still very important. The regime has opted to call it a police problem rather than political. Nevertheless, there is no doubt that its impact on tourism and on the flow of foreign investments to the island has been quite significant. The really important impact of this underground movement is that it has warned the colonial regime that in their fight for Puerto Rican independence these groups will have recourse to all options, including the most extreme, in the pursuit of their libertarian goals. This tactic is essentially different from that pursued by the old nationalists, who were unfamiliar with the methods of modern urban guerrilla warfare. The regime is not being attacked frontally, but by unexpected blows dealt to its most vulnerable points. The CAL considers itself to be a national liberation movement. As such it has an advanced ideology similar to that espoused by other groups of similar orientation in diverse parts of the world.

Faced with this challenge to its authority, the right has not remained passive. A rightist underground organization has made public a communiqué in which it says it will model itself after the Death Squadron of Brazil. Claiming to be composed of policemen and ex-policemen, the organization has said it will kill an *independentista* for every North American executed by the CAL. On two successive occasions the national headquarters of the PIP was fired upon from a moving car. A socialist leader, Juan Antonio Corretjer, was shot at near his home. The car of the secretary-general of the MPI, Juan Mari Bras, was dynamited in front of his residence. The pattern of intimidation has also manifested itself in the burning of the printing press of the newspaper *Claridad,* the official organ of the MPI.

All this suggests participation of the CIA and the Cuban exiles. In fact, in Santo Domingo Juan Bosch has recently denounced a general plan directed by the CIA, with the participation of Cuban exiles, to assassinate radical leaders in the Antilles. If, moreover, one remembers the fascist attempt against the headquarters of the MPI on November 7, 1969, and the collusion of the police in that act, the matter takes on a still clearer aspect. In addition to this rightist terrorism, the persecution of patriotic organizations by the police and the FBI has been intensified. Those persons who have put up posters referring to political acts have been arrested and tried. The Riot Squad has been strengthened and trained especially for combat with "subversive" organizations. In the public schools, the persecution of student and teacher *independentistas* is at its height under the direction of the Secretary of Education, Ramón Mellado. The same can be said for the Río Piedras campus of the University of Puerto Rico under the present administration. The University Guard has become an instrument of aggression and repression, directed against the progressive students and faculty of the university. All this forms part of a pattern; a general plan of repressive character forged by the colonial government and its chiefs in Washington to thwart the Puerto Rican struggle for independence.

The repression itself is testimony to the present increase in strength of the patriotic struggle on our island. We are living an historic moment analogous to the one lived in the thirties, for once more there is before us the ultimate question which Albizu Campos articulated so simply: "Yankees or Puerto Ricans?" The difference, of course, is that 1970 is not 1930; the entire world is on the eve of profound revolutionary changes. And against these changes we see rising everywhere the dinosaurs of the counter-revolution. Puerto Rico today (1970) is an excellent example of the inevitability of this clash. In the confrontation between these two forces the crisis of colonialism in our country will be intensified and from here will the clarion call for its final liquidation ring out and be answered.

IV THE NEW PUERTO RICAN INDEPENDENCE PARTY
    (PIP) AND THE DEVELOPMENT OF THE PUERTO
    RICAN REVOLUTIONARY VANGUARD (MPI)

One of the most significant events in the fight for independence during the course of the last two years has been the radicalization of the Puerto Rican Independence party (PIP). As I pointed out earlier in my book, the PIP was unable to maintain its official standing as a political party during the 1968 elections. The position of this party appeared to deteriorate with the breaking-off of one of its most prominent leaders, Dr. Antonio J. González, and the creation by the latter of a new political party clearly conservative in character, the Puerto Rican Union party (PUP).

The leadership of the PIP, now under the presidency of Rubén Berríos Martínez, has imparted a new radical tone to the group through the introduction of two basic issues: socialism on the one hand and civil disobedience on the other. Although this radicalization originally took the form of Christian democracy, today it has refined its ideas, although some of its public stances often appear to conflict with its philosophy. This ambiguity may be inherent in the nature of the PIP as an organization determined to go to the electorate or, on the other hand, it may be considered a concrete illustration of what Marx called utopian socialism. Or perhaps it is the result of both factors operating together. Whatever the case may be, the PIP has succeeded in creating a strong base among Puerto Rican youth—above all, among university and high school students. Its militants have resorted to acts of civil disobedience frequently. During the academic year 1969–70 they held a hunger strike in protest against the presence of ROTC on the Río Piedras campus. In addition, they have attempted to obstruct the entry of North American seamen to the exclusive beaches, to hang posters in open violation of the law, and to invade the firing ranges of the North American Navy in Culebra.

Should the vote for eighteen-year-olds be approved in next November's referendum, there will be a quarter of a million new voters in Puerto Rico.* The PIP is confident that it can gain the support of a considerable number of these young people. As the consequence of both a strong

* The referendum showed a majority in favor of the eighteen-year-old vote. (Author's note to the English edition)

injection of youth into the heart of the party and the new focus which characterizes the PIP, by 1972 it should become a powerful force in Puerto Rican elections. However, we should not lose sight of the fact that the polarization we are witnessing now is forcing the PIP more and more to the left. This could cause many elements of the "old guard," who do not see eye to eye with the new radical posture of the PIP, to abandon the party. On the other hand, those who have begun the process of radicalization could become impatient with the electoral posture of the PIP and enter the MPI or some other political group with a clearer leftist position. As I have already said, we are dealing with the problem which confronts every political party: if it is too doctrinaire, it runs the risk of losing the votes of the undecided, and if it is too indecisive, it runs the risk of losing the more doctrinaire. The 1972 elections will allow us to observe if the PIP has truly succeeded in taking the bull by its horns.

The Pro-Independence Movement (MPI) has evolved—according to its secretary-general, Juan Mari Bras—from a "patriotic vanguard" to a "revolutionary vanguard." This posture was recently defined as an application to Puerto Rican political reality of the Leninist principles of "democratic centralism" and "revolutionary vanguard." It is a national liberation movement wherein are gathered all the most progressive sectors of the patriotic Puerto Rican struggle. By its very nature, it is a multi-class movement, although it is based firmly on the premise that only the working class can firmly cement the socialist character of the Puerto Rican revolution.*

The MPI has directed its campaign of resistance to

---

* The MPI has now made public its intention of becoming a socialist labor party. It has now changed its name to Partido Socialista Puertorriqueño (PSP) and is avowedly Marxist–Leninist.

colonialism to three fundamental issues: compulsory military service, the surrender of our mineral wealth, and the fight to maintain the beaches for the general use of the Puerto Rican people. All these campaigns are directed toward the creation of a crisis that will checkmate the prevailing colonial system in Puerto Rico, a condition necessary for the achievement of our independence.

At the celebration of the one hundred and second anniversary of the Cry of Lares, the MPI and other patriotic organizations sponsored a massive burning of selective service cards of the U.S. armed forces. This act brings a maximum sentence of five years in a North American prison. Moreover, the MPI has abandoned its previous practice of resisting compulsory military service in the last phase of the process of recruitment; instead, it exhorts its militants and sympathizers not to register for the draft in the first place. This act of resistance also brings a five-year jail sentence. In addition, the MPI has openly supported the underground struggle of the Armed Liberation Commandos (CAL).

By means of a lot of hard groundwork in the towns of the mining zone (Lares, Utuado, and Adjuntas), the MPI has succeeded in creating a strong resistance to the surrender of our mineral wealth among the sectors most directly affected by the possible exploitation of the copper mines. Using the slogan, "Puerto Rican mines or no mines," the MPI has begun a campaign to resist at all costs the surrender of our mineral wealth to North American partnerships eager to exploit it.

A similar campaign has been directed toward the recovery of our beaches, many of which are used today for the exclusive enjoyment of San Juan's luxury hotels. The militants of the MPI have invaded the "private" beaches of hotels like the Caribe Hilton to demonstrate to the Puerto Rican people that the beaches belong to the people.

All these acts, of course, are an indication of how the very dialectic of liberation has polarized Puerto Rican society and has contributed to the radicalization of the independence movements—with the consequent reaction of the annexationist and colonialist groups. The increasingly repressive attitudes and acts of the present government against the *independentistas* is a palpable illustration of this last assertion. The polarization of our country is intensifying. I have tried to enumerate the positive effects of the polarization in this prologue but must also warn of the consequent oncoming intensification of the activities of the repressive colonial machine.

No people struggling for its liberty has been able to achieve this liberty without the sacrifices that marked all other patriotic struggles. At this moment of ascending power in the *independentistas'* struggle, it would be naïve to expect that independence and national liberation will be achieved peacefully. We have the example of the Puerto Rican liberation movement of the thirties as a solemn reminder of the extent to which the regime will react once it feels threatened. Therefore, as I said in the first edition of this book, those who will decide between a peaceful and violent nature for this struggle will not be the *independentistas,* but those who oppose independence.

HATO REY, *Puerto Rico*
October 1970

Addendum | A Socio-Economic Interpretation of the Puerto Rican Migration*

It would be a futile intellectual exercise to see Puerto Rican migration to the United States as abstracted from the social and historical conditions within the island itself that have fostered such a migration. It should be evident even to those that submit a policy of "benign neglect" with respect to nonwhite peoples that *something* must have happened in a country in which almost one-third of its population has now settled in the United States, a social phenomenon that has occurred at a hectic pace during the last two decades. As a matter of fact, the problem of Puerto Rican migration should be seen as part of a problem that transcends the relationship between Puerto Rico and the United States, to become a problem concerning the much broader one that hinges upon mass migratory movements within the context of the international division of labor in capitalist countries. The situation of the Puerto Rican migrant in New York allows us to reflect on the nature of the American capitalist system itself, as well as on the very nature of the relationships between the United States as a world colonialist power and those countries that are subject to its domination.

* Text of the keynote address delivered at the Conference on Puerto Rican Studies held at Princeton University on November 5–7, 1971.

Seen within this context, the depressed condition of the Puerto Rican slum dweller or migrant laborer is not an aberration or a direct consequence of certain hereditary or cultural traits, but a situation that is rooted in structural conditions that have their origins in Puerto Rican society itself. That is to say, the shifting from Puerto Rico to the mainland merely prolongs, and at times aggravates, the basic problems that the Puerto Rican faces in his own country: collective impotence, cultural and personal aliena-tion, intellectual and moral colonization. As the Puerto Rican migrant learns the hard way, the situation he faces in the United States generally takes a turn toward the worst. Whether or not he achieves consciousness of this fact hardly affects the objective conditions which he faces when he arrives in the mainland.

Compared to all other migrant groups, Puerto Ricans are the only ones who come from a territory annexed by the United States at the conclusion of the Spanish-American War. It is misleading, to say the least, to compare those white migrant groups who entered the mainstream of American life by assimilation and who have been incorpo-rated or co-opted into positions of power, and Puerto Rican migrants who come from an overseas extension of U.S. territory. The former were Americans by choice; the latter became American citizens because they had no other alter-natives, given the political status of the island as a colony of the United States. Thus the whole of Puerto Rican territory was ceded by Spain as a war booty, opening the door wide open to American economic, military, and cultural penetra-tion of the island. By that time (1898) Puerto Rico was already a distinct nationality, a Latin-American country in terms of its history, language, and culture. It was also an island endowed with great strategic value, an abundant and cheap labor force, and open to the thrusts of the great sugar corporations and the tobacco trusts. At the end of what John Hay called "our splendid little war" the markets and raw materials of the Caribbean, as well as Asia, were now fair game for the expansion of American economic interests. The expansionist pattern of American rule was already set and the whole of Latin America—but above all the Caribbean—became a vast scenario for the emergence of a vast international proletariat which provided the surplus that fed the ever-growing profits of American capitalism.

In contrast to the older Mediterranean, the "American Mediterranean" was populated by vast black and *mestizo* populations. Imperialism was thus justified in terms of racist doctrines, of the Spencerian dogma of the social "survival of the fittest." Puerto Ricans were among those peoples that Senator Beveridge alludes in the rhetoric proper of his times when he exclaims:

"We will not renounce our part in the mission of our race, trustees under God, of the civilization of the world . . . God has not been preparing the English-speaking and Teutonic peoples for a thousand years for nothing but vain and idle self-contemplation and self-admiration. No! He has made us the master organizers of the world to establish system where chaos reigns. He has made us adept in government that we may administer government among savages and senile peoples."[1]

This messianic complex—an attitude which Americans have never really shed even down to the present day—provided the essential leitmotif for the process of cultural assimilation of Puerto Rico, one of the few possessions within its vast neocolonial framework that the United States decided to annex formally as a "territory."

[1] As quoted in Richard Hofstadter, *The Paranoid Style in American Politics and Other Essays* (New York: Knopf, 1965), p. 176.

The year 1898 marks the formal entrance of the United States as an imperialist power and attests to the belief of its leaders that it, too, had to participate in the "scramble for empire" initiated by the European countries. This was essentially a scramble for new markets and raw materials, as well as for cheap labor. The author of Puerto Rico's first "organic act," passed by Congress in 1900, candidly states his preoccupation:

We have reached the point in the development of our resources and the multiplication of our industries where we are not only supplying our home demands, but are producing a large surplus, constantly growing larger. Our greatest present and prospective need is for markets abroad. We cannot find them in the countries of Europe. Their demand upon us is limited. They strive to supply themselves and to compete with us in the markets of the world. Our opportunity (and theirs also) is the "Far East."[2]

The first forty-odd years of American colonial rule in Puerto Rico illustrate very well what Senator Foraker had in mind. Not only was Puerto Rico to become a captive market for the surplus of manufactured products of the United States, but its agricultural economy was to suffer under the impact of the tariff barriers that were meant for the protection of American goods. At the moment preceding American occupation of Puerto Rico, our island's economy centered around three basic commodities: coffee, tobacco, and sugar. Most of the land belonged to the peasants that cultivated it. According to the study made by the Diffies, Puerto Ricans were owners of 93 per cent of the farms that existed in Puerto Rico in 1899, so that "a great number of persons belonging to the rural population were

---

[2] Statement by Senator Foraker (Ohio), *Congressional Record* (Senate), April 30, 1900, page 4856.

homeowners and permanent residents of the Island."[3] The authors also point out that out of the total area of the island (3,535 square miles = 2,198,400 acres) 41 per cent was devoted to coffee, 15 per cent to sugar cane, 32 per cent to foodstuffs, and 1 per cent to tobacco. But by 1930 the sugar industry raised its area of cultivation from 70,000 to 250,000 acres, this being 44 per cent of the total cultivable land. At that juncture 60 per cent of all sugar production was monopolized by four great absentee corporations, and the same held true for tobacco (80 per cent), public services and banks (60 per cent), and maritime lines (100 per cent).

The move toward the concentration of property in the hands of a few absentee corporations went hand in hand with the creation of a cash-crop, monoculture, plantation type of economy. The demise of the coffee plantations, heralded by the closing of the traditional European markets as well as by the devaluation of the Puerto Rican peso that came on the heels of American occupation, led to the unfolding of a process in which the *campesinos* of the coffee plantation subculture were forced to seek jobs on the great sugar plantations and *centrales*. This led to the creation of a rural proletariat whose life chances were geared to the sugar factories, and by the conclusion of the first three decades of American rule Puerto Rico had become—within the international division of labor—an economy basically dependent upon the price of sugar in the world market.

It is worthy of note that this role of sugar producer was also shared by Cuba and the Dominican Republic, our next-door neighbors. As a matter of fact, this lopsided character

[3] Bailey W. and Justine Diffie, *Porto Rico: A Broken Pledge* (New York: The Vanguard Press, 1931), p. 150.

of our economy must be seen as part of a broader scheme whereby the great sugar cartels were extracting the surplus from an Antillean proletariat that worked on a seasonal basis for subsistence wages. The *tiempo muerto** that inevitably followed as a sequel to the end of the *zafra*† kept the sugar-cane worker in a state of forced unemployment. It is no wonder that a study made by The Brookings Institution in 1930 gives this bleak picture of the Puerto Rican laborer: "Generally speaking, birth, sickness, accident and death are suffered with little attempt at alleviation. In the mountain homes of the *jíbaro* one all too commonly finds illness and suffering accepted with helpless fatalism."[4]

Statistics concerning migration to the United States during this period show that in 1910 about fifteen hundred Puerto Ricans were living on the mainland, whereas in 1920 there were twelve thousand, in 1930, fifty-three thousand, and in 1940, some seventy thousand. It is difficult to determine within this context the nature of this early migration to the United States. The extreme impoverishment of the Puerto Rican rural proletariat, the lack of a speedy and cheap means of transportation to the mainland, the language barrier in a context of widespread illiteracy—all of these factors would tend to suggest that the small number of migrants that are accounted for during this period were not primarily from those sectors of the Puerto Rican population that were the hardest hit by the *tiempo muerto*. But this is a period of Puerto Rican migration that has not been studied by scholars with the same intensity as that of the postwar

---

* Literally, "dead time." It meant the period of forced idleness after the sugar-cane season ended.

† The sugar-cane harvest and processing process.

[4] Victor S. Clark, ed., *Porto Rico and its Problems* (Washington, D.C.: The Brookings Institution, 1930), p. 37.

period. Be that as it may, it is altogether evident that the number of Puerto Ricans living outside of the island during these first forty years of American domination constituted but a small percentage of the total population.

This should not obscure the fact, however, of the existence within American territory of a sizeable number of American citizens—whether they liked it or not Puerto Ricans were made American citizens by an Act of Congress in 1917—whose objective conditions vis-à-vis their equivalents on the mainland were well below the standard held valid and legal for the latter. This was, and is, essentially what colonialism is all about, and before long we were to witness a process whereby the Puerto Ricans who came to the mainland as American citizens were soon faced with a situation of discrimination and impoverishment that was not much different from their lot on the island. Exploitation shifted from a geographical viewpoint, but certainly not from an economic and social perspective. The fact that the new situation on the mainland could be labeled "internal colonialism" instead of "classical colonialism" did not alter one iota the plight of Puerto Ricans, blacks, chicanos, and other so-called ethnics constituted the most downtrodden and discriminated-against groups within American society.

But let us return once more to Puerto Rico in 1940. The decade of the thirties is an extremely important decade in the history of twentieth-century Puerto Rican society. The Great Depression that shattered the optimism of the "Gay Twenties" and "rugged individualism" in the United States hit the island with extraordinary force. A colonial economy so tightly wedded to that of the colonial power aggravated the problems faced by Puerto Ricans. It is in the thirties that we witness the emergence of nationalism as a political force in Puerto Rico, and it is also in this decade that the cry for urgent social reform is heard more loudly and clearly. The crisis of the thirties helped to bring to the fore all those problems that had hitherto been submerged in the consciousness of Puerto Ricans: the colonial problem, the cultural problem, the economic problem, and others. The thirties also serve to dramatize what Professor Gordon K. Lewis has labeled "the imperialism of neglect": a characterization of the first three decades of American colonial policy with respect to the island.[5]

During the thirties the Puerto Rican protest movement focused its attention upon the dual problems of colonialism and misery. The movement was divided in two: the revolutionary sector and the reformist sector. The first, led by the great nationalist leader Pedro Albizu Campos, became the spokesman for a radical solution to Puerto Rico's colonial problem via a nationalist revolution. The second, led by Luis Muñoz Marín, became the advocate of a postponement of the solution to Puerto Rico's colonial status until the basic economic problems of Puerto Rico were solved. Rhetorically, it spoke the language of nationalism and socialism, but without truly antagonizing the powers that be. These powers, however, were truly antagonized by the nationalists, and a period of violent repression of the Puerto Rican independence movement culminated in the jailing of the top leadership of the Nationalist party and the persecution and physical limitation of many of its cadres. By 1938 the colonial government had things under control in Puerto Rico.

In this same year the Popular Democratic party (PPD) was founded under the leadership of Luis Muñoz Marín.

[5] Gordon K. Lewis, *Puerto Rico: Freedom and Power in the Caribbean* (New York: Monthly Review Press, 1964).

Consistently backed by the New Deal administration on the mainland, the PPD came to power in 1940. A new, reformist era was heralded by the party who made the *jíbaro* its symbol and *Bread, land and liberty* its motto. Until its demise in the 1968 elections the PPD became one of the most significant mass movements in Puerto Rican history. Its main base of support came from the peasantry, although after 1944 it managed to count upon other significant sectors of the Puerto Rican population, such as the working class, the intellectuals, and the professional middle class. In a sense, it may be said that the PPD attempted to steal the thunder and the lightning from the Nationalist party, whose program for basic social reforms was frequently clouded by its elitist approach to politics and by its repeated emphasis upon the solution of the problem of colonialism as the *sine qua non* for the solution of all other problems. But the men who were to hold sway within the Popular Democratic party after the consolidation of its power base were not the nationalists and socialists within its fold, but rather the pragmatic, technocratically oriented liberals who naturally would put "economic development" within an unaltered colonial framework.

Rexford Guy Tugwell, whose stint as a colonial governor of Puerto Rico helps to reveal the absurd pretensions of a liberal working within an illiberal system, saw clearly where the rub was. In his rambling autobiography, which he has had the nerve to subtitle "The Story of Puerto Rico," Tugwell writes contemptuously of the "romantics" in the PPD, and leaves no doubt as to his conviction that the continued American presence in Puerto Rico depends upon the "pragmatists," the practical men, that is to say, "mostly those who had . . . worked in the States, who to a degree, at least, recognized the difficulties and dangers involved in the situation. It was they who possessed the power to transform. They recognized that the balance of power in the Puerto Rican community must pass from the politician and the landed and moneyed dons to the technically trained and realistic younger group whose ambition was not to exploit the *jíbaro* and the *obrero* for the benefit of himself and his connections but to develop as a people in one co-operative effort, with leadership but not with dictatorship. *This was the American idea* [my emphasis]."[6] So it was indeed the "American idea" and those willing to seize upon it who were already firmly in control of the PPD in 1948. The early attempts at nationalization of the cement and bottle factories gave way before Operation Bootstrap, probably the single most important program within the PPD. Its first administrator, Teodoro Moscoso, was precisely the kind of technocrat that Tugwell had in mind when he spoke about the "American idea" and its application in Puerto Rico.

The "rationale" for Operation Bootstrap can be found in the 1952 special number of the *Annals of the American Academy of Political and Social Science* that, in a way, gives the clarion call for the Puerto Rican equivalent of what C. Wright Mills called "the American celebration." The same postwar era that heralded Operation Bootstrap provided the main impetus for the massive exodus of Puerto Ricans destined for the mainland. The essence of this economic program consisted in the luring of industrial enterprises to Puerto Rico through a system of tax exemption for a period of from ten to seventeen years. Cheap labor and the provision of overhead capital in the form of roads, electricity, physical facilities for the factories, etc., made the

---

[6] Rexford Guy Tugwell, *The Stricken Land* (New York: Doubleday, 1947), page 489.

proposition attractive for investors from the mainland. In its beginnings, Fomento was successful in attracting to the island the type of light firms that were mostly labor-intensive rather than capital-intensive enterprises. A considerable proportion of the labor force employed in this program was composed of women. The upsurge of the construction industry that marches hand in hand with a rapid process of urbanization attracted a considerable proportion of laborers from the countryside. As an inevitable sequel to its policy of industrialization and its neglect of the agricultural sector of the economy, Fomento altered the balance of the rural-urban continuum in favor of large-scale concentration in urban areas. Many of the displaced *campesinos* that flocked to the urban areas did so as an intermediate step towards migration to the mainland. As the scholars that contributed to a special number of the *International Migration Review* devoted to the Puerto Rican experience suggest, the labor shortage in the postwar United States served as a magnet for Puerto Ricans, who in increasing numbers migrated to the mainland. Several other factors contributed to this exodus: a high rate of unemployment in Puerto Rico, the postwar economic boom in the United States, the stiffer immigration laws passed by Congress, and the policy of the Puerto Rican government to foster widespread migration to the States as a kind of "escape valve" for a supposed surplus population considered an endemic Puerto Rican problem.

The existence of a large reserve army of unemployed has always been one of the great "attractions" of Fomento for mainland investors. On the other hand, the policy of discouraging by all means possible the syndicalization of the Puerto Rican labor force has meant that only 18 per cent of the Puerto Rican workers are unionized. This, of course, reduces to nonexistent the real possibility of collective bargaining. Within this context an abundant army of unemployed has a depressive effect upon wages and thus perpetuates the very nature of Puerto Rico as a cheap labor area. A clear understanding of this fact led *The Wall Street Journal* to write with great satisfaction about the rosy prospects for private investment in the island: "The appalling rate of unemployment [in Puerto Rico]—variously estimated at between 12 per cent and 30 per cent—is helping industry at a record clip from the continental U.S., where the labor pinch is currently severe. For one thing, local income and property taxes, as well as license fees, are often suspended for up to 17 years, depending on a company's product and the extent to which it aids industrialization of the area. In addition, the Puerto Rican Government doles out generous subsidies for everything from transportation to training."[7]

Today the picture of widespread unemployment is still bleaker than that presented by *The Wall Street Journal* five years ago. There has been, on the one hand, the shifting from labor-intensive to capital-intensive industries, as illustrated by the great petrochemical complexes of CORCO, Sunoco, etc. These factories are highly technified and require a very skilled labor force. On the other hand, a sizable number of American corporations have closed up or are on the verge of closing. Some of them have been affected by the Kennedy Round and its lowering of tariffs for European products such as shoes, lingerie, etc. Others are leaving simply because they have come to the end of the road in tax exemption. This has created a severe condition of unemployment, particularly among small towns in the interior of the island. With the closing down of factories in

7 *The Wall Street Journal,* December 27, 1966.

these towns, a wholesale exodus is occurring from some of them that before long is bound to lead to the existence of ghost towns in our midst. This enforced idleness drives the unemployed to the urban slums and to the mainland in search of work. Needless to say, the human cost of this situation is appalling. As a matter of fact, the whole Operation Bootstrap seems to be running out of steam and faces its worst crisis since its inception in 1948.

It is no wonder if under such conditions unemployed Puerto Ricans go to the mainland to search for work. Like their Algerian counterparts in France, they are frequently hired to perform the kinds of jobs nobody else wants. And yet they are "the last to be hired and the first to be fired" in present-day American society. This in turn aggravates the problem of dependence. A very recent study points out that nearly half of the welfare recipients in New York are Puerto Ricans. This is not a reflection upon Puerto Ricans, but a reflection upon the system that allows such a situation to occur. Surely the solution is not, as the study suggests, to make welfare payments higher in the island. The problem is of a structural nature, and the authors really come up with the answer when they point out: "The principal beneficiaries of these current welfare policies are American corporations with plants in Puerto Rico, which are able to capitalize on cheap Puerto Rican labor and gain tax exemptions, and New York City sweat-shop operators who pay sub-standard wages. The principal victims are the Puerto Rican migrants and New York City taxpayers."[8] Anybody who knows two beans about Puerto

[8] This study, made at the request of Assemblyman Andrew J. Stein of the New York Municipal Assembly, was made by Professor Kingsburg of the Fordham University School of General Studies. I refer to its summary as it appears in *The New York Times*, October 25, 1971.

Rican cultural patterns has to shudder before the consequences of what being on welfare means to the Puerto
Rican male and female. This vicious circle extending from
Puerto Rico to the mainland and back again is a vivid
reminder of the bankruptcy of the policies of colonial
administrations on the island during the past thirty years.

But not all the causes for massive Puerto Rican migration are of a structural nature. There is also the "escape
valve" theory of Puerto Rican migration that was one of the
Popular Democratic party's favorite themes during its
twenty-eight-year-long administration. The "escape valve"
theory was frequently hushed up, as was the birth control
program. Nevertheless, the essence of the theory was the
deliberate fostering of Puerto Rican migration to the mainland as a way of "decongesting" the island of its excessive
population.

The ideological underpinnings of this theory were dual:
on the one hand, the high density of the Puerto Rican
population per square mile; on the other hand, the unabat-
ing fertility of Puerto Ricans and the consequent fear of a
"population explosion." Within this context, migration was
one side of the coin and birth control the other. The
creation of a Migration Division in New York under the
authority of the Secretary of Labor of the Commonwealth
of Puerto Rico was a direct result of this policy.

The massive postwar exodus has been described by one
of the most prominent of Puerto Rican demographers as
"one of the greatest exoduses of population registered by
history," and its results have been that "if we add to the
total number of migrants the number of children that they
would have given birth to if they had stayed on the island,
we reach the conclusion that between 1940 and 1960 the
island lost nearly one million people as a result of this mass

migration." To this he adds that from 1950 to 1960, 70 per cent of the migrants were persons from fifteen to thirty-nine years of age.[9] The problem of the "excessive" number of Puerto Ricans was thus solved by allowing the "escape valve" to function unimpaired, although naturally with help of the Puerto Rican government.

The natural outcome of this policy has been what we have now: namely, a country in which a third of its population is living outside of its territory. As José Hernández Alvárez' study concerning return migration to Puerto Rico has shown, it is true that there has been a continuous process of people coming back to Puerto Rico after spending several years on the mainland. These, however, are mostly those that "have made it" on the mainland. The contrast between those who return and those who stay is aptly stated by Hernández Alvárez when he points out:

Within the present context of Puerto Rico as a developing country, return migrants generally represent a middle class element bordering on the Island's educational, occupational, and financial elite. Many have taken advantage of opportunities becoming available as a result of modernization, resuming life in Puerto Rico under favorable circumstances—as professionals, white collar workers, and highly skilled technicians . . .

In the middle of the 1960's, the large group of emigrants remaining on the mainland are mainly oriented toward the same economic activity which attracted them a decade or more ago. Although earning substantially more than most people in the homeland, they are experiencing industrial displacement resulting from the mechanization and automation of the routine and repetitive task they are accustomed to perform. Also caught

[9] José Luis Vázquez Calzada, "La emigración puertorriqueña: ¿solución o problema?" *Revista de Ciencias Sociales de la Universidad de Puerto Rico*, Vol. VII, no. 4 (December, 1963).

by the "leveling up" of educational requirements for employment, as well as difficulties related to language and ethnic identity, the Puerto Ricans in the United States are encountering serious difficulties in finding and keeping jobs.[10]

The average Puerto Rican migrant is thus stuck with living on the mainland without much chance of economic and social advancement. And yet the desperate need for work makes the tide of migration ebb, but with the prospect of rising once more at any indication of an upswing in the economic cycle.

While Puerto Ricans are forced to migrate to the mainland, nearly forty thousand Cuban exiles have entered freely into the island. The Puerto Rican people can do nothing about it, since immigration is a matter of the exclusive competence of the U.S. Federal Government. Thus, the Pill, widespread sterilization of Puerto Rican women (recent figures show that one out of three have been sterilized), and migration are supposed to be the answers to our problem, while at the same time thousands upon thousands of Cuban exiles suit themselves to the Puerto Rican labor market. Yet our exiles are condemned never to return to their fatherland, even though it was not their fault if they were forced to emigrate. This is the higher immorality involved in the attempt to solve the economic and social problems of a society saying goodbye to one-third of its people.

Up to now, we have attempted to describe in what must necessarily be schematic form the social and economic conditions within Puerto Rican society that served as a framework for the massive exodus of Puerto Ricans we

[10] José Hernández Alvárez, *Return Migration to Puerto Rico* (Berkeley: University of California Press, 1967), p. 104.

have just mentioned. It goes without saying that the uprooting of such a sizable number of people is not something to be taken lightly or dismissed as just another ranting of a Puerto Rican radical. What this whole process has meant to our people—both those residing on the island and those living on the mainland—in terms of alienation, exploitation, problems of identity, racism, and so forth, is something which only our own people can describe faithfully. If, as the great nineteenth-century Apostle of Cuban liberty José Martí once said, one must live within the monster in order to know his entrails, then in all justice it must be said that the Puerto Rican émigrés living in the United States are truly the ones that have witnessed and felt firsthand the nightmare that has shattered the American dream.

It is only recently that Puerto Ricans on the island— above all those among us that are in favor of independence for Puerto Rico—have come to realize that for all practical purposes we had forgotten about our brothers on the mainland. This problem can be seen from a dual perspective. On the one hand, our defense of Puerto Rico's Hispanic-American heritage made us ill-at-ease with those of our brothers in the United States who through no fault of their own spoke a kind of garbled Spanish. For too long we had a kind of conditioned reflex approach concerning Spanish as a tool in the resistance to colonialism, and many times we were turned away by what we considered—wrongly, we now realize—a less-than-honest effort to speak our vernacular correctly. On the other hand, Puerto Rican radicals from the island came face-to-face with a new generation of Puerto Ricans born during the postwar period in the United States, who eagerly attempted to identify with the radical trend in Puerto Rican society and history. We soon realized that there was a schism between us, a schism that tended to reveal more or less openly the class differences that divided the petite bourgeois leadership dominant within the political scene of the island's independence movements and the essentially proletarian character of the groups on the mainland whose consciousness of Puerto Rican-ness led them to identify with the independence struggle on the island.

In a sense it can be said that in a fit of temporary absent-mindedness many Puerto Ricans on the island had forgotten about those on the mainland and vice-versa. It is only recently, particularly with the creation of a Puerto Rican Studies Program in the City University of New York, that a heightened awareness of the problem has surfaced and is being discussed.

The problems faced by a Puerto Rican in his society are magnified and multiplied when he migrates to the United States. Regardless of what Glazer and Moynihan argue in *Beyond the Melting Pot,* the American ethic is a messianic one, and all ethnic groups are required to assimilate culturally as a condition for achieving a share in the material and spiritual goods of American society. This is particularly true for Puerto Ricans, whose process of assimilation to what Glazer and Moynihan call the "Anglo-Saxon Center"[11] starts in the Island of Puerto Rico itself. The intellectual and moral colonization of Puerto Ricans is merely continued and intensified on the mainland, but what I have called elsewhere "the colonialist syndrome"[12] is the result

[11] Nathan Glazer and Daniel Patrick Moynihan, *Beyond the Melting Pot,* 2nd ed. (Cambridge, Mass.: The M.I.T. Press, 1970), pp. 20, 311.

[12] The colonialist syndrome is "that aggregation of attitudes, orientations and perceptions which magnifies the power, wisdom and achievements of the colonizer while minimizing the power, wisdom and achievements of the colonized." *Annals of the American Academy of Political and Social Science,* Vol. 382 (March, 1969) pp. 26–31.

of a deliberate policy on the part of the American and the colonial government geared towards the destruction of the trend in Puerto Rican society that has historically been the main obstacle to the complete cultural assimilation of our country: namely, the trend towards independence. Frantz Fanon's insights into this problem are extremely useful for the understanding of Puerto Rican society, not from the point of view of the colonizers like Tugwell, but from that of the colonized themselves.

I have spoken about alienation and identity. These problems are generally dismissed by the defenders of the colonial system as a tendency to fossilize Puerto Rican society, as a static view of our dynamic body politic. Nothing could be further from the truth. The problem is real, agonizingly so. What is involved is the achievement by part of our people of an end to the ambiguity and schizophrenia involved in not knowing what or who they are. The problem is particularly acute with respect to second-generation Puerto Ricans living on the mainland. They have come to realize that they live in a society which rejects them, which despises them as an inferior ethnic group. But when in a search for roots they return to Puerto Rico they find that they are not at home on our island; they are frequently rejected in Puerto Rico not because they are not American enough, but because they are not Puerto Rican enough. The dilemma that leads to an agonizing reappraisal of one's true identity has been the subject of many literary works, prominent among these being the novel by Pedro Juan Soto, *Ardiente Suelo, Fría Estación*. The fact that a talented Puerto Rican poet like Pedro Pietri must communicate willy-nilly in English illustrates the dilemmas and difficulties inherent in our own condition as Puerto Ricans. It is perhaps extremely difficult to establish a causal nexus, but I have the feeling that the abnormally high rate of mental illness among Puerto Ricans living on the mainland is directly or indirectly related to this problem of identity and alienation.

As I have said before, the process of assimilation on the mainland merely magnifies this same process on the island. It is silly to argue that this is a universal process that is tied to the modernization of backward societies and that it extends also to advanced industrial ones. For this would imply the putting of colonialism in parentheses, an incapacity to behold the nature of that collective impotence which is the very essence of colonialism. The experiences of New Mexico and Hawaii should serve as grim reminders of the messianic attitude inherent in the American ethic—the average American is brought up to believe that the whole world yearns to follow and ape the "American Way of Life." In a sense they are not mistaken, for it is a fact that the American style of consumerism has a great attraction for the elites of underdeveloped countries, but this merely demonstrates the international character of class interests and not the inherent superiority of American capitalism. In other words, being pro-American in the Third World means being against any threat to the status quo that keeps the masses oppressed. Puerto Rico, a kind of inflated version of a colonial society having a middle class endowed with a *nouveau riche* mentality, is understandably enough of a society in which the American world-view runs rampant. It is precisely when Puerto Ricans come to the United States that they are confronted with the shock of rejection and the consciousness of ethnicity. For here Americans are not seen from a distance—idealized in terms of myths coming from an education in a colonial society—but seen in terms of how they really behave in their relations with blacks, chicanos, Puerto Ricans, and other groups.

It can perhaps be argued that this problem of identity is

essentially one that provides Puerto Rican intellectuals with a perpetual source of grievance, while the flesh-and-blood Puerto Rican does not worry about this subject. Yet the fact remains: In contrast to other Latin American nations, we are in an extreme condition of political dependence, a condition that tends to aggravate the problem concerning the question "What are we?" It is indeed a sad reflection upon our colonial situation that we should still state the question as our great essayist Pedreira did in 1934: "What are we and where are we going?"

There is, of course, one possible answer to this question: assimilate totally to American society by approaching the "Anglo-Saxon Center." Deny that we are Puerto Ricans and become more and more like the Americans, in the same way that a black decides to whiten his skin and straighten his hair so that he can "pass" into white society. In this sense, a person may speak perfect Spanish—as many annexationists do in Puerto Rico—while at the same time submitting to an interpretation of our past and a view of our future that would lead us eventually into the cultural oblivion of other ethnic groups that have migrated to the United States. On the other hand, a person may speak Spanish only haltingly and at the same time feel that he has to identify with the affirmation of Puerto Rican nationality and culture; that he must take his bearings not from what the colonialists have taught him about our historical development, but from what truly represents the struggle of Puerto Ricans to liberate themselves of all colonialist ties.

The problem is thus not simply a "cultural" one, but rather a political one. It involves no more and no less than a question of power. It is power—particularly the power to determine our own destiny without foreign interference—that constitutes the *sine qua non* for the liberation of Puerto Rican society and of Puerto Rican man.

Of all the ethnic groups that migrated to the United States, Puerto Ricans are the only ones that never completely cut their ties with their fatherland. They never did like Cortés in Veracruz, whose determination to keep himself and his men from returning to Spain was symbolized by his burning of the ships that brought them. Puerto Ricans have never burned their ships. They continually go back to their island, to their homeland. Unlike the blacks—for whom Africa is not truly a home—Puerto Ricans do have a place, a nation, a culture that they can look to.

Insofar as Puerto Rico is a colonial society, insofar as Puerto Ricans in the United States are suffering from exploitation and discrimination, they are one people united by the same conditions of dependency and lack of self-determination. In this respect, Puerto Ricans are part of the Third World, no matter how much the colonial elite and the middle-class parvenus may try to cut themselves off from this reality. Our struggle is thus an international struggle that must be seen from two vantage points: as an anticolonialist struggle and as a class struggle, imperceptibly blending into one.

Historically, this quest for self-determination has taken the road of independence and national liberation. The antihistorical trend leads away from these goals and towards assimilation and annexation to the United States as a State of the Union. This last alternative amounts to national suicide and to the definitive triumph of the colonialist forces in our country.

The two alternatives are clearly drawn in historical and sociological terms. This is a decision that must be made by all Puerto Ricans—those on the island and all those on the mainland. The very awareness of the problem is a step in the attempt at its solution.

A new generation of Puerto Ricans with a consciousness

of their Puerto Rican-ness and a desire for affirming Puerto Rican nationality and negating American values is emerging on the mainland. A similar process is taking place in Puerto Rico. This postwar generation is a hopeful sign of revolutionary change.

The crisis of imperialism as a system of world domination is also evident in Puerto Rico, as it is evident in the United States itself. The inherent contradictions of the system will inevitably require that it take the necessary measures from their solution. As far as Puerto Rico is concerned, the crisis of colonialism on the island and its ramifications among Puerto Ricans on the mainland could well be the definitive indicator of the breakdown of legitimacy and the beginning of a revolutionary process.

Max Weber said that it was not the function of the social scientist to carry the marshal's baton in his knapsack. Prediction is surely not a province of the social sciences. Nevertheless, it is quite proper for the social scientist to analyze the trends and tendencies that he sees in his society, and for him to diagnose the ailments and their causes from a scientific perspective. But above all, the social scientist is a man and as such must take sides and commit himself in the very social process he seeks to analyze. For those of us who believe in the revolutionary transformation of Puerto Rican society, our motto thus will not be the Weberian *Sine ira et studio* (without anger and without partiality), but rather Marx's famous dictum in his *Theses on Feuerbach:* "The Philosophers have interpreted the world. The important thing, however, is to change it."

List of Abbreviations

APPU   *Asociación Puertorriqueña de Profesores Universitarios* (Puerto Rican Association of University Professors)

AUPE   *Asociación de Universitarios Pro Estadidad* (Association of University Students for Statehood)

CAFU   *Comité de Acción Feminina Universitaria* (University Committee of Feminine Action)

CAL   *Commandos Armados De Liberación* (Armed Liberation Commandos)

CES   *Consejo de Educación Superior* (Council on Higher Education)

CIC   Local political police

ELA   *Estado Libre Asociado* (Commonwealth of Puerto Rico)

FNEP   *Federación Nacional de Estudiantes Puertorriqueños* (National Federation of Puerto Rican Students)

FUPI   *Federación de Universitarios Pro Independencia* (Federation of University Students for Independence)

JIU   *Juventud Independentista Universitaria* (University Youth for Independence)

MPI   *Movimiento Pro Independencia* (Pro-Independence Movement)

PIP   *Partido Independentista Puertorriqueño* (Puerto Rican Independence Party)

PLP   *Partido Liberal Puertorriqueño* (Puerto Rican Liberal Party)

PNP   *Partido Nuevo Progresista* (New Progressive Party)

PPD   *Partido Popular Democrático* (Popular Democratic Party)

STACOM   Joint Committee of the United States and Puerto Rico to Study the Status of Puerto Rico

Bibliography

Abbad y Lasierra, Fray Íñigo, *Historia geográfica, civil y natural de la isla de San Juan Bautista de Puerto Rico.* Estudio preliminar y notas por la Dra. Isabel Gutiérrez del Arroyo (Río Piedras: Editorial Universitaria, 1959).

Álvarez Nazario, Manuel, *El elemento afronegroide en el español de Puerto Rico* (San Juan: Instituto de Cultura Puertorriqueña, 1961).

Anderson, Robert W., *Politics in Puerto Rico* (Stanford, Calif.: Stanford University Press, 1965).

Andic, Eaut, *Distribution of Family Incomes in Puerto Rico* (Río Piedras, 1964).

Andreu Iglesias, César, *Independencia y socialismo* (San Juan: Libería Estrella Roja, 1951).

————, *Los derrotados.* Segunda edicion (Río Piedras: Editorial Cultural, 1964).

————, *Luis Muñoz Marín: un hombre acorralado por la historia* (Editorial Claridad: 1964).

Arce de Vázquez, Margot, *La obra literaria de José de Diego* (San Juan: Instituto de Cultura Puertorriqueña, 1967).

Azcárate, Pablo de, *La guerra del 98* (Madrid: Alianza Editorial, 1968).

Babín, Maria Teresa, *Panorama de la cultura puertorriqueña* (San Juan: 1958).

Baran, Paul y Sweezy, Paul, *Monopoly Capital* (Nueva York:

Monthly Review Press, 1966). Edicion española: *El capital monoplista* (México: Siglo XXI, 1968).

Bemis, Samuel F., *The Latin American Policy of the United States* (New York: Harcourt Brace, 1943).

Benítez, Jaime, *La universidad del futuro* (Río Piedras: 1964).

Berbusse, Edward, S. J., *The United States in Puerto Rico 1898–1900* (Chapel Hill: The University of Carolina Press, 1966).

Bernstein, Barton J., *Towards a New Past: Dissenting Essays in American History* (New York: Pantheon Books, 1968).

Blanco, Tomás, *Prontuario histórico de Puerto Rico* (San Juan: Biblioteca de Autores Puertorriqueños, 1935).

————, *El prejuicio racial en Puerto Rico* (San Juan: 1952).

Bolívar, Simón, *Documentos* (La Habana: Casa de las Américas, 1964).

Bonafoux, Luis, *Betances* (Barcelona: Imprenta Modelo, 1901).

Brameld, Theodore, *The Remaking of a Culture: Life and Education in Puerto Rico* (New York: 1959).

Brau, Salvador, *La colonización de Puerto Rico*. Edición anotada por la Dra. Isabel Gutiérrez del Arroyo (San Juan: Instituto de Cultura Puertorriqueña, 1966). Este libro se publicó originalmente en 1907.

————, *Disquisiciones sociológicas*. Compilado y con una introducción por el profesor Eugenio Fernández Méndez (Río Piedras: Universidad de Puerto Rico, 1956).

————, *Historia de Puerto Rico* (San Juan: Editorial Coquí, 1966).

Brenan, Gerald, *El laberinto español* (Paris: Ediciones Ruedo Ibérico, 1962).

Cabrera, F. Manrique, *Historia de la literatura puertorriqueña* (Río Piedras: Editorial Cultural, 1965).

Caplow, Th., Stryker, J., y Wallace, S. E., *The Urban Ambience: A Study of San Juan, Puerto Rico* (Totowa: 1964).

Carmichael, Stokely, y Hamilton, Charles, *Black Power* (New York: Random House, 1968).

Carreras, Carlos N., *Betances, el Antillano proscrito* (San Juan: Editorial Club de la Prensa, 1961).

Carroll, Henry K., *Report on the Island of Porto Rico* (Washington, D.C.: Government Printing Office, 1899).

Castro, Paulino, *Historia sinóptica del Partido Nacionalista de Puerto Rico* (San Juan: 1947).

Clark, Victor S., (editor), *Porto Rico and its Problems* (Washington, D.C.: The Brookings Institution, 1930).

Coll y Cuchí, Cayetano, *La Ley Foraker* (San Juan: Tip. del Boletín Mercantil, 1904).

Coll y Toste, Cayetano, *Boletín histórico de Puerto Rico*, 14 volumes. (San Juan: 1914–26).

Corretjer, Juan Antonio, *La lucha por la independencia de Puerto Rico* (San Juan: Publicación de Unión del Pueblo Pro Constituyente, 1950).

Cruz Monclova, Lidio, *Historia de Puerto Rico en el siglo xix.* 3 volumes (Río Piedras: Editorial Universitaria, 1957–1964).

————, *Baldorioty de Castro* (San Juan: Instituto de Cultura Puertorriqueña, 1966).

Dalmau Canet, Sebastián, *Luis Muñoz Rivera, su vida, su obra, su carácter* (San Juan: Tip. Boletín Mercantil, 1917).

De Diego, José, *Obras completas.* 2 volumes (San Juan: Instituto de Cultura Puertorriqueña).

Díaz Soler, Luis M., *La esclavitud negra en Puerto Rico* (Río Piedras: Editorial Universitaria, 1965).

————, *Rosendo Matienzo Cintrón: orientador y guardián de una cultura.* 2 volumes (Universidad de Puerto Rico: Ediciones del Instituto de Literatura Puertorriqueña, 1960).

Díaz Valcárcel, Emilio, *El Asedio y otros cuentos* (México: Ediciones Arrecife, 1958).

―――, *Proceso en diciembre* (Madrid: Taurus, 1963).

―――, *El hombre que trabajó el lunes* (México: Ediciones Era, 1966).

Diffie, Bailey and Justine, *Porto Rico: A Broken Pledge* (New York: The Vanguard Press, 1931).

Dinwiddie, William, *Porto Rico. Its conditions and possibilities* (New York: 1899).

Dos Santos, Teotonio, and others, *La crisis del desarrollismo y la nueva dependencia* (Lima: Moncloa Editores, 1969).

Enamorado Cuesta, José, *El imperialismo yanqui y la revolución en el Caribe* (San Juan: 1966).

Fanon, Frantz, *Los condenados de la tierra* (México: Fondo de Cultura Económica, 1963).

Fernández Almagro, Melchor, *Historia política de la España contemporánea*. 3 volumes (Madrid: Alianza Editorial, 1968).

Fernández de Castro, Ignacio, *De las Cortes de Cádiz al Plan de Desarrollo* (París: Editions Ruedo ibérico, 1968).

Fernández Méndez, E., *La identidad y la cultura* (San Juan: 1959).

Fraga Iribarne, Manuel, *Las constituciones de Puerto Rico* (Madrid: Ediciones Cultura Hispánica, 1953).

Francis, Roy G., *The predictive process* (Río Piedras: 1960).

Friedrich, Carl J., *Puerto Rico: Middle Road to Freedom* (New York: 1959).

Furtado, Celso, *La economía latinoamericana desde la conquista ibérica hasta la revolución cubana* (México: Siglo XXI, 1969).

Gang, Peter, y Reiche, Reimut, *Modelos de la revolución colonial* (México: Fondo de Cultura Económica, 1970).

Gauthier Dapena, José A., *Trayectoria del pensamiento liberal puertorriqueño en el siglo xix* (San Juan: Instituto de Cultura Puertorriqueña, 1963).

Gómez Acevedo, Labor, *Organización y reglamentación del trabajo en el Puerto Rico del siglo xix* (San Juan: I.C.P., 1970).

Gómez Robledo, Antonio, *Idea y experiencia de América* (México: Fondo de Cultura Económica, 1958).

González, Antonio J., *Economía política de Puerto Rico* (San Juan: Editorial Cordillera, 1967).

González, José Emilio, *Profecía de Puerto Rico* (San Juan: 1954).

González, José Luis, *Paisa* (México: 1955).

————, *En este lado* (México: 1954).

Gould, Lyman Jay, *The Foraker Act: the Roots of American Colonial Policy* (University of Michigan Ph.D. Dissertation, 1958).

Granda Gutiérrez, Germán, *Transculturación e interferencia lingüística en el Puerto Rico contemporáneo* (Bogotá: Instituto Caro y Cuervo, 1968).

Guerra y Sánchez, Ramiro, *La expansión territorial de Estados Unidos a expensas de España y los países hispanoamericanos* (La Habana: 1964).

Hernández Álvarez, José, *Return Migration to Puerto Rico* (Berkeley: University of California Press, 1968).

Hofstadter, Richard, *The Paranoid Style in American Politics and Other Essays* (New York: Knopf, 1965).

————, *Social Darwinism in American Thought* (Boston: Beacon Press, 1944).

Hostos, Eugenio Mariá de, *Obras completas,* 20 volumes (La Habana: 1939).

Iglesias, Santiago, *Luchas emancipadoras.* Volume 1 (San Juan: Cantero Fernández, 1929).

Jaguaribe, Helio, and others, *La dependencia político-económica de América Latina* (México: Siglo XXI, 1969).

Junta de Planificación del Estado Libre Asociado de Puerto

Rico, *Informe Económico al Gobernador, 1967* (San Juan: Junta de Planificación, 1967).

————, *Informe Económico al Gobernador, 1966* (San Juan: Junta de Planificacíon, 1971).

————, *Informe de recursos humanos al Gobernador, 1970* (San Juan: Junta de Planificación, 1971).

La Feber, Walter, *The New Empire: An Interpretation of American Expansion, 1860–1898* (Ithaca: Cornell University Press, 1963).

Laguerre, Enrique A., *Cauce sin río (Diario de mi generación)* (Madrid: 1962).

————, *Pulso de Puerto Rico* (San Juan: 1956).

Lewis, Gordon K., *Puerto Rico: Freedom and Power in the Caribbean* (New York: Monthly Review Press, 1964).

————, *The Growth of the Modern West Indies* (New York: Monthly Review Press, 1969).

————, *Puerto Rico: A Case Study in the Problems of Contemporary American Federalism* (Trinidad: 1960).

Lewis, Oscar, *La Vida* (New York: Random House, 1966).

Magdoff, Harry, *La era del imperialismo* (México: Nuestro Tiempo, 1969).

Maldonado Denis, Manuel, *Puerto Rico: Mito y Realidad* (Barcelona: Ediciones Península, 1969).

Marqués, René, *La víspera del hombre* (Club del Libro de Puerto Rico: 1959).

————, *Ensayos (1953–1966)* (Editorial Antillana: 1966).

————, *Otro día nuestro* (San Juan: 1955).

————, *En una ciudad llamada San Juan* (México: 1960).

Mathews, Thomas G., *Puerto Rican Politics and the New Deal* (Gainesville: University of Florida Press, 1960).

May, Ernest F., *American Imperialism, a Speculative Essay* (New York: Atheneum, 1968).

Medina Ramírez, Ramón, *El movimiento libertador en la historia de Puerto Rico.* 3 volumes (Santurce: Imprenta Borinquén, 1954).

————, *Patriotas ilustres puertorriqueños* (San Juan: 1962).

Meléndez, Concha, *José de Diego en mi memoria* (San Juan: Instituto de Cultura Puertorriqueña, 1967).

Mesa, Roberto, *El colonialismo en la crisis del XIV español* (Madrid: Ciencia Nueva, 1969).

Mills, C. W., Senior, C., y Goldsen, R. K., *The Puerto Rican Journey* (New York: 1951).

Mintz, Sidney, *Worker in the Cane: A Puerto Rican Life History* (New Haven: Yale University Press, 1960).

Muñoz Morales, Luis, *El status político do Puerto Rico* (San Juan: Imprenta El Compás, 1921).

Negrón de Montilla, Aida, *Americanization in Puerto Rico and the Public School System 1900–1930* (Río Piedras: Edil, 1971).

Nieves Falcón, Luis, *Diagnóstico de Puerto Rico* (Río Piedras: Edil, 1971).

————, and others, *Puerto Rico: grito y mordaza* (Río Piedras: Editorial Libería Internacional, 1971).

Pagán, Bolívar, *Historia de los partidos políticos puertorriqueños.* 2 volumes (San Juan: Libería Campos, 1959).

Parrilla, Antulio, *Puerto Rico: supervivencia y liberación* (Río Piedras: Ediciones Librería Internacional, 1971).

Pedreira, Antonio S., *Insularismo.* Segunda edicion (San Juan: Biblioteca de Autores Puertorriqueños, 1942).

————, *El año terrible del 87.* Tercera edicion (San Juan: Biblioteca de Autores Puertorriqueños, 1948).

————, *Un hombre del pueblo: José Celso Barbosa* (San Juan: Instituto de Cultura Puertorriqueña, 1965).

————, *Hostos, ciudadano de América* (San Juan: Instituto de Cultura, Puertorriqueña, 1964).

Pérez Moris y Cueto, *Historia de la insurrección de Lares* (Barcelona: 1972).

Perkins, Whitney T., *American Policy in the Government of its Dependent Areas, A Study of the Policy of the United States Toward the Inhabitants of its Territories and Insular Possessions* (Fletcher School of Law and Diplomacy, Ph.D. dissertation, 1948).

Perloff, Harvey S., *Puerto Rico's Economic Future* (Chicago: University of Chicago Press, 1950).

Petrullo, V., *Puerto Rican Paradox* (Philadelphia: 1947).

Pichardo Moya, Felipe, *Los aborígenes de las Antillas* (México: Fondo de Cultura Económica, 1956).

Picón Salas, Mariano, *Apología de la pequeña nación* (Río Piedras: 1946).

Quintero Rivera, Angel (editor), *Lucha obrera en Puerto Rico* (Río Piedras: CEREP, 1972).

Rexach Benítez, Roberto y Celeste Benítez, *Un pueblo en la encrucijada* (Humacao: 1964).

Rivero, Ángel, *Crónica de la Guerra Hispanoamericana en Puerto Rico* (Madrid: 1922).

Roberts, Lidia J., and Stefani, Rosa Luisa, *Patterns of Living in Puerto Rican Families* (Río Piedras: 1949).

Robles de Cardona, Mariana, *Búsqueda y plasmación de nuestra personalidad* (San Juan: 1958).

Rosario, Rubén del, *La lengua de Puerto Rico* (San Juan: 1956).

Ruiz Belvis, Acosta y Quiñones, *Proyecto para la abolición de las esclavitud en Puerto Rico.* Edición con introducción y notas del Dr. Luis M. Díaz Soler (San Juan: Instituto de Cultura Puertorriqueña, 1959).

Salinas, Pedro, *Aprecio y defensa del lenguaje* (Río Piedras: 1948).

Sánchez Tarniella, Andrés, *Nuevo enfoque sobre el desarrollo político de Puerto Rico* (Río Piedras: Edil, 1970).

Sartre, J.-P., *Colonialismo y neo-colonialismo* (Buenos Aires: Losada, 1968).

Seda Bonilla, E., *Los derechos civiles en la cultura puertorriqueña* (Río Piedras: 1963).

——, *Interacción social y personalidad en una comunidad de Puerto Rico* (San Juan: 1964).

Senior, Clarence, *Self-Determination for Puerto Rico* (New York: 1946).

——, *The Puerto Ricans: Strangers—Then Neighbors* (Chicago: 1965).

Silén, Juan Ángel, *Hacia una visión positiva del puertorriqueño* (Rió Piedras: Edil, 1970).

Soto, Pedro Juan, *Spiks* (México: 1956).

——, *Usmail* (México: 1959).

——, *Ardiente suelo, fría estacion* (México: 1962).

Stein, Stanley J. y Barbara H., *La herencia colonial de América Latina* (México: Siglo XXI, 1970).

Steward, Julian (editor), *The People of Puerto Rico* (Urbana: University of Illinois Press, 1956).

Suárez Díaz, Ada, *El doctor Ramón Emeterio Betances: su vida y su obra* (San Juan: Ateneo Puertorriqueño, 1968).

Tapia y Rivera, A., *Mis memorias o Puerto Rico como lo encontré y como lo dejé* (San Juan: 1946).

Todd, Roberto H., *Desfile de gobernadores de Puerto Rico.* Segunda edicion (Madrid: 1966).

Traba, Marta, *Propuesta polémica sobre arte puertorriqueño* (Río Piedras: Ediciones Librería Internacional, 1971).

Tugwell, Rexford G., *The Stricken Land: The Story of Puerto Rico* (New York: Doubleday, 1947).

Tumin, Melvin, and Feldman, Arnold, *Social Class and Social Change in Puerto Rico* (Princeton, N.J.: Princeton University Press, 1961).

Tuñon de Lara, Manuel, *La España del Siglo XIX* (Paris: Libería Española, 1968).

U.S.—P.R. Commission on the Status of Puerto Rico, *Report of the United States—Puerto Rico Commission on the Status of Puerto Rico.* (August, 1966).
————, *Selected Background Studies* (1966).
————, *Hearings—Senate Document No. 108.* Vol. 1: "Legal-Constitutional"; Vol. 2: "Social-Cultural"; Vol. 3: "Economic."

Van Alstyne, Richard W., *The Rising American Empire* (Chicago: Quadrangle Books, 1965).
Varios, *Memoria de los trabajos realizados por la Sección Puerto Rico del Partido Revolucionario Cubano: 1897–1898* (Nueva York: Imprenta A. W. Howes, 1898).
Vientós Gastón, Nilita, *Comentarios a un ensayo sobre Puerto Rico* (Ediciones Ateneo Puertorriqueño, 1964).

Waggenheim, Kal, *Puerto Rico—a Profile* (New York: Praeger, 1970).
Wallerstein, Immanuel (editor), *Social Change: The Colonial Situation* (New York: John Wiley, 1966).
Weinberg, Albert K., *Manifest Destiny* (Chicago: Quadrangle Books, 1963).
Wells, Henry, *The Modernization of Puerto Rico* (Cambridge: Harvard University Press, 1969).
Williams, Eric, *From Columbus to Castro—The History of the Caribbean 1492–1969* (New York: Harper and Row, 1970).
Williams, William A., *The Contours of American History* (Chicago: Quadrangle Books, 1969).

Zahar, Renate, *Colonialismo y enajenación: contribución a la teoría política de Frantz Fanon* (México: Siglo XXI, 1970).

About the Author

MANUEL MALDONADO-DENIS was born in Santurce, Puerto Rico, in 1933. He received his B.A. from the University of Puerto Rico and his M.A. and Ph.D. in political science from the University of Chicago. In 1959, he started teaching political science at the University of Puerto Rico (Río Piedras), where he is at present professor of political science. For the academic year 1972–73 Dr. Maldonado-Denis will be professor of Puerto Rican studies at Queens College of the City of New York.

In 1968–69 the author was a John Simon Guggenheim Fellow. In May of 1972 he was awarded the degree of *Doctor Honoris Causa* by the University of the Atlantic of Barranquilla, Colombia, "for his scholarly contributions and his devotion to the cause of Puerto Rican and Latin American liberation." Dr. Maldonado-Denis is currently president of the Puerto Rican Sociological Association. He is the author of two books: *Puerto Rico: Myth and Reality* and *Portraits of Four Revolutionaries.* He has published numerous articles in scholarly and political journals in Latin America, Europe and the United States. In addition, he is now working on a book about Pedro Albizu Campos, one of Puerto Rico's most ardent nationalists.

Dr. Maldonado-Denis is married and has two daughters.

About the Translator

ELENA VIALO was born in Tucson, Arizona, and received her education in Mexico and the United States. In 1963–64 she was a U.S. Fulbright grantee to Spain. At present she lives in San Francisco.